LONG
ROOD
FROM
JARROW

By the same author:

Cider with Roadies
Pies and Prejudice
Adventures on the High Teas
Hope and Glory
The People's Songs
The Pie at Night

LONG
ROAD
FROM
JARROW

A JOURNEY THROUGH
BRITAIN THEN AND NOW

STUART
MACONIE

EBURY
PRESS

1 3 5 7 9 10 8 6 4 2

Ebury Press, an imprint of Ebury Publishing
20 Vauxhall Bridge Road
London SW1V 2SA

Ebury Press is part of the Penguin Random House group of companies
whose addresses can be found at global.penguinrandomhouse.com

Penguin
Random House
UK

First published by Ebury Press in 2017

www.penguin.co.uk

A CIP catalogue record for this book is available from the British Library

ISBN 9781785030536 (hardback)
ISBN 9781785036316 (trade paperback)

Typeset in India by Integra Software Services Pvt. Ltd, Pondicherry

Printed and bound in Great Britain by Clays Ltd, St Ives PLC

For Tracy Brabin and Jo Cox, Members
of Parliament for Batley and Spen, West Yorkshire

CONTENTS

PROLOGUE

'Going far, son?'

I turn to meet the voice, somewhat awkwardly since I'm still getting used to the graceless choreography required when travelling laden with a large, bulky modern rucksack. It's made in Colorado and according to the manufacturer, 'delivers serious function while looking great, featuring Axiom 5 technology, front entry and stretch mesh front and side pockets'. It can hold '65 litres' should I ever be tempted to fill it with liquid. Nonetheless, it's this highly visible piece of kit which has presumably prompted the question from behind me. That and my remorseless, solitary plod along an unlovely stretch of northern trunk road on a quiet weekday morning.

'London,' I answer.

'Bloody hell!' he replies.

He's a big man in his late fifties, I'd guess; Geordie accent, close cropped hair, brisk, active. He moves alongside me, clutching a thick rope leash wound around his wrist at the end of which strains a large German Shepherd dog; enthusiastic, curious, increasingly aware I feel that there is half a meat and potato pasty in either the stretch mesh front or side pocket (I forget which) of my great-looking, yet seriously functional pack.

It's 5 October 2016 on the A167 between Pelaw Grange and Chester-le-Street. A rinsed fresh autumn morning in Northumberland; a sky of rippled, downy cloud and a low gauzy sun over the far blue smudge of fells. Nearer to hand, less lovely, the buffeting, thunderous, continuous rush of articulated lorries along the noisy arterial road.

'London?' There's pity in his voice, with a hint of disbelief and perhaps a dash of admiration. 'Elsa!' He yanks the boisterous dog to heel.

'Yes, I'm retracing a famous journey ...' I pause. 'If I were to say "the Jarrow march" to you, would that mean anything?'

He smiles and looks me up and down, as if wondering what kind of response might go down best. Over the next month of walking almost the length of England, I'll ask many people this question and get all kinds of responses to that word 'Jarrow' and the famous march of 1936. Some will be knowledgeable, some vague, some apologetic, some impassioned, many wildly inaccurate. A few faces will be blank and sheepish, offering an embarrassed shrug or a wild guess. Others will have learned about it at school, especially up here on this first northern stretch, where many will have treasured, polished stories to tell. Some will have had family members on the march. Others will claim to.

I'll meet people whose granddads cooked the marchers breakfast in a drill hall in Leicester and a lady whose mum watched them stride past her cottage down a country lane near Bedford. A taxi driver in Darlington will talk of knowing old miners who had walked with them through Manchester and Birmingham. A sweet, older woman in Newton Aycliffe will tell me that she still has a tent peg that she found as a girl left behind after they had taken down their camp in her village. They didn't pass anywhere near Birmingham or Manchester and they never pitched a tent in Newton Aycliffe but as Frank Lloyd Wright once said, 'the truth is more important than the facts'.

The man on the A167 between Pelaw Grange and Chester-le-Street thinks for a second or two, then with a jutting jaw, a sly look and an eye on my reaction says, 'Aye, it means something. A bunch of bloody left wingers who went to London to stir up trouble because they had nothing better to do.'

Certainly the last of this is true. It was having nothing
to do – no work, nor money, security or purpose, just long,
empty repetitious days of hardship, boredom and despair
– that sent the marchers all the way down to London 80
years ago. In a sense then, my dog walking companion is
absolutely right. He registers my surprise though, which is
genuine. You don't find many north easterners who'll 'trash'
the Jarrow marchers. Respect for Jarrow's great collective
effort is coiled into the DNA of the region, embedded in its
still proud sense of self.

'Every bugger in County Durham claims their dad or
granddad or budgie was on that bloody march. Sorry, son, but
I'm a bitter man. Worked in the steelworks in Consett and it
was never the same after nationalisation in '67. Labour let me
down. I'm a rarity round here in talking like that. This is Labour
country, Country Durham. Mining country ... with no mines.
Well, I wish you luck. You'll see some places ... I almost wish I
was going with you ... Cheerio, son.'

He crosses the road gingerly, Elsa recalcitrant still, odour
of pasty still lingering on the breeze perhaps. As he gets to
the other side he yanks on the dog's chain, halts her and turns
around on the opposite verge. He shouts something across the
road back at me with a wry grin.

'I hope you get a better welcome than they did anyway ...
all five hundred thousand of them.'

A joke. A good one. I want to ask him more, but a speeding
convoy of huge vehicles flicker and rumble past like a strip of
film, and when they have passed he too is gone. But to answer
his first question, which I don't think I did: yes, I am going far.
Three hundred miles, give or take.

To London. A long road from Jarrow.

*

They denied us the future we wanted, but that doesn't mean they can deny us our past ...

Matt Perry, *The Jarrow Crusade: Protest and Legend*

'Who cares? The world's moved on ...'

Software Consultant, Kent, via Twitter

The *Shields Gazette*, established in 1849, is the oldest evening paper in Britain. It still appears nightly, in print and online, and remains the voice of home and the journal of record for generations of Geordies, Mackems, Wearsiders and for thousands across the north east of England. On New Year's Day 2013, in amongst details of the Queen's Honours List and drunken revelry in Hebburn, it carried these notices:

SHIELS Con. Died aged 96.

Dad, you had a long life. We are so proud to have been a part of it. Love and miss you always, Moya & Brian x

Dad, you will always be near us. Con, Eileen, grandchildren and family.

Con Shiels, a widower of Jarrow, South Tyneside died on Boxing Day 2013 after a short illness, mourned by his son, two daughters and several grandchildren and great-grandchildren. He'd been a fitter by trade and had served 12 years in the Royal Navy. But it was the events of one late October day in 1936 that Con spent the rest of his long life being asked about, interviewed by earnest academics, TV comedians and politicians, appearing on scores of documentaries, speaking to classrooms full of eager schoolchildren.

On 31 October 1936, aged just 20 and enrolled on a work scheme in London, Con joined his father, an unemployed riveter, and nearly two hundred other men from his home town to walk the eight or so miles from Edgware to London's Marble

Arch. They were on the final leg of a protest over the decision to close their steelworks, to publicise the plight of their dying town and to ask for government assistance in creating new jobs. They'd been on the road on foot for three-and-a-half weeks and covered almost 300 miles by the time young Con Shiels joined them. The youngest present, he went on to outlive every other man on that walk and thus when he passed way, he held a claim to be the last of the Jarrow marchers.

A decade before, on 14 September 2003, another nonagenarian and another 'Con', Cornelius Whalen of Hadrian Road, Jarrow, died at the Queen Elizabeth Hospital in Gateshead. He was the last man alive to have walked the whole 291-mile route from Jarrow to London amongst that famous body of men. In commemoration, the Jarrow Brewery named a beer after him, the Old Cornelius. But it was Con Shiels who was actually the last survivor to have walked among them, if only for that final dour, rain-lashed day along the Edgware Road. At a packed requiem mass for him at St Matthew's RC Church, Jarrow, parish priest Father Peter Martin said: 'This is the closing of a chapter of history. There can't be any others who can say they took part.'

Except that there might have been. There might still be even, though this is extremely unlikely of course. The truth is we just don't know. The Jarrow march of October 1936 is an event which, although lit by fires of memory and the glow of romance, has many an obscure and shadowy cranny and corner. That's decidedly strange when you consider that we are not amongst the Vikings or the Saxons here. We are not in the realms of Camelot or Sherwood Forest. We're talking of twentieth century Tyneside and modern Britain. Here is an event that happened relatively recently and within living memory, had two 'embedded' journalists in its number and was covered by the national press, radio and newsreels. It was a fairly straightforward undertaking; a three-and-a-half-week march to deliver a petition to parliament. But it has attained the status of a national myth akin to the stories of Robin Hood or King Arthur, and like those, has become negotiable, malleable, debatable. While its status is unarguable, its details are anything but.

For instance, above my desk as I write this is a laminated copy of the original schedule of the walk drawn up by the organisers and lodged at the time of the march with the BBC and the National Archives. It is hard to conceive of a more august or official document of the trip. It is also quite wrong. Two overnight stays are recorded in Thirsk and Boroughbridge. These never happened. The marchers didn't even pass through these towns, though they did lodge in nearby Ripon. Ripon, however, doesn't appear on the itinerary. During his 2005 bid for leadership of the Conservative Party, David Davies claimed his grandfather had marched with the Crusade from York to Aldermaston. His grandfather may well have marched somewhere with someone. But the Jarrow marchers passed through neither York nor Aldermaston.

Famously, a dog accompanied the march. Many of the press reports dwelt somewhat sentimentally on this adorable pooch, presumably to provide some cute human (or rather canine) interest and distract from any awkward political dimension. Depending on whose account you read, this was either a setter, a retriever or a terrier. But even a cursory glance at the pictures would suggest that it's actually a Labrador. Whatever its breed, this plucky, uncomplaining companion was called Paddy. Or perhaps Peter. Then again, some people say it was called Blackie. Others say Jarrow.

Anyway, what is certain is that it walked all the way with the men, all 200 of them. That's 'two hundred' according to the police and the march organisers in any case. We can only find corroborating evidence and names for 176. And when I say 'names', there's another complicating issue here because many of the men gave false ones so that they wouldn't have their benefit stopped by the National Assistance Board. For instance, marcher Thomas Downey was probably actually Thomas Dobson.

While the marchers covered the miles, their equipment went ahead in a van. No one knows the driver's name or the make of his vehicle. On arrival in London, they were taken on a river boat trip and the 10,000 signature petition they had carried in a box for the entire route was hurriedly taken from them at the House of Commons. It has never been seen since. No one knows where it is, or if it still exists. It might be mouldering in a forgotten cabinet in the bowels of Westminster, or lying in its wooden box on the muddy bed of the Thames.

Some may find all this vagueness and fudge dispiriting. But apart from that last properly shameful detail, I think it entirely in keeping with the march and its legacy. 'Jarrow' (the whole matrix of events reducible to one word like 'Aberfan', 'Hillsborough' or 'Orgreave') has become mythic, storied; a thing of lore and romance as much as hard fact, one whose details and legacy are still debated today. Many of the 'facts' surrounding the march may be opaque or contentious, but the 'truth' of the Jarrow march, its emblematic significance as a piece of Britain's social history, is as enduring as it's contested. Douglass in the *New Statesman* in 1996 said, 'it is a story told and retold …. The ghosts of Jarrow's Crusaders still march into Jarrow's consciousness.' The Jarrow march casts a long shadow, and you invoke the name lightly at your peril.

In 2000, a collective of disgruntled road hauliers, the self-styled 'People's Fuel Lobby', announced their plans to send a slow-moving convoy cum blockade of lorries down the A1(M) from Jarrow to London to force the government into lowering duty on fuel thus safeguarding their profits. Spokesperson Andrew Spence declaimed, 'I don't know if anyone has heard of the Jarrow Crusade? Well, it's starting again, only bigger. We want as many vehicles on the road as possible.' Spence's crass attempt to usurp this icon of working-class struggle for such selfish, disruptive, acquisitive ends was a PR disaster. Denounced everywhere, it lost the People's Fuel Lobby what little public support they had.

Whilst the 1930s produced many marches, protests and outpourings of anger and dissent, none are as well remembered, beloved or lionised as the Jarrow Crusade. When discussing the

Jarrow march, be it with Geordies, Labour movement stalwarts, working people of the north or British people of a certain vintage generally, it's wise to remember that you're on hallowed ground and dealing with emotive, if not entirely accurate, memories. Tread softly, as W B Yeats asked the famously unfussed Maud Gonne, for you tread on my dreams, or in my case, lacing up my Size Nine Meindl Respond GTXs and treading on a whole romantic cultural icon, over community and place and memory.

I have no connections with Jarrow. I've no link to the march or any of the marchers. I'm from the north west, not the north east, and Geordie friends have never tired of reminding me that my bit of 'the north' is more like the Midlands to them. But something appealed about retracing the Jarrow march.

Firstly – and I wouldn't want to downplay this element – I just fancied going for a really long walk. I liked the idea of passing through unfamiliar landscapes, experiencing the character and thrill of towns, villages and cities never visited, meeting, eating, drinking, soaking the country in. I like Britain and British history. I like the people and I like hanging out with them. I like random eavesdroppings, chance meetings and unexpected encounters and I had many on this journey, from the rosy cheeked Women's Institute ladies who gave me a bag of apples to Albanian builders tearful on grappa late at night, and from concert pianists to chip shop waitresses.

Being British, I was also drawn to the notion of heroic failure. At the end of his life, the last surviving man of the march Con Shiels said of it that it 'had made not one ha'porth of difference' and been a 'waste of time'. But some think the constant, largely supportive publicity for the Jarrow march, the effort and endurance of the men and the focus on the plight of the town and conditions in industrial Britain, helped shape public attitudes into a fresh and keen desire for change. This new national mood may well have contributed to the Labour landslide of 1945 and thus to the setting up of the Welfare State and the NHS, those imperilled secular sacraments of modern Britain that are part of our self-image and identity. As long as Jarrow's remembered, 'the struggle' goes on. Even growing up half a century later and a hundred miles south, my nana would bring up the Jarrow march whenever industrial disputes or economic crisis were in the news, which they often were in the seventies and eighties. It was a crusade; the men were heroes, their treatment a scandal. These days, we didn't know we were born, us modern softies with hire purchase fridges and central heating. We hadn't known the deprivation and squalor of that grim decade, the 1930s. Even the term 'the thirties' has a ring to it, and it's more a tolling bell than a dainty tinkle.

Unless you're one of those enormously irritating people who says 'before my time!' when receiving a question about the Marx Brothers or the Suez crisis in Trivial Pursuit, certain decades call forth an immediate mental image. The eighties: a girl with a bubble perm in legwarmers listening to a Walkman on rollerskates, or a yuppie banker in Sloane Square with a brick sized mobile. The seventies: a bovver boy in half-mast trousers eating a Findus Crispy Pancake during a power cut. The sixties, a couple in kaftans singing Donovan's 'Catch the Wind' round a campfire, or pushing flowers down a National Guardsman's rifle barrel or rolling naked in some mud whilst doolally on acid. And so on. The 1930s, should they conjure anything, will suggest a downcast man in clogs, flat cap and muffler standing on a street corner. At his knee, perhaps, two filthy kids who look beseechingly into the camera whilst playing with a hoop and stick or a lump of coal. Words and phrases that spring readily to mind might include 'Means Test', 'Rickets', 'Hitler', 'Diphtheria' and, of course, 'Jarrow'.

The thirties get a really terrible press. Though recent revisionist historians have proposed a different view of the decade citing the relative affluence of the south and such, this has yet to gain much popular traction outside academia. 'A low, dishonest decade' was W H Auden's famous verdict, badmouthing the thirties almost before it was over in his poem 'September 1, 1939'. That poem was written on the eve of war of course, and our view of the end of the thirties is inevitably coloured by it being the grim prelude to years of global carnage. In 1973, Claud Cockburn called it 'the Devil's Decade' which quickly gained purchase as the accepted view of the times. In 2009, Richard Overy named it 'the morbid age'. Most recently, Juliet Gardiner in her hefty, magisterial study *The Thirties: An Intimate History* claims, 'the thirties is a statement as well as a decade because whilst those years are gradually slipping from our grasp what they have come to represent are ever more present; confusion, financial crisis, rising unemployment, scepticism about politicians, questions about the proper reach of Britain's role in the world'.

With no grand regnal designation such as the Elizabethan, Georgian or Edwardian age, the thirties have become simply part of what we blandly compartmentalise as 'between the wars', suggesting a hiatus, a pause, an interval between the two great defining conflicts of our modern world. But there's another point of view, one building up a credible intellectual head of steam that cites the thirties as the shaping decade of the world we live in today. It's the decade in which we start to voraciously consume mass media such as the new-fangled BBC, which was powered by the smart new National Grid; one where we become obsessed with personal fitness, fashion and sport and greatly more hedonistic, going to the movies, drinking, dancing, 'clubbing' and staying up late. The thirties in some ways start to look very much like Britain today, once you've wiped away the snot and coaldust.

Other thoughts occurred to me too, casting Jarrow's legacy in a different and less rosy light. In a modern world fixated on anniversaries – happy and tragic – and in a cultural milieu where the passing of a moderately successful pop musician or minor sitcom actor creates the torrents of grief once seen for dictators (and with sometimes, it seems, the same whiff of compulsion), Jarrow's eightieth anniversary made barely an appearance in my 'timeline'; no hashtags, no videos, no campaigns. Jarrow's anniversary was not trending. It was not going viral. We had not reached peak Jarrow, or anything like it. For this reason alone maybe, it was a trip worth making.

Of course, any writer with a gleam in their eye and a nose for a good 'state of the nation' story will find rich loam in this doleful era, and richest and most fertile of all is the seedbed of the Jarrow march. It resonates down the years and like all good myths you can bend it to your own ends in any era. From the moment the Crusade reached Marble Arch, writers and commentators have been finding echoes and parallels in their own age, and I clearly am no different. But even so, the particularly weird, fissile state of England in October 2016 seemed to have so much in common with the England of 1936 that a notion long nagging at me suddenly became compelling. When I realised that a significant anniversary loomed, I had the idea to re-trace the walk on its eightieth anniversary day by day as the marchers did, visiting the same towns and comparing the two Englands of then and now.

Some parallels between then and now suggest themselves immediately: A Conservative government recently returned to power with an increased majority. A Labour Party led into disarray by a leader widely seen as divisive and incompetent. The rise of extremism here and abroad fired by financial disasters, a wave of demagoguery and 'strong man' populism. Foreign wars driven by fundamentalist ideologies leading to the mass displacement of innocent people. A subsequent refugee 'crisis'. The threat of constitutional anarchy with conflict between government, parliament and judiciary. Manufacturing industries, especially steel, facing extinction. Marches and mass rallies resurgent as popular but questionable forums for political debate. Explosions of new forms of media. Inflammatory rhetoric stoked by a factionalised press. Football a national obsession; its wages, profits and morality constantly debated. A country angrily at odds with itself over its relationship to Europe, the elephant in the nation: Brexit.

David Cameron's decision to hold a snap referendum on our membership of the EU on 23 June 2016 was both for him

and, so many think, the nation a disastrous, vainglorious mistake.
Margaret Thatcher hated referenda, feeling that they gave up
parliamentary sovereignty and put national policy at the whim
of a protest vote. This is precisely what occurred. Misreading
the national mood entirely (and not helped by Jeremy Corbyn's
near-invisibility) the Remain campaign ignored concerns over
immigration and talked dryly of economic competency and
trade tariffs. Saatchi and Saatchi designed two stunning posters
for the Remain campaign; one showed Boris Johnson looking
twerpish in a woolly hat knocking on the door of Number
Ten with the caption 'Be careful what you wish for', another
featured a grinning Nigel Farage lying smugly in a crumpled
bed captioned 'Don't do something today that you'll regret in
the morning'. Strategists think they could have proved decisive.
But they were never used.

In the aftermath of the referendum vote to leave the
European Union, the reaction from some liberal metropolitans
was disbelief, disgust and not so much rage as a kind of pricked
hauteur. Those boors and idiots up north had gone and spoiled
it for everyone. This generalised shock and bafflement was not
shared by those of us who come from these towns or had spent
any time outside London and the home counties this decade.
In the run-up to the vote, and in the absence of any genuine,
cogent explanation of the issues involved, the intelligentsia,
especially on the left, had simply snorted their contempt and
dismissed any opposing views as 'racist' and held only by 'little
Englanders'. In truth, whether your England is little or large
and whether you want its borders iron clad or porous, Brexit
proved that one thing is not in doubt: we are a divided country,
chiefly along lines of geography and class.

The referendum result was so truly appalling to some in
Britain probably because they had grown used to viewing the
world through the filter of their Twitter timeline, hearing only
the echolalic voices of those who thought like them. Thus was
assumed a general soothing consensus about race, nation, work,

power. The only dissenting voice I heard from the creative industries post Brexit came from socialist comic Jeremy Hardy who said, 'the centre of British politics is so incredibly Europhile. They seem to base their entire view of the EU on the welcoming attitude to children in continental restaurants'.

Brexit was such a shock to the metropolis because it broadcast and amplified the authentic voice of an England they had nothing to do with and probably didn't much want to; not the warming, agreeable multicultural glow that came with chatting to your Senegalese neighbour, Nepali shopkeeper or Latvian plumber, but a different, chillier, altogether less genial acknowledgment of diversity that is the realisation that not everyone thinks, lives or acts like you do. Brexit proved that there is not one England. We are not all sweetly alike really when you get down to it. We are not all in this together, and in that too, we have much in common with the fractious and divided 1930s.

As the shampoo ads once had it, here comes the science bit. The Gini coefficient was developed by an Italian statistician in 1912 to describe the income distribution of a nation. It's the most commonly used measure of inequality. Before 1979, inequality in the UK was actually fairly low in terms of income, but through the 1980s income inequality began to rise. Apart from a brief pause during the recession and financial crisis of 2008–2010, the UK's Gini coefficient has steadily increased to an all-time high. We are now the most unequal country in Western Europe and at a level of income inequality unheard of since the setting up of the Welfare State.

Just as in 1936, the old centres of industry in the north – Britain's 'rust belt' – have been hardest hit. Not everyone and not every town has felt the bite and sting of austerity or experienced the raw downside of globalisation and technology as keenly as some have. Thus metropolitan Britain could scarcely believe that the post-industrial north would be so insular as to baulk at warm notions and comforts as easy travel, study and work opportunities, access to continental markets and affordable mini-breaks to Budapest and Lisbon. However, having never properly enjoyed any of these, it was easy for Wakefield, Oldham and Skegness to reject them.

A brilliant but atypical article in the *Guardian* by the LSE sociologist Dr Lisa Mckenzie bucked the trend, asserting in its title 'Brexit is the only way the working class can change anything'. In it, she wrote:

> As a group of east London women told me: 'I'm sick of being called a racist because I worry about my own mum and my own child,' and 'I don't begrudge anyone a roof who needs it but we can't manage either.' Over the past 30 years there has been a sustained attack on working-class people, their identities, their work and their culture by Westminster politics and the media bubble around it … In the last few weeks of the campaign the rhetoric has ramped up and the blame game started. If we leave the EU it will be the fault of the 'stupid', 'ignorant', and 'racist' working class. Whenever working-class people have tried to talk about the effects of immigration on their lives, shouting 'backward' and 'racist' has become a middle-class pastime.

In the midst of the post-Brexit hand-wringing, navel-gazing and fist-shaking, this struck a bracing chord. Whilst no Brexiteer, I'd been dismayed at how whole areas of Britain and all kinds of people I'd grown up with and lived among could be so easily, so lazily, so insultingly dismissed. When I saw that the Jarrow area had voted 'leave' by 62 per cent, I wondered what the Jarrow men would have thought, how they'd have voted and why, and what the world would have made of their march then. Heroic stand for the native community, or petty protectionism maybe?

One enraged tweet I saw frothed about how the inhabitants of 'these boring towns' had done us all a terrible injustice and inflicted an act of suicidal revenge on blameless London,

Brighton and the likes. Another message I received when I stated my intention to 'do' the Jarrow march again was the response from the software consultant quoted earlier viz, 'Who cares? The world's moved on.' Our Kentish friend may well be right and, if so, I was about to find out exactly how. But I wasn't so sure. As for those derided 'boring towns', in many ways, this is their story. But for me they are only boring if you are bored of history, people, politics, sex, death, religion, art and culture. Life, in other words. I'm very much hoping you're not.

The 1930s may have been a dire period for Britain's coal mines, shipyards and steel mills but they were a boom time for travel writing and the solo literary traveller. Adventurous young men like Patrick Leigh Fermor and Laurie Lee packed tiny knapsacks of pitifully small litreage with neither Axiom 5 technology nor front entry mesh and stomped across Europe. Leigh Fermor trekked from Rotterdam to Istanbul getting into scrapes, sleeping in hedgerows, monasteries and the odd inn, sketching, talking, drinking and generally having a wonderful, character building time that would later make him a famed war hero. His magical account of his teenage odyssey *A Time of Gifts* is a classic of the genre. Laurie Lee 'walked out one midsummer morning' and that was the title he gave to the book of his journey, one that would ultimately take him to the battlegrounds of the Spanish Civil War. That bloody conflict was a darkening stain across Europe as the Jarrow men marched through England.

At home, two colossi of English letters were making journeys through England that would prove just as vivid and celebrated, if less gilded, with smoke and rain and muck instead of wine, fruit and Mediterranean sun. In the first half of 1936, just before the Jarrow march, George Orwell spent three months in the north of England researching what would become *The Road to Wigan Pier*. Orwell lived in Wigan, Barnsley and Sheffield but his experiences in these towns – in whose deprivations and squalor he immersed himself completely – are those of Jarrow too. The remorseless, sapping, daily grind of poverty is described to haunting effect and those middle-class, left-wing intellectuals who will not dirty their hands with it are excoriated in a closing tirade which his publisher Victor Gollancz was extremely nervous about. (I would have loved to have read Orwell on Brexit and its treatment; he was an internationalist but he was both a patriot and fiercely supportive of the working people of England.)

Orwell took some of his inspiration for *The Road to Wigan Pier* from a very successful and similarly motivated book of three years previously. J B Priestley's *English Journey* was one more comfortably travelled than Orwell's road (by chauffeured Daimler and pleasant hotel room rather than the trams and tin baths of Wigan) – but the sentiment was the same. The two writers, of different backgrounds and mien, laid bare an England of harsh contrasts and lives of constant desperation, one in which the plight of the industrial working class could only be remedied by democratic socialism. The success and impact of both books, along with and the Jarrow march, may well have contributed to the Labour landslide of 1945.

So with both *The Road to Wigan Pier* and *English Journey* as daunting, humbling antecedents, I decided to embark on the *Long Road from Jarrow*. I wanted the title to have an echo of both and a hint of the metaphorical as well as the actual. I would start the walk eighty years to the day after the Jarrow marchers did, 5 October, and cover the route day by day as they did, staying in the same towns. I would do it on foot by and large, but if I needed the time to research and explore those towns – some of their daily stages covered 22 miles – I'd hop a passing bus if it took their route. I didn't have a chauffeured Daimler but I did stay in hotels with reasonably fluffy duvets, trouser presses and complimentary tea and coffee making facilities. I would aim to get to London on 31 October and hopefully succeed where the march was fobbed off, not to say duped, by getting inside the House of Commons and actually meeting an MP. How this eventually turned out was sadder and sweeter than I could ever have imagined.

My intention was to compare the England of now and then, to see if the shadow of 1936 really did fall across 2016, but also to get to the heart of England today first-hand. Commentators and chatterers across the media are fond of airy generalisations in think pieces composed in what Priestley described as, 'warm, well-lighted book-lined apartments'. These 'state of the nation' prognoses and editorials are often written from one very particular part of that nation, and with a view partially obscured by the Gherkin and the Shard. I wanted to see, hear, smell even what England was like close up by walking it, moving along its length at a speed where I could look it in the eye, shake its hand, maybe buy it a drink. You can cover the distance I would travel on a high-speed train in three-and-a-half hours. But I was going to take three-and-a-half weeks; still brisk going on foot, but with time to linger, delve, look around and 'mooch', to use a good, descriptive old dialect word.

This is not then a book about the Jarrow march as such, in the way that Matt Perry's excellent aforementioned study is, or the powerful, evocative *Jarrow March* by Tom Pickard (out of print but findable). What follows here, and what I'm more interested in with this book, is where we have been since then and how we have got here. I'd like to know what the country looks like now from the roads, tracks, streets and riverbanks they walked, and to see the pews, pubs, cafés and halls they visited; a picture of now overlaid with a filter or gauze of 1936. If a journey of nearly a month can be said to be a snapshot, then it is that; a picture of a country with a long history, a volatile present and an uncertain future – vivid and real, if sometimes blurry and breaking out of the frame.

'THE TOWN THAT WAS MURDERED'

You can tell a great deal about a place and a time by the names it gives to its tower blocks. In the Futurist architectural reverie of the 1960s, when designing the new estates was as much 'civic art' as 'town planning' and more about 'cities in the sky' than reeking stairwells and intermittent lighting, they were given titles as lofty as their elevated walkways.

In the opening shots of the 2011 alien invasion thriller *Attack the Block*, the names glimpsed on the map of the sink estate where the action takes place (Wyndham Tower, Huxley Court, Clarke Court, etc.) tell us that director Joe Cornish knows his classic British sci fi. The renaming of the Peckham tower block in *Only Fools and Horses* from Walter Raleigh to Nelson Mandela House cleverly reflects changing British cultural touchstones. This trend was parodied in the Judge Dredd comic books where tower blocks are named with desultory ordinariness after Enid Blyton, Ricardo Montalban, and Rowdy Yates of TV western *Rawhide*.

When I was a teenager, I hung out with two punk girls with vermilion hair who lived in one of the three 16-storey tower blocks that loomed over my council estate. These impressive edifices were called Dryden, Thackeray and Masefield House respectively and were clearly christened by a council apparatchik with eclectic taste in literature and a touching high-mindedness (in every sense). Similarly, Dublin's heroin-ridden Fatima Mansions were named after a miraculous visitation of the

Virgin Mary in rural Portugal. In the decaying concrete heart of Ordsall, Salford, stood the fabulously misnamed Orchards, comprising Apple, Peach and Pear Tree Court. These sardonic anomalies and juxtapositions were once common and many remain. Unless you live on a Shetland croft or in a thatched Cotswolds idyll, there will be a tower block somewhere in your town called Rembrandt Court, Coleridge House or Johann Sebastian Bach Gardens. It will be covered in crude drawings of genitalia and the lifts will be out of order.

In the centre of Jarrow, by the squat red brick town hall, stand two bulky, neatly kept, cream and red concrete tower blocks. These are small by the standards of my old estate but they still dominate the skyline as the shipyard cranes would once have done. One bears the name Ellen, the other Wilkinson. We will come back to why. But they stand almost in the centre of a tough, embattled town, the sort you find across the north of England, maybe the north of everywhere, maybe everywhere. It carries in its streets and its stones the enduring sense that it has taken hard blows in what was not a fair fight, and, whilst unbowed, is still bloody from the fray.

Some hard facts about a hard, defiant town then. Jarrow sits on the banks of the Tyne, watered by tributaries of the Don, nine miles west of Newcastle along the busy A1058 and A19, or seven stops of the Metro line. In the past, it boasted a nine-hole golf course, squeezed in between Hebburn Lakes and the slag heap, although it did not possess a single set of traffic lights until the late 1960s, when this modern flamboyance was installed at Carrick's Corner. Even further back, the world's oldest complete Bible, written in Latin and to be presented to Pope Gregory II, was produced at this monastery – 'the Codex Amiatinus', now under lock and key in Florence. Jarrow's population was 43,431 at the 2010 census, over 97 per cent of which were white British. It is the least ethnically diverse area of Tyneside and its unemployment rates are significantly higher than its neighbours'. Jarrow is not just geographically distant from London (let alone Florence), it is financially, ethnically and culturally remote from the capital's habits and ways of life and walking from one to the other would show me what Britain had in common and what divided it. Ellen Court and Wilkinson Court, 'the Jarrow flats', stand sentinel in the middle of the town at a flat intersection of two main roads. They look down on a Masonic lodge, the town hall, a typically British parade of charity shops and pizza outlets. They hint at no worse and no better than a thousand similar blocks across Britain and look rather smarter than many. Ironically, recent refurbishments were financed by the European Union. Jarrow will not be seeing money like that again any day soon, if ever.

There are other Ellen Wilkinson courts and houses around the country; in Poplar, Dagenham, Bethnal Green and Tower Hamlets for example. Across Britain there are girls' schools named after her and university halls of residence. But here her memorial is most relevant, most rooted in place. Whenever anyone here in these neat ten storey blocks gives their address, they pay tribute to one of the most colourful, significant and enigmatic figures in post-war British politics, the woman who coined the two most memorable descriptions of Jarrow; 'the most famous town in England' and 'the town that was murdered'.

'Red' Ellen Wilkinson, as every biographical note including this one mentions, had fiery auburn hair and politics to match. Born into a poor family in Ardwick, Manchester in 1891, she was a bright and dynamic girl who became a socialist in her youth and a communist after the inspirational events of Russia in 1917. An active trade unionist and feminist, she entered parliament in 1924, one of only four women MPs at Westminster. Part of the National Government during the Second World War, she became Minister for Education in 1945 in Attlee's Labour administration. Always plagued by ill health and bronchial problems, she died of an overdose of medication during the bitter, iron winter of 1947. The coroner declared it an accident but doubts have always swirled around the facts of her demise.

She was worried about losing her post in a cabinet re-shuffle and possibly depressed at the end of an affair with Herbert Morrison, intriguingly a stalwart of the party's right wing.

But Ellen Wilkinson is seared into the popular imagination because of her tenure as the MP for Jarrow and her strong involvement with the Jarrow march. Having become the town's MP the year before, she symbolically led the march – albeit often dashing away to other engagements – and became an icon of it. If you're looking for an insightful exploration of the background to the march and the political climate of the time, you can do no better than her little book *The Town That Was Murdered*. I have it in front of me; a faded red first edition from 'The Left Book Club' bearing the stern injunction 'Not for Sale to The Public'. Wilkinson had a glittering second career as a journalist and her gift for the punchy phrase is evident from the off: 'Jarrow's first export was not battleships but Christianity'.

With this brilliant opening line, Wilkinson reminds us of what made the town famous before it became a byword for industrial decline. She's referring to another of Jarrow's famous old boys, in fact its original local boy made good, not Palmer the millionaire shipwright or any of the marchers but a writer called Bede, who came to the monastery of St Paul at Jarrow in AD 684 as a boy and long before anyone called him Venerable. 'First among English scholars, first among English theologians, first among English historians, it is in the monk of Jarrow that English literature strikes its roots … he is the father of our national education.'

She goes on in her brisk entertaining style to describe the ebbing and flowing of different waves of capitalism and industrialisation on the spunky little town; often watched jealously by its large, overbearing neighbour Newcastle. She describes the coming and the going of the pits and mining life. She notes with a narrow, suspicious gaze the arrival of the 'vain and vigorous' Charles Mark Palmer the shipping magnate and the various moguls of steel. For Red Ellen, these men were not the admirable civic benefactors who now lord it paternalistically from statues and pedestals all over our towns, but avaricious fat cats for whom profit was all, even when they weren't up to the job. 'Business men denounce the very idea of planned socialism as inefficient and wasteful. But under capitalism, shipbuilding seems to be as wasteful as could be.'

Palmer's shipyard gave the town work and a great and dirty deal of it between 1851 and 1933. But Sir Charles was no Titus Salt, no George Cadbury or Lord Lever. He gave his town little in the way of concert halls or public baths, no temperance bars, nurseries, libraries or clinics, no carillons playing merry tunes on Sundays in well-tended parks. He stretched to a tea stand that would sell them a hot drink while they queued for work at five-thirty on freezing winter mornings. Jarrow was no Saltaire, Bournville or Port Sunlight built on decent principles, non-conformist faith and a desire to do right by one's fellow man. Here the religion was profit and Sir Charles's god was Mammon.

Wilkinson's verdict is damning:

> There is a prevailing blackness about the neighbourhood. The houses are black, the ships are black, the sky is black, and if you go there for an hour or two, reader, you will be black ... Sir Charles Palmer regarded it as no part of his duty to see that the conditions under which his workers had to live were either sanitary or tolerable.

Like many of his peers, Palmer made the task of making a living as hard as the men could stand. 'Lying like a dockyard clock' is a phrase you can still hear used by some old timers in the region, referring to those exploitative and unscrupulous owners who would keep the clocks slow to wring more labour out of the men.

Pretty bad even in the 'good old days', life was about to get appreciably worse for the working folk of Jarrow. By 1933, profits were down in the shipyards due to overproduction and cheap imports, and Palmer's yard closed. When Jarrow's one main industry was destroyed, in Wilkinson's ringing phrase, the town was murdered. In an attempt to rein in the 'excess capacity' in British shipbuilding, 37 other yards were to suffer a similar fate. None though was left so damaged as Jarrow. In a harsh twist that was impressively badass even for big business and government, the shipyards were not only closed and dismantled; powerful vested interests then 'salted the land' in a manner that Hannibal and the Assyrians would have whistled approvingly at. Government and bosses colluded to set up a body called the NSS, the National Shipyards Security Ltd, to protect profits by closing and dismantling sacrificial yards like Palmers (the word 'security' here carries a certain black humour). The NSS, the government and the shipyard owners decreed that once yards like Palmers were closed, none could be established again there for forty years to keep ship production low and profitable nationwide. The earth was salted. Jarrow was murdered. (Eighteen months later, with war looming, there was a shipping shortage. The orders went to Belgian shipyards who had bought first-rate machinery from yards like Jarrow at knock down prices.)

Unemployment soared to 80 per cent. Houses were overcrowded and infested with vermin. To the misery of unemployment was added the humiliation and degradation of the Means Test, a harsh inquisition intended to determine whether the unemployed deserved any benefit. Government inspectors would come to the house armed with lists and notebooks, spying into the family's material circumstances in the most prurient and invasive ways. Mothers were checked to see if they breastfed their babies; if they did, their meagre benefit was cut. If one member of a family worked the others received less, so families split up to avoid starvation. So much for the preservation of family values. G K Chesterton, no pinko by any stretch, wrote of it, 'For the first time within mortal memory, the government and the nation has set out on a definite deliberate attempt to make the poor poorer.' Forty years later, as a child in the seventies, watching *Crown Court* or *The Cedar Tree* with my Nan, any mention of the Means Test would make this reasonably genial old lady scowl and curse contemptuously. I shudder to think what she had seen as a girl.

The future Edward VIII had declared, shocked, that 'something must be done' when he saw the plight of the working classes in Wales and Tyneside. When Priestley visited Jarrow just before the march he saw a town ruined and a vision of urban hell on earth:

> Wherever we went men were hanging about, not scores of them but hundreds and thousands of them. The whole town looked as if it had entered a perpetual penniless bleak Sabbath. The men wore the masks of prisoners of war. A stranger from a distant civilisation, observing the condition of the place and its people would have arrived at once at the conclusion that Jarrow had deeply offended some celestial emperor of the island and was now being punished. He would never believe us if we told him that in theory this town was as good as any other and that its inhabitants were not criminals but citizens with votes.

Decades later, Ritchie Calder, one of the journalists 'embedded' with the march, recalled the state of the town that they found. 'In the story of Jarrow, we have the story of the face of hunger … you weren't seeing it on a poster, you weren't seeing it on the telly, you know, Biafra or the Congo or something like that. You were seeing the face of hunger in your street. Or even in your own mirror.'

Whatever your politics, it's hard to conceive of a more perfect stitch-up and sell-out of a community than the one perpetrated in Jarrow in 1934. When a delegation of workers from the shell-shocked town met with the head of the board of trade, Walter Runciman (in Wilkinson's words, 'a figure of ice … apparently completely indifferent to the woes of others') his response to their requests for aid was to coldly announce, 'Jarrow must work out its own salvation' – a remark described by historian Ronald Blyth as 'the last straw in official cruelty'. Runciman's chilly indifference and callous response 'kindled the town', according to Wilkinson.

In July 1936, a packed council meeting convened in the town hall at which Ellen Wilkinson, Mayor David Riley and councillors like Paddy Scullion all spoke. The town should ask again for government help, specifically in the form of a new steelworks, but this time the appeal should be backed up by a petition. Signatures should be collected from Jarrow and beyond. While the meeting debated what to do after this, an unknown voice in the crowded public gallery shouted, 'Let's march down with it.' Within days, plans were afoot to do just that, to the acclaim of Jarrow and to the shrinking terror of the Labour Party, the Trade Unions and the socialist Establishment. The Jarrow march was on.

Hunger marches, as they were known, were very much in vogue in the 1930s. Communists, ex-servicemen, blind communists, blind ex-servicemen, strikers and the unemployed of Rotherham, Sheffield, Bolton and all points north, agricultural workers from East Anglia, all could be found criss-crossing the nation under various banners demanding various reforms and with varying success, i.e. usually none. Though support was immediate and widespread for Jarrow's march to London, there were a few dissenting voices from within the working-class community, and perhaps for good reason. Councillor Dodds of Jarrow was one of many unconvinced about what merely marching could achieve:

> I am not so ready as I was to support an ordinary march to London. I am willing enough to march, God knows, and there was a time when I would have suggested that we put the women and children on buses while the men of the town marched with the Council at their head. But now I think we should get down to London with

a couple of bombs in our pockets. Oh Christ, yes, I am
perfectly serious. We should go down there with bombs
in our pockets. These people of Westminster have no use
for us anyway. These people do not realise that there are
people living in Jarrow today under conditions which a
respectable farmer would not keep swine. Do not put
any limits on your demonstration. Get down there.
And I think we should go to the absolute extreme.

In more conciliatory mood, and with reference to the other
political protests that had gripped Britain, David Riley later
admitted that he felt that, 'Hunger March would not be a very
nice name to have and Crusade would be better. And of course
we adopted the idea; called it a Crusade instead of a march. At the
time, there was quite a number of marches being held all over the
country and they weren't being too well received in many places.'

Riley was a decent and principled man but his words show
how, right from its planning stages, the organisers of the Jarrow
march were obsessed with public relations and fearful of offending
or antagonising the media or Establishment. 'Crusade' also
struck the right churchy note of piety and godliness. Perhaps it's
understandable that the marchers should have worried about how
the Conservative Party and its press would receive them. In fact,
they should have been more concerned and dismayed at how the
Labour Party would react. Essentially, Labour washed their hands
of the march, as they did its predecessors, panicky about possible
infiltration by communists. The Trades Union Council actually
issued a circular denouncing it. Ramsay MacDonald, the Labour
leader, begged by Ellen Wilkinson to offer support, said wanly,
'Ellen, why don't you go and preach socialism, which is the only
remedy for this?' She called this bland response 'sham sympathy'.

And so Jarrow marched, and stitched itself into the warp and
weft of British history. Questions on the march or 'crusade' have
been included in the British Citizenship Test and it remains a central
module of the GCSE syllabus and the Learn English network. In

Jarrow: Protest and Legend, Matt Perry cites some of the crazily
varied array of items the march can be said to have inspired:

> Five plays, two musicals, an opera, three pop songs, two
> folk songs, several paintings and poems, a short story,
> performance art, a mural, two sculptures, glassware,
> four television documentaries, four radio programmes,
> a children's story, a cuddly toy, a real ale, a public house,
> an election poster, street names, innumerable pieces
> of journalism and historical references and of course
> hundreds of often reproduced photographs.

Popular art has kept the name of Jarrow and its complex
associations – struggle, hardship, heroism, failure even – alive
down the decades. Nevil Shute's novel *Ruined City* concerns
the plight of a town in the north east called Sharples, a thinly
disguised Jarrow, left devastated by the closure of the 'Barlow'
shipyard which is clearly modelled on Palmers. Later in 1974,
as an economic and energy crisis gripped Britain and the lights
flickered on and off in offices, homes and factories, the nation's
pop pickers cheered themselves by singing along to Alan Price,
formerly of the Animals, and the most famous musical tribute
to the Jarrow marchers. 'Jarrow Song', which reached number
six in the charts, came from an album called *Between Yesterday
and Today*, in which Price delved into working-class life in the
north east for inspiration. Born just six years after the march and
an old boy of Jarrow grammar school, Price's jaunty brass band
number masks a message substantially more militant than the
ethos of the march itself. It starts with Geordie McIntyre, whose
wife tells him to go to London, where:

> . . . if they don't give us half a chance, Don't even give
>   us a second glance
> Then Geordie, with my blessings, burn them down.

Actually, the notion of burning anything down, or indeed any inflammatory or revolutionary fervour, was something the march organisers were desperate to avoid. Price's lyric though has no such qualms and ends by concluding that 1973 finds the working-class north as disadvantaged as it was in 1936 and in the same need of salvation.

There's a musical, *Cuddy's Miles*, based on the Jarrow march, written by John Miles; a seventies rocker probably best known for his grandiose hit 'Music', whose granddad Cuthbert (or Cuddy) was one of the march's two cooks. Just in case you think the kids are missing out, a New Zealand company produced a cuddly bear toy called Jarrow which the little 'uns could play with whilst reading *The Road to London*. Andrew Matthews' slim book was produced in conjunction with the National History Curriculum in 1997 and tells the tale of Clogger, a little lad from Jarrow who stows away on the march. While loosely based on real events, the real stowaways never got out of the north east and certainly didn't make it all the way as Clogger does. Along the way, he gets a few terse lectures about the essentially inequitable nature of capitalism and specifically the failings of Stanley Baldwin's Conservative administration. Produced just as New Labour were sweeping to power, the tone of the book is decidedly partisan. It ends with Clogger's dad explaining Baldwin's refusal to meet the marchers (you can still pick up the book quite easily on eBay, so clearly not all were pulped by incoming Conservative education secretaries post 2010):

> 'He's frightened. The whole governments afraid there'll be a revolution like the one they had in Russia ...'
>
> On the train back to Jarrow, Clogger was quiet for a long time.
>
> 'Dad,' he said eventually, 'isn't there a way of sharing things out, so that rich people aren't quite so rich but people like us have enough to get by?'

On the small screen, Peter Flannery's epic TV drama *Our Friends in the North* began life as stage play for the Royal Shakespeare Company in 1982. As writer in residence when the RSC staged a cycle of Shakespeare's history plays, Flannery was seized by the thought that his Newcastle background – the legacy of the Jarrow Crusade, housing, industry, corruption – could form the basis of a large-scale work based on life in England in the 1960s, 70s and 80s. Initially keen, the BBC then dragged its feet for literally years. Flannery said later, 'I remember pitching it to BBC executive Alan Yentob as a drama about post-war social housing, probably because I'd spent the day writing one of those scenes. He looked alarmed. Two days later, I'd have said it was all about sex and Soho. It got through eventually.' When it did come to the screen, it was recognised instantly and widely as one of the greatest achievements of British television of any era and made stars of its young cast Gina McKee, Mark Strong, Christopher Eccleston and Daniel Craig. Thus the Jarrow march can claim to have indirectly shaped the creation of two other legends in the pantheon of British romantic myth, Dr Who and James Bond.

In the opening episode of *Our Friends in the North*, it's 1964 and Nicky, played by Eccleston, has returned to Tyneside after a summer's activism in the USA with the civil rights movement. Almost immediately, his new-found political zeal brings him into conflict with his disillusioned dad Felix. Felix shows no enthusiasm for the future Labour government that seems likely after the forthcoming election. 'The Labour Party of which I was once proud to be a member were the first to condemn the Jarrow marchers as hooligans. They stabbed us in the back before we got to Durham. We were sold down the river long before you were born, son.'

Nicky's reply across the kitchen table echoes the dog walker on the Pelaw Grange road.

'Here we go. It never takes long, does it? … The Jarrow march.'

Flannery is from Jarrow, had family members on the march, and the scene is clearly drenched in memory and meaning. About four months before setting off on my march, I spoke with Peter Flannery about representations of working-class life in the media. *Our Friends in the North* treated such people with a Tolstoyan depth and, despite that note of exasperation in Nicky/Peter's attitude to his father's generation, there's a real pride and loyalty to the values of an older era which drove Flannery to get his work on screen despite the misgivings of commissioning editors in offices in W1.

> One very famous controller of BBC 2 said, 'Does it have to have the word "North" in it? And does it have to be about the Labour party? They're failures. I don't want it to be about failure.' So isn't it interesting that they only agreed to make it when Labour were almost in power and fashionable again? In our hearts, we knew that my dad's generation were right but we didn't want to trade on the old gripes and grudges. I looked at my parents – why are they so gloomy and cynical about political purpose when I felt so optimistic? In my youth it felt like a sea change was coming. Doors were opening in your own head. We felt on the brink of something better, not like Jarrow, but a real change. But you can't divorce that from an era that's gone now – the era of funding. That's what makes things possible. What made it possible for me wasn't my role models like Courtney and O'Toole and Richard Burton, brilliant though they were, it was the fact that Durham County Council were willing to give me a grant of twelve pounds a week.

Thanks to social media and a few posts of mine, I had some new friends in the north. Their tweets and messages ping into my timelines over the weekend. Graeme Fenwick tells me that his 93-year-old next-door neighbour waved off the marchers as a little girl in a Jarrow street. Laura Perlmann remembers being hugely proud to play Ellen Wilkinson in her school play about the march. A few correspondents, like Peter Flannery, actually had relatives on the march. Joanne Hackett-Smith's granddad, John 'Smiler' Harney, wrote a poem about his experiences on the march that she says she'll send me a copy of. Iris Walls wrote:

> Hi Stuart, my uncles Edward Stead and Sammy Needham were two of the marchers. Sammy looked after the dog which joined the march and stayed with them right throughout the journey until back in Jarrow. Are you going to be at the Civic reception on 5 October at Jarrow Town Hall? It's only 60 or so yards from Christ Church. It starts at 12.30, Wednesday.

I wonder whether I should use my years of rock journalist expertise and savvy to 'blag' my way on the guest list. Perhaps not. I'm not on 'official business', nor am I 'Beefy' Botham stomping along mob-handed for charity. Nonetheless I jot down the time and venue in my brand-new Jarrow notebook specially purchased for the journey (with small concealed pen in the spine), place it with laptop, shoes, soapbag, maps, carefully rolled and folded shirts and trousers, phone, chargers, cables, replacement contact lenses and other assorted paraphernalia inside my rucksack. Noting with some satisfaction that I still have several litres to spare, I settle back as the train makes the long pull over Shap Fell from my soft north of silent mills and damp valleys into the high lonely north of sea and mountain and, once, of steel and ships.

PRE-AMBLE

There are some cities one never enters without a gladdening of the heart and a quickening of the pulse. Newcastle ranks high among them, possessing that dazzling alchemy of fine buildings and big, open water that always works a certain magic trick. Just as no man ever felt more glamorous or sophisticated than when rounding a corner in his water taxi motor boat with a wake of foam, turning onto the *Gran Canale* and seeing the *palazzos* of Venice or the bridges of Rialto or Accademia rise up before the prow, so (in a quite different way admittedly) it's always a palpable thrill to cross the Tyne by the high line over the King Edward VII bridge and see the best-looking city in England spread alluringly below me as the weekend begins.

The train is indubitably the best way to arrive. All the 'Toon's' most thrilling features crowd and elbow each other sideways to get into shot like those daft excitable kids you see behind sports reporters on TV. At the Ouseburn end there's the stately brick edifice of the Baltic Warehouse, now a fabulous art gallery, glowering grandly across at the huge, sleek, curvaceous silver snail of the Sage Concert Hall. In between is the posh apartment block whose two adjoining rooftop penthouse flats are owned – so a Geordie once told me – by local lads made good, Ant and Dec, which is probably far too cute to be true. The star of this particular show though, as always, is the Tyne itself and its various bridges – graceful and slender, muscular and imposing, funky, functional, old, new – each echoing its neighbour along the broad, silky muscle of the river.

In four days' time, my Jarrow march starts in earnest and I've arrived in the north east early to meet people, do some research, attend a couple of events, mull, acclimatise, buy plasters and toothpaste and generally do all the things that I'm sure I won't have time to after I stride optimistically out of Jarrow on Wednesday morning to spend the next month trekking the long miles to London. I breakfast at a busy greasy spoon tucked below the giant arches of the Tyne Bridge, built by Dorman Long of Middlesbrough in 1928; pure architectural Gotham in green metal and tensile steel. Two council workmen come in, paint spattered and chalky – that's their appearance, not their names – and proceed to put themselves efficiently and remorselessly outside two large breakfasts whilst gutting and filleting the morning's tabloids. They dispense swift, terse, unrepeatable judgements on Theresa May, global warming and Ken Bruce's PopMaster. I ask them if they have they heard of the Jarrow march. They tell me they know the song, and after some debate and rehearsal, proceed to sing me a challenging, atonal version of 'Fog on The Tyne' by Lindisfarne.

I head from the waterside to town proper up the steepening curve of Grey Street, the most elegant thoroughfare in England according to John Betjeman. I pop into Newcastle's finest department store Fenwick's for last minute supplies. Foot balm, a flat cap (a nod of solidarity to Jarrow's marchers), some new socks and some shaving oil. This being the modern world – and me wanting to keep people apprised as to my progress – I tweet a picture of my purchases. A trollish home counties dentist posts, 'If the Jarrow Marchers could see this, they would give you a righteous shoe-ing.' No they wouldn't, I tweet back, tetchily perhaps. This sort of stuff riles me though; the implication that one should 'know one's place' and that working-class people deserve no better than spittoons and scrag end. I attach to my reply my favourite quote from Nye Bevan when challenged about his love of lobster and champagne, 'Only the best for the working class'.

Once installed in my room, I go through a long-practised routine. Turn off the wall mounted TV with the boomingly loud dance music satellite channel the chambermaid had on, boot up the MacBook and log on (oh, the simple, unalloyed joy of hotels that don't require you to fill in an online questionnaire or decipher those weird hieroglyphics), turn down the aircon temperature (you can grow rubber in most British hotel rooms, and in those that you can't, you could cryogenically store Walt Disney). Then I start an afternoon of research. This begins with a dip into the labyrinthine depths of the BBC's fabled Redux website and archive.

The British Broadcasting Corporation was still a fledgling operation in 1936. It was gearing up to broadcast its first television programmes during the march, actually commencing them the day after the marchers reached London. Perhaps this is why the BBC appears to harbour such a crush on the Jarrow Crusade. This has shown itself through many documentaries, plays and features down the 80 years since. Looming large during the corporation's formative years, the march is now bound up in some way with what Hollywood would call the BBC's 'origin story'. The Jarrow Crusade fits well with the BBC's remit and ethos; national stories that emphasise consensus and moral example rather than conflict, dissent and entrenched interest. A more cynical take on this might be that Jarrow is the BBC's favourite protest because it was the meekest and most obliging to the powers that be.

Redux is one of the BBC's more secret services. When I was first tipped off about it, it was very much Auntie Beeb's Fight Club, in that the first rule of Redux seemed to be that you didn't talk about it. A verbal invite was whispered to me in a TV green room by a producer friend and after that I had to apply to join by writing to the shadowy cabal of technocrats who administer it. After a week or so, I received an anonymous email saying that I was in. I was elated. I felt like I'd been accepted into a more benign version of the Freemasons or a less metrosexual Groucho Club. The Magic Circle perhaps, or Big Chief I-Spy's Club.

Redux is an archive of BBC TV and Radio programmes. But what an archive. Invented by boffins in the BBC's hidden techno-lair at Hook Norton on a day off from the official corporation business of spreading communism and undermining decent British values, it is a vast, bottomless resource for nerds and pros. Firing up my laptop, I enter the search term 'Jarrow march' and look up the most recent result on the subject, a BBC TV documentary *The Road From Jarrow* on the march and its legacy dating from 1996.

It was with the most profound sinking of the heart that I make out, through the juddery visual tape hiss, the unmistakable features of presenter Sir Bernard Ingham, Margaret Thatcher's former press secretary and once ubiquitous bluff pontificator of the loony right. Much of my dismay rests on aesthetic considerations. Sir Bernard is a hard man to gaze comfortably upon for any length of time and such discomfort is only heightened by his belligerent, nasal 'Zippy from *Rainbow* on helium' vocal delivery. My other complaint is more substantive, however; namely that inviting a right-wing ideologue to author a piece on a leftist protest is perhaps not the best guarantee of fairness or accuracy. (A reader called David Walker tweeted me wryly about the choice of Ingham as presenter on the Jarrow march: 'Blimey, did he advocate using unidentifiable policemen on horseback to break it up?' – an Orgreave joke.) This perverse booking would seem a perfect illustration of a malaise of the modern media, that of 'false balance', the notion whereby kneejerk gainsaying is equated with truth. At least they just give Michael Portillo documentaries about old railway lines and steam engines.

Anyway, it's not long before Sir Bernard deviates from historical analysis into one of his trademark riffs of irascible windbaggery. 'Discipline has given way to indiscipline. Family, the one thing that sustained the Jarrow marchers, has gone to pot.' When Ellen Wilkinson is mentioned, it is through gritted teeth, and she is described as 'Fiery Helen' or 'Wee Ellen' when her nickname was universally 'Red Ellen', a designation that presumably stuck in Bernard's throat. It soon became very clear that not only was this rubbish, it was self-serving, ahistorical rubbish, although there were some good contributions from Peter Flannery and marcher Con Shiels. A few minutes though were enough to make me blithely unconcerned that the other two episodes of this have been wiped. I make another 'advanced' pass though the archive and happily I find a more recent and insightful looking radio documentary about the Jarrow march from 2008. Naturally, it is presented by Michael Portillo.

Despite the perverse choice of presenter once again, it is really very much better; more sociological, less opinionated, and in essence a consideration of why the Jarrow march lives on whilst the many hunger marches of the era have been forgotten. The documentary touches upon what would seem to me to be the obvious explanation; the men of Jarrow essentially came politely and with cap in hand, without the dangerous whiff of revolutionary sulphur of the older communist marches.

That night I walked in the dusk across Newcastle to one of its cultural and historical landmarks, the Literary and Philosophical Society. Newcastle is proud of the Lit and Phil and it's as much a part of the cultural fabric of the city as the Big Market, St James' Park or the Angel of the North, and rather older than any of them. Established in 1793, it is the largest private library outside London. It is where Joseph Swan first demonstrated the electric light bulb. It received Britain's first wombat and duck-billed platypus and notable current members include Alexander Armstrong and Neil Tennant. In the beginning, it was styled as a 'conversation club', albeit one in which discussion of religion and politics was strictly forbidden. That has since been relaxed and so there are no awkward moments or angry shushing tonight during Matt Perry's lecture on Ellen Wilkinson, of whom he has written a comprehensive biography. It's compelling stuff and Matt doesn't gloss over some of the anomalies of her career and mysteries of her life: though initially a staunch supporter of Indian liberation, when in government, she thought we should put the troublesome Gandhi in gaol, and of course there are the vague and cloudy circumstances of her sad premature death.

Matt kindly gives me a copy of his book and tells me I should visit the Jarrow Crusade eightieth anniversary exhibition at South Shields Museum that he's curated. We also make a tentative arrangement to meet at an event I am very much looking forward to, the tempting if queerly named Jarrow March Eightieth Anniversary Fun Day at Monkton Stadium in the town. How could anyone resist? Tombola, food, brass bands, stalls, activist fun and special guest star, one Jeremy Bernard Corbyn, MP for Islington, leader of Her Majesty's Opposition, the Labour Party, and saint or fool depending on your point of view. I tell Matt I'm looking forward to it.

Geordies are proud of their Metro transport system, and Jarrow particularly so as it was the brainchild and passion of Michael Campbell, the so-called Statesman of Jarrow, leader of Tyne and Wear council who managed to champion the project to completion at a time when Britain was in hock to its eyeballs and could barely keep the lights on. When work began in 1974 it was the biggest urban transport project Britain had attempted in the twentieth century. Tunnels were driven beneath the city's streets and viaducts thrown airily across the Tyne and Ouseburn valleys. It has always been non-smoking and wheelchair friendly and classical music was piped into stations to improve the 'passenger waiting environment'. It opened in the summer of 1980 to instant acclaim and popularity. When my Geordie mate Stod came back to college for the autumn term that year, he talked of little else.

The Metro's sixty stations are a potted history of British transport architecture from late Victorian at Tynemouth and art deco at West Monkseaton to the 1980s minimalism of Park Lane and Ilford Road. At South Shields station, a fruit and veg stall has blossomed under its brutalist steel girders which is a neat bit of civic adaptation. Having certainly got the rucksack capacity but not the desire for a few heads of cauliflower, I pass it by and head to the South Shields Museum and the Jarrow exhibition.

Celebrations of local culture are of variable entertainment value, as anyone who's ever broken their leg at a Gloucester cheese rolling or attended a potato picking festival in Kent can attest. But they seem ever more crucial as municipal Britain takes wave after wave of battering from central government. Despite grand speeches about 'devolving autonomy' and a 'northern powerhouse', we are the most centralised country in the Western world. Westminster has the nation's purse strings in a grip of iron and for every pound raised by tax, 91p is allocated by central government. Towns like South Shields and Jarrow have been hardest hit.

Put baldly, the north east is the poorest region in Britain. In an essay of December 2016 entitled 'The Strange Death of Municipal England', Tom Crewe states that, 'almost a billion pounds have been sucked out of its economy since 2010 [and] it has the highest percentage of deprived neighbourhoods in the country ... Newcastle City Council has reduced its budget by £221 million with another £100 million in cuts planned for the next two years. Leader Nick Forbes told the *Guardian*, "people went white ... at the prospect of it".' So this is a northern power house that cannot afford the electricity bill.

At South Shields Museum though, however embattled, there's a flutter of excitement among the staff as a film crew from the BBC's *Look North* magazine show are upstairs in the exhibition hall. 'I'm afraid that the museum is closed to the public at the moment,' says an earnest, diligent, young staff member. 'Ah, I see ...' and produce my BBC pass, always a useful thing to have in one's pocket, even if the picture makes one look like Alan Titchmarsh's idiot younger half-brother. I am waved through under false pretences which makes me feel rather a heel and so, once upstairs, I lurk outside the inner door until the filming is over.

The interviewees are Matt Perry (who's having a busy week) and Tom Kelly, a local writer and poet who along with Matt has been working with school kids in the town to produce some excellent, inspiring work about community and history. Matt is a boyish academic in mod casuals, Tom a genial silver-haired Geordie in a stripy jacket. Matt and Tom are hoping not just to keep alive the memory of the march but to use it as a springboard for all kinds of creative activities. A workshop in which:

> Pupils will examine archive material, photographs and personal accounts to bring the story to life as they think about the lives, hopes and feelings of the men, as well as thinking about the general morale and conditions. Afterwards, they will put themselves in the shoes of the marching men, to write either a poem, diary entry, song or newspaper article. The day can also include a session making banners, posters and badges.

It's easy to mock such well-intentioned efforts at educating kids about 'people's history'. But after one workshop, five kids came back and said they had found out that they had relatives, great-grandfathers and great uncles on the march and that it had made them feel 'ten feet tall', and had sparked long conversations between generations in the family. I remember grim, pointless field trips spent brass rubbing the tombs of long dead viscounts. Keeping the stories and culture and sacrifices of their granddads and grandmas alive for these kids is surely just as valid a way to spend a Tuesday afternoon.

In the exhibition, portraits and testimonies bring the marchers vividly to life. James Henry Walters hadn't worked since being gassed twenty years before at the front (62 per cent of the men were First World War veterans) and was keeping a wife and four children on 36 shillings a week. Touchingly, he commented, 'The march will be a success ... the country's behind us.' Philip McGhee was one of the lucky ones in that he had only been out of work two years when the march took place. There is a sweet picture of the oldest and youngest marchers: John Farndale who at 18 had worked two weeks since leaving school at 14 and Geordie Smith, 62 and a veteran of the Boer War. Framed on the wall is the original of John 'Smiler' Harney's poem (my correspondent Joanne's granddad), touching in its defiantly high spirits.

Playing on a continuous loop are the two brief fragments of surviving newsreel footage of the march; the men on their way to Darlington ('great sympathy for this orderly march' says the narrator, plummily) and their sodden final entry into London. The Metropolitan Police had originally tried to prevent all filming of the march fearing it would create too much sympathy for the men but in the end they grudgingly relented. Seeing Ellen and the tired, soaked phalanx on this grainy monochrome film, trudging across London in the dreary, pouring rain, water cascading from their antique sou'westers and capes, reminds me of just what I've got in store over the next month. I make a mental note to check the long-range weather forecast, through splayed fingers possibly.

The morning of the Fun Day though dawns bright and warm across the north east and, though I don't know it yet, it's a herald of a mercifully mild October to come. There is for sure a rich, easily mined irony in styling the commemoration of a hunger march as a 'Fun Day'. Wags across social media have clamoured to point this out when I mentioned the event. 'Relive those heady days of the Means Test and rickets with a go on the bouncy castle and a jumbo hot dog' and so on and so on. They have a point. I thought it was important that I was there though. I wanted to sense the mood of the community, I wanted to see how Labour's newly re-elected leader acquitted himself and I really like hot dogs, especially the al fresco variety.

Having initially been distinctly cool on the idea of the Jarrow march, not to say positively obstructive, the Labour Party, like the Beeb, have spent much of the intervening eight decades getting enthusiastically on board. The Jarrow memorial in the town (one of them anyway) has been unveiled not once but twice by successive leaders Michael Foot and Neil Kinnock, both seeking glory by association and presumably glossing over the lack of party support back in the day. Carrying on in this vein, the Labour ruling executive of 2016, unlike that of 1936, are keen to express their solidarity with the sacralised memory of the march. So much so that they have sent their top man up from London for the job, rather like the dispatching of Michael Caine in *Get Carter* except hopefully without anyone getting pushed off a multi storey car park or shot and dumped in a massive coal scuttle

The Jarrow Fun Day on 1 October 2016 is the first public appearance of Jeremy Corbyn since being re-elected as leader of the Labour Party with an increased majority a week earlier; which is a sentence that no sane person could have envisaged reading or writing before 12 September 2015. Though an MP for over 30 years, he had never held any position of authority or responsibility and during the party's 13 years in power, when he might have been expected to help with the business of government, Corbyn voted against the whip 428 times – more than any other Labour MP. Then he was regarded, as one unnamed Labour insider told the *New Yorker*, as 'a quaint irrelevance'. His relevance may be arguable but his quaintness is not. In a paroxysm of either stupidity or optimism depending on one's point of view, Labour introduced a system whereby three quid bought you a vote in their leadership election. Corbyn was washed to power on this unleashed tide of activism, and some mutterings of chicanery.

Many of those who'd been vaguely aware of him as a bearded antediluvian spear-carrier of Labour's London left have been baffled, not to say appalled, by Corbyn's ascent. Not just by his rise to power – stranger things have happened in Westminster – but his elevation to Che Guevara style counter-cultural icon among some young and not so young. (I gave the piece I wrote for the *New Statesman* on the Fun Day the title JC Un Rock Star but they didn't use the headline, perhaps unfamiliar with Bill Wyman's solo hits.) Corbyn is a phenomenon that seemed to have disappeared along with Benny Hill, Red Wedge and student union bars named after Steve Biko. He's a variety of political animal most thought had become extinct, a Spartist dinosaur reeking of hummus and hemp and definitely not the smoky fires of industry.

As a Corbyn agnostic with a strong disposition towards downright atheism, I wanted to see how the north east took to the new Messiah. Over his first year in the job, I'd found him weak and disengaged, especially on issues close to the heart of the working-class north. He had been almost silent on Orgreave and Hillsborough; both emotive events back powerfully in the news. Conversely, you couldn't shut him up on the Middle East and Arab–Israeli matters, and believe me I had wanted to.

There was another flavouring in the mix. Tony Blair was the longstanding MP for nearby Sedgefield. Many in the north east still regard him as one of their own and had never enjoined with the now prevalent view of him as slick warmonger. The New Labour love-in of 1997 now makes some rather embarrassed. Power corrupts, but it also makes others uncomfortable, particularly those who'd prefer a state of continual carping but largely impotent opposition. There was much muddled and dubious logic surrounding the Iraq war. But Professor Peter Clarke, author of the *Locomotive of War* put it well when he told *BBC History* magazine, 'Blair took a very moral view of why the British and Americans should invade Iraq. Something he had reason to rue afterwards but even if it was a terrible mistake, we should not doubt his sincerity'. Many brilliant voices of the secular left – Christopher Hitchens most famously – thought that, in essence, it was a just war. Also it seemed to me that in the revisionist rush to excoriate Blair and his legacy, we had forgotten SureStart schemes for working-class families, the now-abolished AIM education grants that supported many poor ethnic minority students, the introduction of the minimum wage and many other achievements which no one should be ashamed about.

In this conflicted, sceptical state of mind, I make my way through the sunny, pleasant suburban streets of South Tyneside between Hebburn and Jarrow to Monkton Stadium. Along Dene Terrace, the houses and gardens are well kept, the streets clean, the people busy. Eighty years ago, when the last-minute arrangements for the near military planning of the Jarrow march were taking place here, Dene Terrace would have looked and felt very different. The faces thinner, the streets grimier and the houses grimmer. Monkton Stadium wouldn't have been here either, since this fine local landmark and resource was built as a direct result of the Jarrow march. In June 1937, unemployed men from the area (including some marchers) rebuilt a derelict sports ground with money from the Surrey Fund, established after the Jarrow march by Sir John Jarvis, MP for South Shields. In the years since it's become one of the crucibles of north-eastern athletics and distance running, training ground of Steve Cram, David Stephens and more.

When I arrive at the gate to pick up my wristband from councillor Audrey, I am told, a little breathlessly, that 'he' is already here: 'We gave him a dinner at the Lakeside pub last night. I think he enjoyed it.' Inside, there's a low-level buzz of activity. As well as the usual Fun Day stalwarts – stalls selling smelly soaps and wonky home-made craft items, the aromatic burger van and the little kids serenely orbiting in giant teacups – there's a tangible if cordial political dimension and presence; trade union groups hoping to save the local hospital, a lively contingent of ladies from Women Against State Pension Inequality dressed as suffragettes. Various local politicians are waiting for their chance at the mike, but they all know that they are the support act. The star here is slightly younger than Mick Jagger and has become a slightly odder kind of rock star politician.

The stands are full-ish of Jarrow and Hebburn families. Many have the names of a Jarrow marcher on small placards that they wave. Congratulating myself on recognising her from her tiny Twitter profile photo, I spot '@JoHack', or Joanne Hackett-Smith, one of the first people to contact me when I 'reached out' (in the modish parlance) for people with Jarrow march stories. Jo is smart, blonde, 30-something and rightly proud of her march associations. She's a civil servant, a local girl, and her great-grandfather ('Granda' as Geordies have it) was John 'Smiler' Harney whose sweet poem is in the South Shields exhibition. He lived in Lime Street Jarrow with wife Eleanor and was father to ten children, though only eight survived (at the time of the march, Jarrow had one of the worst infant mortality rates in Britain).

When Smiler reached London, he met a woman who said she could offer his family work, particularly his daughter who could clean for her. He continued to write to the woman and he eventually received a fancy coat in the post. She said if his daughter wore the coat and travelled to London, she would hire her as a live-in housekeeper. 'This was a bribe I suppose,' reflects Jo.

'So he sent Florrie, my granny, aged 13 to London on the train alone. She arrived at a posh house in London where the lady of the house was a doctor's wife. They had one child and the mother didn't work. She was awful to my grannie apparently; she had to scrub all the floors before she would feed her on a morning. She was also made to eat alone, with no interaction with the family whatsoever and she could only use the tissue paper from oranges for the toilet.'

Florrie was desperately unhappy, but didn't dare tell her father John because she knew the family back in Jarrow needed the money. Such experiences were not uncommon. Many young, working-class girls from industrial Cumbria, Lancashire, the north east and Wales were sent down into domestic service with well-to-do London families that was effectively little more than slavery and certainly not as benign as the world of *Upstairs Downstairs* or *Downtown Abbey*. Eventually, one day, some old Jarrow friends also in service in London called for Florrie and the doctor's wife refused to let her leave the house, demanding she went to her room. 'Imagine the anxiety and fear of a 13-year-old girl being controlled by a complete stranger,' says Jo.

The Jarrow girls went to the local bobby on the beat and explained the situation. By happy coincidence, he was from Sunderland. He went to the house and demanded Florrie come to the door with her suitcase packed. Florrie went home to Jarrow and lived into her nineties. 'But granny always said she was "sold down the river for a bliddy coat!"' remembers Jo. We could have talked much more, but at this point I had to take my leave of Jo as, with a discernible rustle of excitement, the Fun Day's main attraction was passing beardedly amongst us.

While it would be wrong to say that Corbyn's presence created the same scenes of unhinged mania that might attend the arrival of Beyoncé, or Barack Obama or one of the judges on *Strictly Come Dancing*, there was a definite buzz in the air. As he was led around the grassy enclosure, patiently and amiably nodding as various things were pointed out to him, a small but intense knot of admirers tailed him closely. I fell into their wake and together we circumnavigated the arena like a clump of drifting frog spawn.

If I was expecting dazzling bon mots, Bevanesque oratory or high wattage charm, I was to be disappointed. His visible mood as he was corralled into several selfies was that of a man who would much rather have been at a polytechnic sit-in or an airless council chamber in Haringey debating sanctions against South Africa, both of which I imagined he did enthusiastically 'back in the day'. Eventually, with a flourish by the brass band, activities proper commenced.

The host of the event was a local TV anchorman who was well known to the crowd, and by far the best dressed of the various people to take the stage that day. His daughter, a budding pop chanteuse, also provided some musical entertainment, although the song she sang was one of those enervating John Lewis advert ballads rather than 'The Red Flag' or an inspiring anthem about Soviet steel production, both of which I'd have enjoyed more.

Jarrow's MP Stephen Hepburn gave a doughty and on-message speech by way of introduction to the Labour leader which was as much about JC (Jeremy Corbyn) as JC (Jarrow Crusade). This reached a weirdly obsequious climax as he evokes the trials of the marching men. 'Had he been at the side of the road when those marchers passed by, Jeremy would have shared his sandwiches with them,' he says, and at least one audience member found the faintly Christ-like tone of this eulogy somewhat creepy.

The *New Yorker* compared Corbyn to Chauncey Gardiner, the simple-minded gardener embraced as a guru in Peter Sellers's *Being There*. But soon after the man himself takes the mike it becomes very clear to me that JC is not so much Chauncey or that other JC (Jesus Christ) as JP (John Peel), the late radio presenter and alternative music guru. The two men have many things in common. They share a physiognomy; both bearded, softly spoken, mildly drony. Both were educated at private school in Shrewsbury and acquired greatest affection and fame in middle age. But there's more than that. JC and JP deftly cultivated images as principled mavericks and saintly rebels despite long, comfortable careers in two of the cosiest berths in the British Establishment – the BBC and the Labour Party. All the while though, they presented to the world a much-admired resistance to being sucked into the mainstream, even whilst being at its very heart. (There are few places more mainstream or 'Establishment' than the Palace of Westminster or the *Top of The Pops* studio.)

Both exhibit(ed) a haughty disdain for the shallower, slicker elements and personalities of their chosen worlds. Peel routinely made sport of people like Tony Blackburn, a genuine soul fan who did more to promote black music on BBC radio than anyone else in his era, and the admittedly sickly/sinister Bates/ Edmonds axis at 'wonderful Radio One'. In Corbyn's case, he has billed himself as polar opposite and antidote to the stage-managed spin machinery of New Labour, Blair and Alastair Campbell. By hiding their not inconsiderable egos behind a gentle wooliness, Corbyn and Peel are 'National Treasures' for the kind of liberal who bridles at the idea of national treasures, considering them painfully 'little Englander' and celebrated by the likes of the *Daily Express*. My grumbling discontent (occasionally flaring into incandescent rage) with Corbyn is that it is not his beard, allotment or even politics that make him the polar opposite of Blairism but his electability. (As I write this, his poll ratings are miserable, though admittedly the last year has taught us to be wary of the pollster.)

JC's speech was cogent and thoughtful if short on emotional fireworks. He gave a genuinely fine tribute to 'Red Ellen' whilst brandishing a well-thumbed first edition of *The Town That Was Murdered* from the Left Book Club. He went down well of course; this is Labour's heartland and these people are loyal. In private, a few I spoke to were downbeat about his electoral clout and competence but others said that they found him fresh and inspirational. I acquired a coffee and a bag of donuts and decided to listen to the other speeches before going back to the hotel to pack.

Next up was an executive of public service union Unison who'd come straight from central casting circa 1984 with a strident, staccato delivery and a range of 'off the peg' agitprop ('and let us be clear that we say as a movement to THIS Tory government'). There followed a smooth LibDem, then a pleasant lady from the Greens whose lengthy factual re-telling of the march read from a piece of paper was lovely whilst smacking of an earnest school project ('This term we have been studying the Jarrow Crusade which took place in October 1936 ...'). Funniest by far was the nonagenarian Conservative candidate who sat on a folding chair beaming and said, 'I am from Jarrow and I live in Jarrow and naturally I haven't agreed with a thing I've heard here today ...'

I watched as Jeremy was hustled very gently into the changing rooms and I assume out to a waiting car, since I didn't think even a cyclist of his commitment could have come on his folding Brompton. The week before, his share of the Labour members, vote grew to 68 per cent. A huge influx of new members have made Labour the biggest political party in Western Europe. All this proves to some that he is destined to be our next Prime Minister. As many have pointed out, however, this is rather akin to saying that Liverpool will win the Premier League because the Kop want them to. As I set off for my three-hundred-mile trek to London, Downing Street seemed a long way off for me and JC.

STAGE ONE

JARROW TO CHESTER-LE-STREET

5 October, 12 miles

We are a nation besotted with statuary. Latterly, our near immediate response to the passing of a beloved celebrity is to demand a disturbing, generally unrecognisable facsimile of them somewhere of local significance; Eric Morecambe leaping like a salmon on that town's seafront, Harold Wilson pipeless outside Huddersfield station, the John Lennon with the tiny body and alarmingly large head outside the Cavern, Liverpool. At the time of writing there are campaigns to erect statues of Victoria Wood in Bury, various suffragettes outside Parliament and David Bowie in Brixton, Bromley and seemingly everywhere he ever booked into a Travelodge for the night. There was briefly a campaign to commission a 300-feet-high golden statue of former Dr Feelgood singer Lee Brilleaux in Southend which sadly failed.

For every 'controversial' abstract bronze on the windswept piazza of a new town, or geometric fibreglass scalene triangle in front of a Midlands police station that creates local kerfuffle, there are thousands of silent sentinels that we bypass every day without a thought. And, ignoring the occasional celebrated Peter Pan or Sherlock Holmes, most of these stolid figures are the sons of empire; straight-backed, moustachioed, mercantile, magisterial, military and nearly always men (only 2.7 per cent of

British figurative statues are women and they are mostly either allegorical, royal or nude).

The statue of Sir Charles Mark Palmer on the main street in Jarrow leaves you in little doubt as to who once bossed this town like a personal fiefdom. He stands above the main street puffed and proprietorial, gazing out over the hard little town. Below his feet is a lengthy, boastful CV graven into the stone: 'Sir C Mark Palmer, baronet, born South Shields, November 3rd 1822. Founder of the Palmer works and of the town of Jarrow of which he was the first mayor in 1875 ... originator of the first steam screw ... Member of Parliament for North Durham ... this statue erected in 1903 by the workmen of Palmer's company and a few friends commemorates a life devoted to the social advancement of the working classes, the prosperity of Jarrow and the industrial progress of Tyneside ...' Whether the working classes of Jarrow would still have coughed up for a statue to Sir Charles 30 years later is very much open to debate.

The Jarrow marchers have their own memorials of course, scattered around their home town; a crude and often vandalised mosaic in a grim underpass, a bronze of Red Ellen at the head of a group of men in Morrison's car park. (At its unveiling, surviving marcher Con Whalen was persuaded to wear a Morrison's badge for the pictures.) There's a stark metal silhouette of marching men at Jarrow Metro station too. But while these form part of the everyday street furniture of the area, none is as grandly prominent in Jarrow as Sir Charles surveying what once was very definitely his domain. Everywhere in the town are shades and echoes of his marshalling of the long defunct yards; Palmer Street, the Palmer Hospital, the Palmer Nursing Home, even the Palmer's Tavern pub.

I was last in Jarrow a decade ago, researching an earlier book called *Pies and Prejudice*. I was, I hope, honest and fair but what I wrote was no puff piece or tourist blurb and I've always thought that the least I could do was come back and explore again. A passing Jarrovian in the street reminds me of my earlier visit. He passes by with a wry, not unfriendly smile, a handshake and a swift nod. 'I hope you like it a bit more than last time, Stuart'. And I do. There is still the faint echo of neglect and decline, of hard times being resisted and there is none of the easy, comfortable atmosphere of content that I'll increasingly find as I travel south. But there's life here and people going about their business on a glorious October morning and no sense of a town cowed or beaten. There are, however, signs of Britain's remorseless and bizarre 'hipsterfication', something else I'll see much of on my journey. Jarrow now boasts retro emporiums where a fellow about town can get his tache waxed and his beard mascara'd. You can buy cupcakes and smoothies. Most noticeable of all for me is the transformation (from the exterior at least) of the pub that so unnerved me last time. The Jarrow Crusaders then was a dark, forbidding cave of gassy, pissy lagers, giant booming TVs and clanking fruit machines where everyone stopped talking, *Slaughtered Lamb* style, when I entered. Now it's McConnell's Gin And Ale House and has wood panelling, posh spirits and micro-brews. Who knows? It may still be a place a chap could get a thick ear but at least he could enjoy a chilled Masons Dry Gin (distilled from a small copper alembic still) whilst acquiring it.

It was the early hour rather than nervousness that stopped me popping in. And I was distracted by the appearance on the street corner of a man in a blue serge boiler suit carrying a large tray of sandwiches augmented by what may well have been vol-au-vents and bound for the side entrance of the town hall. This I took as a cue that the Jarrow eightieth anniversary civic reception was about to begin. A local and well-connected contact of mine (who shall be nameless) had tried to wangle me an invite to this event but had encountered stubborn resistance among the local council to 'journalist types'. I wasn't slighted by this at all but I did find it a little strange. From the embedded journalists of 1936 through BBC documentaries through various anniversary pieces, the press treatment of Jarrow's march has never been less than positive. In fact, one might even say, sentimentalised and gushing. So exactly what scandalous and profligate fillings were in those sandwiches. Caviar? Songbirds? Cruel and exorbitant pâtés from endangered species? Just what had they got to hide at that buffet?

Denied entry I may have been, but there was little chance of me starving to death in Jarrow. You would have to be extremely poor or painfully shy for this to occur. Little greasy spoons, prim cafés, pizza outlets, pie shops, chippies and cake shops abound. Rosie's Café. Hetty's Tea Room. Even butcher David C Hodgson ('purveyor of quality meats') will wipe his bloodied hands on his apron and seat you in the window by the hanging sides of beef for a 'delicious Saveloy, pease pudding and stuffing – £1.40' or a 'Full House Bellybuster – £2.95'. Pavement and café society is alive and well in 'Jarra' on a Wednesday mid-morning.

I plumped for beans on toast in Rosie's where, above the sizzle of bacon, the local radio news bulletin was reporting on yesterday's speech by recently installed PM Theresa May, asserting that the Tories were now 'the party of workers', occupying the centre ground vacated by Corbyn's Labour Party. Next was an item on Home Secretary Amber Rudd's proposal to force companies to disclose how many foreign workers they employ, which some business leaders called 'divisive and damaging'. Then it was back to the DJ who was trying to get a phone-in item going on what people thought was the most inspirational sandwich filling. I checked the website of the *South Shields Gazette* where a nice young journalist had written up an interview with me alongside a report on the Fun Day. Against all common sense, I broke an iron habit and dipped 'below the line' into the comments section where the dark things lurk. There was nothing nasty there – this is the north east after all – but one contributor, writing under the name 'Old News', reminded me that many are waiting at the keyboard to grind their personal axe.

There is no comparison between the desperate lives that our ancestors endured in the 1920s and 30s and today's luxury. They had NOTHING – but now even sanctioned lazybones STILL get state and voluntary aid despite being undeserving. So much so that today's Britain has been stupid enough to lavish money and houses even on to 3m workshy foreigners. The poor souls shown above got on with life after their march. Only the Labour Party seeks to profit from their poverty now.

On the way up the street I paused to look in Blackberry Estates's window to check local house prices. A three-bed new build semi is on offer for £110,000 billed as a 'must view', 'perfect for first time buyer, no chain'. Very different from the vertiginous London prices often in the news. But then, as I was going to find, I was a long way from London. I stopped off in Boots to buy some spare batteries and paracetamol and headed up to Christ Church for my 10.30 ceremonial start.

When you consider the loathing and contempt their local bishop held them in, starting the Jarrow march in an Anglican church with a service and a blessing, might seem odd, grovelling even. Though a man of the cloth, Hensley Henson, Bishop of Durham, is one of the undisputed villains of the Jarrow mythos. This pillar of the Establishment and virulently anti-socialist member of the Lords regarded the marchers as a revolutionary mob and condemned several fellow bishops and clergymen for their warmth towards Jarrow and its plight and their 'foolish utterances'. In Jarrow, his condemnation of the march is well known and well remembered.

But then this was a 'crusade', and keen to be seen as such rather than a hunger march or anything similarly inflammatory. The mayor had wanted a minister with a crucifix to lead the march from the front but none willing could be found, which with the benefit of hindsight seems a good thing. Still the pews of the church were crammed with marchers and their wives plus various dignitaries resplendent in their chains of office, wigs and gowns and the clergy of all Jarrow's denominations; C of E, Catholic, Baptist and Presbyterian. From the pulpit, the men were encouraged not to 'drink the wine of violence' en route. They were then blessed by one of the many clergymen present and sent on their historic way to the rousing strains of 'Onward Goes the Pilgrim Band'.

Eighty years later the church is locked and barred so I can't even get in to see the little plaque commemorating the march. There's no signs of life, just a faded cardboard sign for the day nursery and toddler group in a grimy window of an outbuilding at the rear. An elderly lady passes with her dog which sniffs me listlessly, closely followed by a young Romanian mum with a buggy who tells me that the church doesn't open today. Maybe they'll do something special here for the hundredth anniversary, I hope. When I'd been planning my trip, I'd regularly been asked if I was having any kind of send-off or whether anyone would be walking with me. No, I'd answer, perhaps a little piously. This wasn't a sponsored walk or high-publicity charity event. It was research, exploration, discovery with maybe a little adventure along the way. I didn't want any hubristic palaver at the start. But as I stood alone in the deserted back street, the young mum, the old lady and the listless terrier all long gone, I couldn't help thinking that maybe just a tiny bit of palaver would have been nice.

The start of the original march had palaver galore. Almost the whole town turned out to see them off, police forcing crowds back behind cordons on to the pavement. Those lucky few townsfolk who had jobs and watched from their office or factory windows were reprimanded and told to get back to work. For the first time in years, the public gallery of the local court, usually a popular source of warmth and diversion for the unemployed, was empty. A thousand men had applied to be marchers and the round number of 200 were chosen, as well as the Mayor of Jarrow, three councillors, two journalists to record the journey and two supportive medical students to check health and administer any first aid. A second-hand bus was purchased for £20 and converted for their needs. This would go ahead with supplies, cooking gear, sleeping kit and sundries. Every man was provided with waterproofs, 1s 6d. pocket-money and two 1d. stamps a week. Sam Rowan was detailed as 'mail man', collecting and sending post for and from the men in every town (this was an England of four cheap postal deliveries a day where an invite to lunch could be sent at breakfast).

Outside the church, after the service, Mayor Thompson inspected the men. Seven of the original cohort had dropped out, most because of ill health or family pressure, with one fortunate chap having found a job. Substitutes were found quickly though including two neighbours, Bob Burns and Billy Beattie of Morpeth Avenue. Billy's wife was out so he left a note on the mantelpiece saying he'd set off for London and would see her in a month. Nowadays of course he'd text her, Facetime her or leave a post on her Facebook wall. Mine and Billy's Englands are similar in many ways, but only if you discount the astounding advances in everyday technology. I'd be helped in my journey by strange new forces; Google maps, Spotify, YouTube, Dark Sky Weather apps, Uber and Twitter. I was keen to feel resonances of 1936 and so I donned the flat cap I'd bought in Fenwicks and, with a nod to the marchers' mouth organ band, put Vaughan Williams's 'Romance for Harmonica and Orchestra' on my headphones as I left the little houses and narrow streets of Jarrow behind me.

Unexpectedly, the first few miles are lovely. You might even call them leafy. Very soon out of Jarrow a green walkway leads me away from town through Campbell Park, a verdant tract reclaimed for the community from what was once called 'the Crusher', a huge slag heap resulting from smelting iron ore at the Palmer's shipyard. An information board has an aerial shot from the time of the march which shows a vast, scarred muddied tract of prefabricated buildings and hulking machines. Now, in the caption's words, it has 'returned to field' and on this sparkling morning, the sound is that of coal tits and blackbirds rather than grinding and crushing.

I've given myself a few rules for the trip. As said, I will begin and end every day/stage in the same towns they did. I'll walk as much as I can but if a meeting or adventure suggests itself I'll buy time by hopping on a bus for a while as long as it covers the route of the march. I've decided that as I walk, if I can find a pleasanter path than the verges of a busy road I'll take it, provided it runs at least alongside their route. So I walk along the Bowes Railway Path, following the track of the old Bowes line, built by George Stephenson in 1826 to shift coal from the Durham pits to the River Tyne. When the marchers passed by, it was a busy, noisy and viable line and they'd have seen and heard the comings and goings of smoking and laden engines. Now it is part of our post-industrial heritage culture, quietened and retired into a long gentle walking and cycling route.

Springwell Bank is the village and cutting where the marchers made their first stop for lunch on that first day. They arrived by one o'clock to the cheerful light tenor of Councillor Gordon, 'the singing councillor'. They drank a couple of gallons of tea and ate corned beef sandwiches that involved forty pounds of corned beef and fifty loaves; this was a trip requiring military logistics. I stop, sit on a tree stump and try to catch the radio news on my phone, wondering about the social and political context of my trek compared to theirs. I catch the end of a radio magazine show and hear two items; one is about the current craze for spriralising vegetables, the other is about the protocols of group chat on WhatsApp.

I stomp the Bowes Railway Path for several more congenial miles through which, if you ignore the distant thrum of the A1(M) and the Sunderland Road, you get a real sense of how beyond the big population centres, 'the great north' is vast and wild and empty. Eventually this enormous silence and emptiness of green moors and distant hills gives way to the urban edge of Sunderland. This is the land of the Mackems, the nickname supposedly reflecting their manufacturing heritage and gift to the world, as in 'we mak'em and they tak'em'. This was a name given in Sunderland's heyday of mining, shipbuilding and glass – all gone now of course, but the city has seen massive regeneration in recent decades. Nissan came here famously and reset the region's economy. Danish mechanical engineers Grundfos and various service industries have relocated at Doxford International business park.

I walk though Crowther Industrial Park between the large striplit units of Schiedel Chimney Systems and Ronbar Flexible Conduits and Accessories, emerging onto the main road from a subway and into the prim bungalows and mock Palladian columns of Picktree suburb. Somewhere around here, 80 years ago today, borrowing a football from schoolkids who'd bunked off to greet them, 40 or so of the marchers played football in the street. The north east was and is football mad and was once a hotbed of British football talent, even if the area's giants are snoozing a little too soundly for local satisfaction these days. A prominent sign advises that I am entering into County Durham or 'Land of The Prince Bishops'. The Prince Bishops were a ruling class of noble clergymen of the fourteenth century onwards, but they always sound to me like a sixties beat group with bowl haircuts, white sports jackets and winklepickers.

After another hour down the roaring road, I finally enter Chester-le-Street as the sun drops low and slants blindingly across the quiet town. I'm about an hour ahead of the marchers. They arrived at 5pm to be met by local councillor Mr Robson and the women's section of the local Labour Party, who came to greet them with bread and jam. Marcher Sam Rowan said later that he would 'remember to his dying day' that he'd 'never seen men so disappointed in their lives'– presumably at a second round of sandwiches. Ungrateful perhaps, but then these men were tired and hungry and the contrast with the exultant send-off from home must have been marked. Was Chester-le-Street jealous or grudging of its local rival's new fame? Certainly some of the most generous and sympathetic receptions the Crusade would receive were in places you would least expect it; Yorkshire's Tory strongholds and comfortable southern villages.

Though the men felt their reception here was 'cheerless' and 'ambivalent', pushed and 'packed like sardines' into the tiny parish hall for their supper, the *Shields Gazette* put a distinctly upbeat spin on proceedings, mindful of the effect on morale amongst families back in Jarrow. Chester-le-Street's own weekly paper though, the *Chronicle and District Advertiser*, only found room a week later for a brief mention of the marchers in the 'We Know' column, buried amidst Mothers' Union meetings, exam results, the Dean of Peterborough's visit and an in-depth investigative report on the trade in stolen leeks from local agricultural shows. (This apparently silly story had a serious dimension. Allotments were a vital source of food that unemployed men could feed their families with and, as writer Arthur Barton put it, provided 'a refuge where he could get away from the accusing faces of his children and his wife's incessant 'will ye now work again?'') Regardless of Bernard Ingham's homilies, the truth is poverty divides and wounds families and communities, rather than bind or strengthen them.

I enter Chester-le-Street slowly, footsore, squinting, my flat cap pulled down over my eyes against the glare of a brilliant dusk. I fancy I cut rather a dash; a Clint Eastwood-esque man of mystery, making curtains twitch and causing owners to pull down the shutters and spin the signs to 'Closed' in Lloyds Pharmacy, G W Horner's general store and Bridge End Kebabs and Burgers. My first day's march is over and I'm ready for something long and cold. There's a café open on the square and I stride in as they are wiping down the tables and upending the chairs. Sensing my disappointment, the two ladies say they can stay open for a few minutes more (and a few dollars, well, quid more) and I take a seat. One lady brings my order and I launch into an explanation that I hope will prove an overture to an informative and wide-ranging chat.

'I'm a bit hot and thirsty, you see, because I've walked from Jarrow. I'm retracing the Jarrow march. The Jarrow march!'

'Oh have you? Very good. That'll be £2.65 please. I'll be locking up in ten minutes.'

Deflated, I take a long draught of my mango and apple crushed fruit cooler, something that neither The Man With No Name or The Jarra Lads would have ordered I'm sure. But at least I'm on my way.

STAGE TWO
CHESTER-LE-STREET TO FERRYHILL

6 October, 12 miles

Immediately the Jarrow march reached Chester-le-Street on 6 October 1936, Ellen Wilkinson headed north to Edinburgh for the Labour Party Conference which opened that day. In this bald statement is a very striking illustration of one difference between then and now. In the new, devolved UK and particularly since the election of 2010, Scottish Labour could probably hold its conference in a small branch of the Edinburgh Woollen Mill outlet and not unduly inconvenience any customers.

Writing three years later, in *The Town That Was Murdered*, Wilkinson's burning frustration with her 'comrades' in the party still smouldered.

> It was a queer experience, that Labour party conference in Edinburgh in 1936 ... Having got the men well started on their road I dashed to Edinburgh for a couple of days for the unemployment and distressed area debates ... I went from the warm comradeship of the road to an atmosphere of official disapproval. The Trades Union Congress had frowned on the march and the Labour party followed the lead.

There were other good reasons for Ellen to make sure her voice was heard at conference. High on the agenda for debate was the worrying rise of the far right both here and abroad. In Spain, Franco's Fascists were waging war on the democratically elected government and their own people, helped by Hitler. Closer to home, the very day before the Jarrow Crusade set out, Oswald Mosley's Blackshirts, or British Union of Fascists as they were officially known, had attempted to march through predominantly Jewish areas of London's working-class East End and been beaten back by anti-fascist demonstrators, socialists, Irish republicans, Jewish groups and ordinary Londoners in what would become known as the Battle of Cable Street.

According to the *News Chronicle*, 'the greatest East End crowd in living memory – some estimates say 300,000 – awaited the Fascists.' This huge and diverse contingent faced the Blackshirts with a chant of 'They shall not pass', a deliberate echo of the *No Pasaran* battle cry of the Spanish Republicans. All police leave was cancelled and 6,000 foot and mounted police were assembled to escort the 2,000 Blackshirts, at least until the full force of the opposition was known. Tram drivers parked their vehicles across Aldgate to block the Fascists' intended route. Off-duty seamen opened their storage sheds and turned lorries on their side to form barricades. Women flung the contents of chamber pots over the Mosleyites from upstairs windows. Eventually persuaded to abandon their route through Jewish areas, Mosley's crew were escorted by police through deserted back streets. Later Mosley complained that, 'it was the first occasion in which the British government has surrendered to the Red Terror.'

Wilkinson though did not arrive in Edinburgh in time for the conference's morning debate. At it, her secret lover Herbert Morrison (grandfather of Peter Mandelson) condemned the anti-fascist contingent and praised the police, in the same spirit which had seen the parliamentary Labour Party wash its hands of the Jarrow marchers. Morrison and Red Ellen were certainly unlikely paramours, which tells one something about the capricious workings of the human heart as well perhaps as other organs.

Minus Ellen, the marchers were up and off from Chester-le-Street by 7.30am after what seems a fairly cheerless and uncomfortable night on the cold floor of the church institute. I was up bright, if not quite this early, and over a cappuccino in Mr Pickwick's café (random Dickensian posters, brisk mid-morning trade of chatty oldsters) I looked at the news pages of 6 October 2016. Unlike the BUF, the modern British far right were keener on breaking their own heads than that of their enemies. Nigel Farage, a strangely ubiquitous media figure for a man who has failed seven times to be elected to parliament, had once again taken control of the chaotic UK Independence Party following a punch-up in the Strasbourg council chamber which had left MEP Steven Woolfe in hospital needing a brain scan. His alleged assailant, a fellow UKIP MEP, later described the incident as 'handbags'. Wolfe replied that the party was 'ungovernable' and in a 'death spiral'. Elsewhere, more literally and more tragically, a hundred people were killed in a hurricane in Haiti.

I checked my texts, tweets and emails and there was encouraging stuff from friends and strangers alike. My old mate Andrew Collins pointed out that as I was doing this for a book, I was following very much in the Jarrow men's footsteps; a northerner walking to London and hoping to get some work out of it. Other contributors suggested good places to get 'bait' if I was 'clamming' at various pubs and cafés here and in Ferryhill, today's final destination. Strolling through Chester-le-Street as noon approached, I summoned the effort of will required to forgo the tempting if dyspeptic offer advertised in a pub window. 'Pint of Crushed Berries Bulmers served in a glass with ice, cheese burger, chips, onion rings and our home-made coleslaw, all for £7.95.' In the same glass, I wondered?

Today's stage, 12 miles from Chester-le-Street to Ferryhill, would take me through a series of evocative-sounding places.

There was the curiously named Pity Me, lonely and harsh-sounding Framwellgate Moor and Neville's Cross, the site of a famously vicious battle between the English and the Scots. Soon out of Chester-le-Street, the original marchers had discovered two stowaways, a couple of 14-year-old lads from Hebburn who were put on the next bus back home but whose tale inspired the kids' book about Clogger that found its way onto the national curriculum. It took the marchers a while to notice them among the throng, certainly longer than it would have taken me to spot extra companions as I walked alone through County Durham. My spirits were high though. A tweet from a correspondent called Anne Graham said that she would look out for me as I passed through Pity Me and, even if she missed me, I should call in at Taylor's the butcher for 'the best pork pie in the north east'. Surely this was a claim no red-blooded, mildly peckish northerner could ignore. I narrowed my eyes, scanned the horizon and paced another mile or three of long, straight road.

Neither Pity Me nor Framwellgate Moor are as forlorn or desolate as their names suggest. They meld into one; two long, straggly urban villages clinging to the sides of the major road from Newcastle to Darlington. According to the Oxford Dictionary of British Place Names, there are various theories on the origin of Pity Me. It may indeed be 'a whimsical name bestowed in the nineteenth century on a place considered desolate, exposed or difficult to cultivate'. Or it may be an anglicisation of the Norman *Petit Mere*, a small or shallow lake. Most wild and romantic are the folk tales that say the coffin of St Cuthbert was dropped near here en route to Durham, at which point the saint implored the monks carrying him to take pity on him and be more careful (which must have come as a surprise), or that a group of monks, who were similarly surprised to encounter some raiding Vikings, sang the fifty-first psalm, 'Miserere mei, Deus' or 'Pity me, O God'.

Nothing so rum befell me as I made my way along the parade of shops that form a kind of retail border land between the two villages. In a consecutive run come the Ebony Salon, Look Lush Lucy's Nailbar and Terry's Barber Shop. In 1936, these sites would presumably have been hardware stores and grocers, bakers or cobblers and there are two ways of seeing this shift, both of which seem to me partly true. Yes, we have become an image-fixated, self-absorbed, adorned and decorated nation, for sure, but when times are tough, people still want to look good – or at least striking, almost as an act of defiance – and that may be no bad thing. After all, we have been doing these things to ourselves with woad and kohl and pelts almost as long as we have been hunting and skinning stuff and so, appropriately, at the end of this array of beautification, I find the much-vaunted Taylors The Butcher.

The staff in their nylon housecoats and jaunty hats are gearing up for lunchtime but it's already busy; a young goth couple, a clutch of workmen in flecked blue overalls, a man in a suit buying several pasties. I mention my journey and that I've been recommended here by a local gourmet and one lady disappears into the back. A few minutes later, a hearty bespectacled man appears wiping his hands before shaking mine. John Green, head butcher, and I chat by the purple flicker of the Insectocutor. He's well up on the Jarrow Crusade ('it was a time of real deprivation and they were marching to London to show their willingness to find work') though, like many, he places it ten years earlier than is the case, presumably to chime with the General Strike. John lives in Ferryhill where I'm headed today. 'Eight miles you've got left I'd say. Straight down, you can't miss it.' He tips me off about a good pub, the Manor House, and sends me on my way with a pie which is not only gratis, always a splendid seasoning, but hot. Midlanders regard this as sacrilege but it's the way the north likes them. For what can give more solace and joy than the feel of hot grease dribbling down the chin whilst dining on foot *al fresco* and *en plein air*, as our continental friends would have it? Afterwards, freshening up on a bench with a packet of wet wipes bought from the Co-Op, I reflect that this may well be the second best pork pie I have ever had. (The first will always be the one consumed one winter's afternoon in Cromford, Derbyshire in the street outside the pie shop and to which no words can ever do adequate justice.)

On a milky, muggy October morning at a busy intersection around which a few pubs, tanning salons, some maisonettes and the Bella Mamma Italian café bar cluster untidily, one would have no idea that this is a place not only steeped in violence and bloodshed, but one with a very real significance in the history and composition of the modern United Kingdom. What happened here at Neville's Cross 650 years ago still shapes England and Scotland's fractious and intense relationship.

It happened on an October day too, the seventeenth of that month in 1346. Following English King Edward III's resounding victory over the French at Crecy in the summer, the French King Philip invoked the terms of the Auld Alliance between the Scots and asked King David II of Scotland to avenge him and retaliate by invading England. The Scots had it their own way for a few weeks, rampaging south through Northumberland sacking and looting as they went. But when they came to Neville's Cross, a settlement named after the old Saxon Cross here, they camped and waited to be paid protection money that was promised for the next day, unaware that the Archbishop of York had mobilised 7,000 men of northern England into a fighting force that lay in wait in the autumn mists of County Durham.

With favourable ground and better tactics, the English routed the Scots army. Many Scottish nobles perished and the rest fled the field, abandoning King David II and his bodyguard. Legend says that they escaped and hid under a bridge over the nearby River Browney but were given away when their reflections were spotted by a detachment of English soldiers. Already hit twice in the face by arrows – the metal tips could not be removed and gave him pain and headaches for the rest of his life – King David was captured and imprisoned for 11 years, and whilst most of southern Scotland subsequently fell to the

English, David's sacrifice and stoicism was seen as instrumental in securing independent nation status in the long term.

The cross has gone, relocated to Durham town centre now, and the actual battlefield has been developed and built upon; studio flats and garages where a generation of high Scottish nobility was cut down by blades and hails of arrows. But a network of paths and an information board will guide you through a quiet pasture which once ran with blood. As I walk the length of the land on this journey, time and time again I will be reminded that every postcode, every OS square, every parish boundary is packed and freighted with history at its densest and darkest. Another legend of Neville's Cross has it that the English were led into battle by a woman, the dark-skinned Queen Philippa, Edward III's consort of Moorish extraction and a leader every bit as loved and exotic as Red Ellen at the head of her band of men.

A quick glance at the various Macs and Mcs among the roll call of marchers shows that many of Ellen's men were either Scottish or of Scottish lineage and were rubbing alongside their English brethren a deal better than in the fourteenth century. Scottish migrants had been drawn south by the promise of work in the mines, steelworks and shipyards of Jarrow during the town's boom years. Between the wars, Scottish unemployment was always higher than in England, and even when some parts of England (though not Jarrow, for sure) began to experience some economic upturn in the mid and late thirties, Scotland remained poorer. Much of the available work had also been relocated to England where the workforce was seen as more amenable and malleable. This labour drain sapped not just Scotland's economic and industrial vigour but its self-confidence and pride. By the time of the Jarrow march, Scotland was widely viewed south of the border as the sick man of the union – a basket case in modern parlance. But for years this was slow to solidify into any real organised support for nationalism or independence.

Prior to the EU referendum of June 2016, the last convulsion in British politics had been the bitterly, narrowly contested vote on Scottish independence in 2014, which brought forth a turn-out of 84.6 per cent – the highest recorded for any election or referendum in the UK since the introduction of universal suffrage. Its aftershocks were still being felt on the day I arrived in Neville's Cross. Nicola Sturgeon of the SNP was suggesting in that day's paper that Scotland's clear 'remain' majority in the EU vote meant that she had a mandate for a new referendum on independence. Scotland want to be part of Europe, even if England don't. Let's call the whole thing off.

The afternoon was shading into a golden, glorious early evening as I paused on a bench at an intersection provided by Durham City Council 'for the benefit of residents and visitors alike. Pause for a while and enjoy the area'. I tried, DCC, but there's only so much enjoyment to be gained from watching articulated lorries thunder by. But the thought was there. Once rested, I'm off again to the sound of birdsong and down a quiet stretch of road at the bottom of which a little cottage has a pretty sign framed and hung on a gate. It reads, 'Come My People. Enter thou into thy chambers and shut the doors abut thee, Isaiah 26 20. Leave The EU.' I read it several times, undecided whether it's an ironic sneer at 'little Englanders' or a genuine plea for 'drawbridge up' isolationism. This is the weird new febrile, uncertain England I walk through.

A sign tells me I'm five miles from Spennymoor, one from Durham, 12 from Bishop Auckland and 13 from Consett. Ferryhill, my destination, is not mentioned. This is disconcerting. I decide to take a minicab from here to my nearby hotel, drop my bag, and then return and pick up the Jarrow route into Ferryhill proper. I call a local number and the man who comes to pick me up is a Scot. 'If you want a recommendation for local pubs, I should say that I don't go drinking in Neville's Cross. Old habits die hard. It might be another ambush.'

In the taxi, along empty rural back lanes to the soothing backdrop of Smooth FM's liquid melding of Elton John, the Bee Gees and George Benson, I fall into an easy, knackered kind of conversation with the driver. He's smart and funny, silver-haired at the margins of a shiny dome, 60-ish, resembling a more genial Larry David. 'I've always worked away or long hours. Used to work on the pipelines. My wife finally got fed up and decided she wanted me to retire. She says, "I've been married to you for 34 years and only seen you for 18 months." Well, I says, you can either have the big money or me in the house. So I retire and I stay at home with her and we go shopping and on wee errands … well, she soon got sick of that, so here I am again, on the roads.'

Unlike the waitress in the Chester-le-Street café, my driver has not only heard of the Jarrow march but is positively interested. 'I was born 17 years after the Jarrow march but I suppose like them I came south looking for work. A group of mentally disabled people – is it special needs? Learning difficulties? Sorry, I don't know the phrases – they did a stage play about the march just recently. It was in the local papers. Industrial history's a bit of a thing with me. This used to be mining country, County Durham. They say you could once walk from Black Hall colliery just near here all the way to Workington, coast to coast, completely underground in the old mine tunnels. In Ferryhill you'll see a pub called the Dean and Chapter, everyone knows it as the Black Bull, but they changed its name to that of the old pit here. Nice gesture I suppose. Yes, lot of changes in those 80 years …'

At this very moment we hit a pothole and my head grazes the vinyl roof.

'… But the council hasn't finished the road yet.'

He drops me off at my hotel, a queer, rambling but intriguing-looking place in the outlying countryside. 'You're actually slightly closer to Sedgefield here, Blair's old constituency, you know. The Dun Cow is where he took George Bush and 20 armed security officers for lunch. They had the fish and chips I believe. Good pub. Minister's Indian restaurant, that's a nod to him too, superb. Enjoy! Hey you know, we had an oyster festival here last week, and a Bavarian stomping band ... Oh, it all happens round here,' he says with a wry smile. Then his radio crackles and he is called away to Pelaw Green.

With a parting, over the shoulder wave, he leaves me to Ferryhill in the dusk. With the sun dropped behind the distant treeline of Thorpe Larches, it's turning distinctly cold. The lights are on in the bus that pulls into the station, disgorging its homecoming workers back from the factories of Sunderland or the offices of Durham, a gang of kids from the big college there or in Spennymoor. I take a walk along the main street where, up at the eastern end, there's a 'Europe Beacon', a stylised and somewhat ironic gas lamp, considering that this corner of Durham voted overwhelmingly to leave the European Union with the only substantial Remain vote coming from the students of the famous and prestigious university. Outside the Post Box pub, a lad in kitchen whites blows on his hands and pulls on a fag; a real one, increasingly a rarity in the land of outlandishly named vaping outlets. Already I am finding that there are new constants and fixtures of every English high street today, 80 years on from Jarrow, when it would have been tobacconists and butchers. Now it's e-cig shops, retro barbers, cupcake bakers (often defunct, a bewildering craze on its way out), pizza shops where a moustachioed eastern European man stands behind a teetering tower of boxes waiting to be filled, and tattoo parlours. Ferryhill's is called Comfortably Numb, which is actually rather good.

My dog-walking ex-Consett steelworker told me that Ferryhill was 'a pit village with no pit'. It's a simple statement of fact that, like the famed 'pub with no beer', suggests a certain melancholy. The town has a tough and insular air, sitting on a limestone ridge on the former Durham coalfield, its jaw set against the world and the coming winter. It's quiet today, but on

Friday things get livelier for the market and in summer, fetes and galas parade the old miners' banners and celebrate the town's heritage. At the Dean and Chapter pub – the former Black Bull – a young woman sips a bright blue drink as she feeds the kaleidoscopic fruit machine, and a hefty, older man sits hunched at the bar over his pint and *Gazette*. From the outside, it is a north-eastern Hopper scene. The exterior has been redone vividly and rather forbiddingly in slate grey and coal-black livery with ghostly silhouettes of former miners. The legend reads, 'The Dean and Chapter, this pub is dedicated to the 73 miners who lost their lives at the colliery from 1904 when production began until 1929. The colliery closed in 1966.' A long time gone, but where work has been hard, the memories are long too.

Night is properly here now, cloaking the town. The marchers got their first hot meal of the trip by the roadside at Neville's Cross – a stew of lentils, carrots, leeks and turnips. I get mine in a curry house down one of the dark ends of Ferryhill's main drag and where, as I'm the only customer, the waiter comes and sits with me as I finish my carafe of house red, admiring my recording device ('what is that, man?!') and listens thoughtfully as I tell him why I'm here.

'You've walked from Jarrow? From Jarrow?! Today?!'

Yes, and I'm going a lot further. He's never heard of the march but is fascinated and horrified that the men went all the way to London. 'Times must have been hard. I don't think anyone would do that now. Too far. They'd be on their phones haggling on Uber!'

He lives in Sunderland and gets the bus in every day to Ferryhill. 'It's not my restaurant but I sort of manage it. It's owned by my uncle.' He nods towards the kitchen from where some clattering, sizzling sounds and pungent, heady aromas are emerging. 'He's been here five years. I've been here … hmm … about two and, to be honest, now I'm getting …'

He searches a little mournfully for the right word.

'Restless?' I offer.

'I just have this feeling that there must be something more, something else out there ... see a bit of the world. But I suppose I'll stay here,' he concludes with a small resigned smile.

'Well, the food is lovely,' I say, not entirely truthfully. 'The Jarrow marchers wouldn't have eaten bhuna and bhajis.' 'No,' he laughs, and then, in case he thinks I'm presuming them bigoted, I quickly add, 'I mean I bet there was no hot food in Ferryhill at night then.'

'Well, there is now,' he laughs, 'if you like pizza. And they could certainly have got their hair cut,' alluding to the town's glut of cheap independent pizza shacks and mock Edwardian barbers.

The streets of Ferryhill are dark and deserted tonight but things were different 80 years ago. The welcome here was as warm as it had been muted in Chester-le-Street. A message chalked on the road as the marchers arrived read, 'Welcome to the Jarrow Crusade. We are in solidarity with you.' In a letter home from the road, the Crusade's cook, Con Shiels' dad (also called Con, confusingly) said, 'We got a better welcome here, as all the town was out.' After placing the oak petition box (lettered in gold leaf paint from Woolworth's costing a penny) in the council chambers and holding a public meeting in the street, the marchers were fed on scones and ham sandwiches in the Miners Institute. In a famous incident, one marcher was seen carefully lifting the ham from his sandwich and posting it back home. When asked, he explained that his family had not eaten meat for six weeks.

The Manor House has been here several hundred years, but with their strict discipline, I doubt any marchers popped in for a pint. I'm pointed in its direction by two twinkling ladies in their eighties tightly linking each other for warmth as they make their booted way along. 'You can't miss it! We've just come from there!' they giggle, and perhaps their tight embrace is for reasons of stability as well as warmth. I lift the latch and find the pub empty except for a little lively, amiable knot of drinkers at the bar. I find a spot a discreet eavesdropping distance away and order a pint which I promptly knock over, spilling the contents all over the bar. This is embarrassing but it does effect a dramatic entrée into the conversation.

At the bar in a loose circle with pints and white wines are a couple in fleeces, a hearty solo male drinker and a mother and daughter with a fascinating dynamic who I chat to in earnest. Mum is in her forties; denims, check shirt, casual and smart in an alternative, relaxed style. Her daughter though is immaculately coiffured, glamorously made up, salon tanned, tall and catwalk elegant. The differences between them are not just aesthetic I'll find, but both are bright, chatty and personable. Mum moved to Ferryhill some years ago, but was brought up in Jarrow and remains a proud Jarrow lass.

'It's an anniversary tonight, isn't it? They passed through here and stopped the night. They were marching for jobs, not handouts. They wanted to work. And they were given no support at all except from the ordinary people. Their Labour MP pushed their case but the rest of the party didn't want to know. They ostracised her for it. Ellen Wilkinson, she was called. Now everyone wants to claim them for their own. Have you ever studied the Jarrow march, Robin? Robin's doing Government and Politics at college. She'll give you a different view I imagine.'

Daughter Robin tells me that she's a Conservative, 'and that makes me proper weird round here. You never meet anyone who's a Tory. Or at least who'll admit to it. Of course, there are lots of different types of Conservative. There is for instance (and here I think Robin is quoting from her course notes) the One Nation Conservative who believes in the Welfare State and in helping the vulnerable and the less well-off. But even they aren't naive. You have to face the fact that some people are just … higher than others. There's a natural hierarchy among humans.'

Really? I say. Is there? Listening back to the recording they kindly let me make of the conversation, I realise that the speed at which I snapped this back at Robin was ungallant to say the least. But Mum is with me.

'Is that right? A natural hierarchy? So the rich are rich on merit, are they? Not because of inherited wealth or their old school ties or ...'

Robin knows Mum has the better of this rally but attempts a lobbed return. 'Mum, you can't say that ... that ... a teacher, say, has the same intelligence as someone on the dole ...' She drifts back to the baseline as Mum closes in at the net.

'Well, they might well have. And anyway, it's not about where you end up. A society should have equality of opportunity. Look at me and you. When I went to college, I didn't have to borrow or beg from my mum and dad. I got a grant and went to university and I got a degree. You're a bloody talented drama student and you can't tell me that you wouldn't go to uni and study if it wasn't for the money. And, love, I can't afford to pay for you to go ...'

'I don't want it,' interjects Robin, quickly but not completely convincingly. 'We went to parliament on a college trip and some of the politicians told me it was a waste of time. The assistant chief whip of the SNP hasn't been to university, you know ...' she tails off.

My feeling about this is the same now as it was in the pub that autumn night. It may well be right that university is not for everyone, but I would surely like to meet the men in Westminster who, having had the best education money can buy, tell working-class girls from the north east that university is a waste of time.

Inevitably, as talk, beer and wine flow, the conversation glides inexorably towards one topic. 'They're all saying round here this Brexit is a great thing,' says Mum. 'They'll learn. I don't think it's a great thing at all. My cousin is in medical science, he's researching a disease of the feet, not a very serious one but an unpleasant one that could be cured. The research is funded by the EU. Or was. Straight after the referendum, £600,000 of investment cut instantly and 20 people out of work.'

As I leave, each drinker except Robin – who to be fair hadn't heard of it – offered some positive thought about the march that passed through here 80 years ago.

'I don't know if Jarrow would happen again. People standing together, women, children with their husbands, you think – wow! But are we like that any more? On the news tonight they were saying, yes, it's all romantic and all but did it achieve anything? Well, I think it did. It achieved something in that we're talking to you about it now.'

This is the notion that Matt Perry addressed in his lecture; that if Jarrow and by extension the Labour movement forget the march then it certainly has failed. But not if it is collectively remembered. They can take away the future that working people wanted but they cannot deny them their past.

Just down the road from the Manor House there's one minicab in Ferryhill's taxi rank and I take it back to my hotel. The driver is a handsome woman in her fifties, but her eyes are dark and lined and her face is flecked with little scratches and nicks. These are not signs of abuse necessarily, but of someone who isn't looking after herself as well as she should. She asks me what's my business in Ferryhill and when I tell her I'm researching a book, her own story starts to emerge.

'I've thought about writing a book, just to tell about my life.'

After 32 years of common-law marriage and two kids now at university, her partner left her last year and she seethes, 'The bastard is now trying to get me out the house, the house and the home I've built for 32 years. It's dragging through lawyers now. They say you've got rights, but have I? That's why I'm driving this cab. You think you know someone but you don't. I said to the bastard, "All these years, what was I to you?" I know that people split up but he wants me out on the street. It's my home, it's my kids' home. My son wants to kill him. So,' she glances at me in the rearview mirror with a sad smile, 'you think anyone would be interested in my story?'

Maybe, I say. As she's pulling over and reading the meter and I dig for change, I suggest that she starts a blog to see how that feels and to perhaps find sympathetic readers with similar experiences. She turns to me puzzled, awkward. 'What's a blog?' And so I get my phone out, lean into the little space between the two front seats and flip through a few blogs randomly; musings about spiralised vegetables and vinyl records with a nice but angry lady from Ferryhill that I've just met.

'Yours doesn't have to be like this, of course,' I say. 'People blog about family, divorce, kids, all kinds of things.' As I leave, she stays parked, and as I reach the door of the hotel, I look back and see her looking into her lap still, her face uplit in the chilly northern dark by her phone. Perhaps she's found an inspirational blog from a woman sharing her similar story with the world. Or maybe she's just buying a copy of Donovan's 1971 *Mini Monster* EP on Pye. Either way, it was an interesting trip.

I'd noticed while scrolling though the blogs on my phone that Matt Perry had emailed me. So, having kicked off my shoes and with one eye on *Question Time* on the tiny wall-mounted TV in my room (the kind specifically designed for you to bang your temple on), I read his message. At his lecture, we'd been talking about the Jarrow march in the context of other 'iconic' events in Labour and working-class history, prompted by the fact that the 1984 miners' strike is back in the news with calls for a debate on the clashes of Orgreave. The strike was initially about the pit closures enforced by National Coal Board chairman Ian MacGregor doing the bidding of Mrs Thatcher. Matt has been reading MacGregor's memoirs.

Hi Stuart,

You might have missed the topical connection between Orgreave, MacGregor and the Jarrow Crusade. And might want to use it. In his memoirs, he recalls getting a job in 1936 with Sir James Lithgow, who established the National Shipbuilding Securities that bought Palmers and put a 40-year ban on shipbuilding on it. 'Of the half dozen or so men who have influenced my life, he was the one – my first great mentor … I did not take on the Coal Board in order to butcher the industry, or to smash the miners. But there was no way I was going to let their leadership stand in the way of establishing management's right to manage the business and make it a going concern.

At this very moment I look up and catch a glimpse of *Question Time*. When I was a child, this was the BBC's flagship political debate programme, where union and parliamentary titans clashed under the withering basilisk gaze of Sir Robin Day. These days, tuning in, you are more likely to be treated to the political insights of some unspeakable and deranged reality TV show flotsam or the dim but loquacious lead singer of a minor 1990s pop–soul ensemble. But speaking at the moment is Leanne Wood, the leader of Plaid Cymru, who has been pricked into passionate scorn at mention of Theresa May's claim that the Tories are the party of working people. 'I worked as a probation officer in South Wales during the miners' strike,' she says, white-faced with quiet rage. 'I saw the human cost and the legacy of closing those pits. They will never be the party of working people. We should never forgive them. Never, ever forgive them.'

I turn off the TV, turn over, and fall asleep in the quiet arms of a mining town with no pit, just like scores across the land, where the lights are going out. 'No longer a going concern' and definitely no concern of some.

STAGE THREE

FERRYHILL TO DARLINGTON

7 October, 12 miles

Breakfast in Ferryhill must have gladdened the Jarrow marchers' hearts as it hardened the arteries; 70 pounds of bacon, 140 loaves of bread for frying, three boxes of tomatoes for same, all consumed in the Miners Institute. On leaving, they were also given 120 pounds of cherry cake for the journey, and the reporter from the *Shields Gazette*, Selwyn Waller, noticed that some were already putting on weight. Before they set off at 9.30am, some of the younger marchers had an impromptu dance with the girls of Ferryhill in the market place.

Not having been asked to dance, not liking cherry cake much and, moreover, none being forthcoming, I skip breakfast, leave town and pause for elevenses from a van by the roundabout at the Eden Arms in Rushyford. Someone once wrote that a man never feels as free and alive as when he jumps on to the back of an old London bus in motion. I would add the similar feeling engendered by eating a bacon butty and drinking coffee from a Styrofoam cup on a road never taken before and headed somewhere new.

Seated at a plastic table on the layby, I listen back on my recording device to Robin and her mum exchanging views in the pub last night and think about the youngest of the Jarrow lads, early twenties I guess, dancing and flirting with the girls of Ferryhill before setting out with a wink and a spring in their step that October morning in 1936. The year before, the school leaving age had been raised from 14 to 15, but children could be exempted if they could find 'beneficial employment'. This dismayed educationalists but was welcomed by those working-class families who needed the extra wages of their teenage offspring.

Of course they weren't 'teenagers'. No one would have called them that as that designation only really arrived (and then across the Atlantic) with the Second World War, the ubiquity of the automobile and the growth of leisure industries and the mass media. The lads and girls who danced in Ferryhill market place were young men and women; 'youths' as they were called. They were not a separate tribe, there was no generation schism. They were merely younger, sillier and more carefree versions of their mums and dads. But essentially their sights were set on the same targets – houses, jobs, children – and they took the same, long-established route to get them.

Most of the Jarrow marchers were well out of their teens since juvenile unemployment was always low even during the worst of the twenties and thirties slumps. 'Youths' were cheap to hire and pay and easy to get rid of. They were physically different too. According to Branson and Heinemann in *Britain in the 1930s*, the average 16-year-old then was more like a child of today. Most 12-year-olds of the 1960s were as big and strong as a thirties' 'youth' and their lives were similarly constrained and slight compared to the teenager of our times: 'Their horizons were limited, their lives rather bare, their opportunities for enjoyment meagre … there were no special teenage fashions in clothes or cosmetics, no teenage magazines to speak of, few teenage activities or entertainments laid on. It was not the custom to interview teenagers on the radio or to solicit their opinions or explore their attitudes.' While things were slightly better for the 18–25-year-old group at whom much culture, entertainment, sport and recreation was aimed, they were still a marginal section of society compared to the powerful middle-aged middle class who held tight the reins of the law, the economy and the polity.

Eighty years later, that situation would seem to have changed. Pippa Norris of Harvard talks of a 'generational cleavage' running through the new politics and the new populism, young people being (or asserting to be) globalist, progressive and more interested in issues like LGBT rights, multiculturalism and gender equality than the old blue collar concerns of community solidarity, nationhood and working conditions. Jon Cruddas, influential Labour MP and thinker, has talked of a shift in the power centres and bases of the left away from the industrial working class and towards what's called 'Globally Oriented Network Youth'. This new 'radical' sector tends to be found in cities, is well educated and easily embraces technological change, leisure and internationalism. 'You can see it around Corbynism. But if you build a public philosophy and a politics around this network, one that discounts the working class, where are they going to go politically? They're not going to regroup around this new fashionable left. They're going walkabout on the right.'

That's the walkabout that took us away from Brussels, and whilst I don't agree with that decision, I can understand it. In the three months between the seismic shock of the Brexit vote and me setting out from Jarrow, I read and heard countless leftist commentators and writers airily, and I think snobbishly, waving away some of the concerns of older, non-metropolitan working-class voters as racism and bigotry. I couldn't agree with Stephen Bush, a writer I generally much admire, when he said that white working-class people in England had no right to talk about being vulnerable and marginalised. He didn't 'buy it', as he put it. The only people who could legitimately feel this way were, say, Mexican workers in San Diego or Latinos in Miami or ethnic minorities in the UK. Whatever you think of this, this dismissiveness will win you no friends among the old blue collar

labour heartlands, as was proved on 23 June to the apparent
bafflement of some liberal observers. Belatedly perhaps, some
have come to see the error of their ways. As Adam Shatz, *London
Review of Books* contributing editor, said of the liberals' response
to the new populism and the white working class, 'Most of us
have found it easier to hate than persuade.'

Such thoughts occupy me as I stride along, though with
admittedly less strength than my regret at deciding to wear some
rather raffish knee-length shorts on what has turned out to be
the first grey, overcast and chilly morning of my trip. A sign
points right to Newton Aycliffe and, fancying the warmth and
buzz of civilisation for a while, I detour toward it. The marchers
lunched at Aycliffe Village just down the road and I'll head there
later, but Newton Aycliffe is its brasher, younger brother. The
largest new town in the north of England, it was founded in
1947 around a major wartime munitions base which brought
workers from the surrounding regions.

In 2015, against the prevailing economic mood, Hitachi
opened an £82million train-building plant here, bringing the
glory days of rail construction back to the north east, continuing
the grand engineering traditions of George Stephenson and
creating 700 jobs. It was feted by then prime minister David
Cameron and was to be at the heart of George Osborne's plans
for the much vaunted Northern Powerhouse. Cameron and
Osborne are both gone, distant as figures from a bygone political
era like Disraeli or Stafford Cripps. But the trains are still being
built. Head out to the site and you can see the huge, sleek beasts
under vast white sheets awaiting their imminent roll-out. In
Hitachi's promo video for the project on YouTube, you'll find
gleaming hi-tech vehicles, besuited captains of industry smiling
and handshaking through a flickering storm of flashbulbs and
accompanied by a beautiful and elegant female Asian string
quartet in white silk. All dazzlingly glamorous, but it will I fear
give you an unrealistic expectation of Newton Aycliffe, especially
if your first port of call is the town centre, or what passes for one.

The architectural style known as Brutalism is beginning to find favour again amongst some critics after years of hostility from the likes of Prince Charles. The north east has more examples of this harsh but powerfully dramatic style than anywhere else in Britain. You won't go far here without chancing upon looming concrete towers or raw, uncompromising brickwork; Redcar Library, Darlington Town Hall, the Apollo Pavilion in Peterlee, the Wilton Centre, Teesside, Billingham Forum and Owen Luder's iconic, divisive, now demolished Trinity Square car park in Gateshead.

Newton Aycliffe is a whole town built in this rugged and unsentimental mode, a style which divides people. Supporters of Brutalism like the writer Owen Hatherley admire 'its rough surfaces, heavy forms and dissonant, often monumental compositions', and see it as 'an attempt to recharge a modernism considered increasingly ingratiating and polite'. Sometimes though, a little ingratiation is no bad thing, especially towards the people who have to live in your brave experiments and your rough, heavy, monumental dissonance.

The journalist Merrick Winn called Newton Aycliffe 'the town that has no heart' in 1957 and you do feel on arrival at this bleak, windswept promenade that the people here deserved something better. It's hard to imagine anyone but those that created it on a drawing board having much affection for the Thames shopping arcades – the nearest thing Newton Aycliffe has to a town centre. But with the ceaseless energy that people have, for better or worse, the townspeople have colonised this dire space and made it their own. An old chap on a mobility scooter chats about 'regeneration' with a lady with a B&M Bargains bag and a small, angry dog. Office workers dash by with soup and salads and mobile phones held end on away from their faces in the style they've seen on *The Apprentice*. Two goth girls sit giggling on a hideous concrete planter. Given a choice, I doubt this is anyone's idea of a pleasant spot to spend your lunch hour. A regular town centre in all its higgledy-piggledy organic confusion would be preferable to this regimented chilliness.

I find more warmth in every sense in the public library, as is often the case. I sit and leaf though a lever arch file full of pictures of the town's construction and inauguration. Every computer terminal is occupied with people doing whatever it is people do on them all the long afternoon. A young blonde woman in boots and a leather jacket comes in. She's just moved back to Aycliffe village and wants to send a fax to her new employer's head office in New Zealand. While she and the ladies behind the counter establish whether they have the technology to do this, they ask how's she's finding the old place after her time away and I schmooze my way into the conversation by asking about my destination today.

'If you want to know about Aycliffe,' the newly returned young woman tells me, 'go down to the village hall. Every month, there's a community club there and you can get a late breakfast. Ask for Harry Moses. He knows everything there is to know. He's written books.'

Harry isn't around when I arrive at the village hall an hour or two later. But I get a cuppa and a warm welcome from the ladies of the Women's Institute. Brenda, Anne and Gill Atkinson are running a bring-and-buy stall. They all know of the original march and Anne has an actual souvenir. 'I believe they stayed here overnight and camped in the field opposite. When I was a little girl I found a tent peg in the field that must have belonged to them because no one ever camps there. I've still got it. If Harry were here he might tell you more. And one of our members, Muriel, is 95 and sharp as a pin. She might remember them coming through as a girl.' A few phone calls establish that, like Harry, Muriel is away for the weekend, but we manage to rustle up David Lewis from the village's local history society and he takes me on a whirlwind tour of Aycliffe.

It's a pretty place, once on the old Great North Road and hence squarely on the route of the Jarrow march. I mention to

David that I didn't like to contradict Anne, but the marchers didn't overnight here. 'No,' he agrees, 'but they did, as she says, have their lunch in the old cabbage and potato patch just opposite the hall, so they might well have put up some kind of tent or awning. They would have had to come here as there was no bypass then.'

The modern bypass, though, means that the village green is a delight; sun dappled and serene on this warm Friday morning. The only activity is a prowling, indolent cat and a gentleman in a fleece and trainers pottering along to his front door with a pint of milk. David has hit his stride. 'The church is older than Durham cathedral, Anglo-Saxon ... that little red building there is the old toll house ... you had to pay to use the old North Road ... that pub, the Royal Telegraph, would have been here then. And that one, the County. Tony Blair went there for lunch with the President of France, there's the blue plaque. And that river running by is the Skerne.'

David has a story that relates how unassuming Aycliffe has another unique place in industrial relations history beyond being where the Jarrow marchers had their butties.

The village hall used to be a school, opened in 1898. There was a church school here on the green but the head teacher and the vicar's wife were in constant conflict, basically because the head was his own man and wouldn't simply do the vicar's wife's bidding. She was always meddling and criticising him and she managed to get the head sacked by the vicar even though the village liked him and he did a good job. So the villagers got together a petition that said Thompson, the head, had been sacked 'ignominiously and without valid cause' and demanding his reinstatement. It was signed by 162 parents representing 449 children. When that got nowhere, the people were so angry that they built a new school on land bought with their own money. But the interesting thing, historically, is that the dispute was one of the first to be taken up by the National Union of Teachers, one of its very first industrial disputes. It went to parliament and in the end the head was re-appointed.

Our circuit of the village has brought us back to where the school once stood and I slurp another tea before hitting the road. Brenda from the WI sees me off in the bright sunshine and gives me a bag of apples for the journey, which strikes me as nicely 'old school' and makes me feel like a peddler or man of the road in a Thomas Hardy novel. I munch a couple myself (apples, not Thomas Hardy novels) and give the rest to some friendly but skittish horses in a field on High Beaumont Hill, and this encounter is the only eventful moment on an afternoon's gritty, noisy walk along the big new A176 into Darlington. I've never been to 'Darlo' before so I'm looking forward to exploring and from the stuff I read on Wiki last night in the curry house, it has several interesting quirks and claims to fame; the Brutalist town hall, comedian Vic Reeves, Quakerism and the coming of the railways.

If you have ever been hugely, vexedly distracted from the matter in hand by the twee recorded message about what is permissible to flush down the toilet of a Virgin train, or sat becalmed in a Hertfordshire field, the victim of a failure of lineside equipment near Leighton Buzzard, then in some senses you have Darlington to blame. It was the pressing need of the people of Darlington to get themselves and their stuff to Stockton that birthed the railways. By 'stuff' we mean specifically coal, the chief reason hotshot Geordie engineer George Stephenson established the world's first public railway between the two towns, primarily to bring coal from Killingworth colliery to the port of Stockton. This was the really important cargo. People were relegated to being dragged along behind in open carts. For these pioneering rail users, there was also the nagging worry widely reported that one might asphyxiate at the high speeds – in excess of ten miles per hour – that the loco could reach. This was a falsehood encouraged by wealthy canal owners desperate to keep their investments profitable and propagated by their press baron friends.

Work began in 1822 laying track on the 12-mile route between the two towns. Three years later, the railway opened to great fanfare. Large, eager crowds flocked to watch Stephenson himself at the controls of the 'Locomotion' as it pulled its 36 wagons – 22 of coal and flour and 14 of workmen and guests. During the final descent into Stockton, it unexpectedly reached 15 mph, surprising one passenger who fell out of his wagon and was badly injured. Add to this the fact that a few years later, on the maiden voyage of the first regular passenger service between Manchester and Liverpool, a high-ranking MP was run over and horribly killed, and one begins to realise just what excitement and faith there was in this new mode of transport. People like Stephenson were determined to make a success of the railways, whatever the cost.

It seems the accident outside Stockton did not sour the mood a jot. Spectator John Sykes recalled, 'The novelty of the scene, and the fineness of the day, had attracted an immense concourse of spectators, the fields on each side of the railway being literally covered with ladies and gentlemen on horseback, and pedestrians of all kinds ... By the time the cavalcade arrived at Stockton, where it was received with great joy, there were not less than 600 persons within, and hanging by the carriages.'

My entry into Darlington was more low key, it has to be said. Night had fallen and there was a chill in the air. But there was some of that old frisson of transport-related danger. Darlington, like most of our town centres, is now thronged with boy racer cyclists criss-crossing at speed, buzzing pedestrians and proffering the odd obscenity for seasoning. Even the most pacifistic among us surely find themselves fantasising about administering rough summary justice on these occasions, but at least these unlovable scamps have youth and stupidity as mitigating circumstances. Even just three days into my trip as a pedestrian, I am already reserving most loathing for those bulky middle-aged men, often in upsettingly snug lycra and with a little ribbed plastic hat, who ride their bikes on the pavement scattering old ladies and children, being too wussy and precious to ride on the highway as they are legally required. The punishment commensurate with this arrogance is yet to be devised. But I'm working on it.

Such retributory thoughts would not have sat well with some of Darlington's most eminent founders. Quakerism was born in the turbulent England of the Civil War when a young man called George Fox, a firebrand and electrifying preacher, toured the north of England spreading the word about a vision he had had on Pendle Hill in Lancashire. Fox's revelation was that the light of God was within everyone, discoverable within oneself and needing no formal or credentialed hierarchy of clergy. This was a radical notion which brought him into conflict with the established church who hauled him before various inquisitions for blasphemy. As Fox recalled, 'They were the first that called us Quakers, because I bade them tremble at the word of the Lord.' Quakerism grew from its beginnings in the English north to become a global religion and, along with other Nonconformist strains of Christianity like Methodism, part of a radical, dissenting, even socialistic strand in our history. Where Anglicanism and Catholicism are ultimately two different faces of the same conservative coin (and I say that as an ex-altar boy), Nonconformism, as the name suggests, is predicated on a lack of trust in the vicar or the priest, the dog collar or the surplice, on what Larkin called 'the vast moth eaten brocade' of the Establishment religions. Methodism and Chapel are indissoluble from the great Labour traditions of Wales, whilst Nonconformism made Manchester the great radical city of the industrial age.

Nonconformism also made towns like Darlington rich. Prohibited from entering the military, church or university by the powers that be, Quakers in England threw themselves into business and commerce, albeit with a caring and positive attitude to their workforce that set them apart from much of capitalist enterprise. Quaker family businesses created some of our best loved brands, brands redolent of Englishness itself; confectioners like Rowntree, Cadbury and Fry's, Clarks the shoemakers, banks such as Barclays and Lloyds. And in Darlington, Quaker industrialists and bankers like Jonathan Backhouse and Edward Pease supported Stephenson in the creation of the modern railways and a world transport revolution.

Making a TV film about Quakerism a couple of years back, I attended a meeting at the Friends House on the Furness Peninsula that is George Fox's old haunt and the crucible of Quakerism worldwide. Quaker meetings are not like church services; there's no leader, no palaver, no incense or droning, no 'vast moth eaten brocade'. Attendees sit in silence until someone feels moved to speak, and if no one does, that's fine. At mine, some 25 minutes of silence in, a man chirped up with a fairly anodyne remark about world peace and that was it for the whole hour. The film crew said they found it uncomfortable. I thought it was the most relaxing and nourishing hour I'd had in years. And I enjoyed my second visit to a Quaker House here in Darlington even more, especially as they were playing 'Brick House' by the Commodores thunderously loud when I arrived and someone speedily handed me a 7.6 per cent strength New World IPA.

I am indebted to Twitter correspondent Judith Sykes who led a chorus of similar voices in steering me to The Quaker House, Darlington which, as you may have guessed, is these days a pub. In fact, one of the finest pubs I've ever set foot in, and as you may have guessed yet again, there've been a few. It's tucked away in the Mechanics Yard, one of the maze of little alleys and ginnels that bisect the town. When Google maps proved wanting, I just let myself be lured by the throb and clamour of music.

'Brick House' by the Commodores was quickly followed by 'Ace of Spades' followed by the Isley Brothers' 'Behind a Painted Smile', to which most of the glamorous, beaming female bar staff and their adoring clientele cut various kinds of rug and threw a range of alluring shapes. It is hard to say just what the pub's chief selling point is, be it the staff, the beer, the live music, the attitude or the home-made onion bhajis. It is even harder to say after a few pints of the 7.6 strength New World IPA. But let us consider them one by one.

Shelley has run the pub for three years and worked here for seven. She heads a team who clearly love their pub and their job. Tonight the music is recorded rather than live – I have no problem with this at all I should say – and is played by DJ Rob who's seated at the 'wheels of steel' in a rather cramped and ungainly fashion in a corner of the bar as one leg is encased in plaster ('Don't ask'), jutting out at an angle designed for a sitcom mishap. However, this in no way affects his performance this evening. The eclectic opening musical salvo is followed by a selection of infectious northern soul tunes that coax some hard-looking middle-aged blokes in Ben Sherman and Farrah on to the postage stamp of a dance floor. The looks of rapture worn by men who've spent lives doing tough jobs in tough towns, whilst dancing to songs of unrequited love, devotion and heartbreak, is one of the many things I love about soul music and soul fans.

It's Friday night and this is the beginning of a weekend of gigs across the country (I had no idea until Shelley and Rob told me) called WSO or We Shall Overcome and designed to raise awareness and money for charitable causes all centred around the notion of 'anti-austerity'. 'Austerity' and 'austere' used to be words I liked. I applied them to the bleak beauty of upland moors and the poetry of R S Thomas. I hadn't realised that 'austerity' apparently means closing libraries and stopping vulnerable people's benefits. The staff at the Quaker House, in keeping with the traditions of their name, are amongst those generous, decent souls not accepting that the weak should suffer most when times are hard, especially when little of it is their fault.

'This is our second WSO anti-austerity weekend,' explains Shelley. 'There are 260 WSO gigs going on across the country this weekend but there has been no coverage in the press. Help spread the word. We want food for the food banks, sleeping bags for the homeless. Darlington has been massively affected by "austerity". We're a working-class town and the cuts have hit us hard. People simply not capable of work are being told they have to.' Here is another quietly smouldering impetus for Brexit that many commentators have either failed to notice or chosen to ignore: after the economic crisis of 2008, one largely brought about by the wickedness and greed of bankers, it has been ordinary people who have borne the cost, in reduced services and savage cuts. Rightly or wrongly, the EU is seen as aligned to that protected cabal of affluent and seemingly untouchable financiers. Brexit was an attempt, however clumsy and misguided, to land a punch on them.

Battling against the joyous racket of Frank Wilson's 'Do I Love You' (if you've got one on the Soul label, congrats, it's worth about 25 grand), I chat with a clutch of gregarious regulars. Marty's been drinking here for 17 years and has missed just six live bands in all that time. I'd heard that Darlington was becoming a boom town, with some people commuting to London. 'A boom town?' He takes a thoughtful sip. 'Well, there are now 12 pubs in the city centre serving real ale,' he says, this clearly being Marty's quality of life index. Francis is a beaming Indian man who is clearly loved by all. 'I am Francis! I am the Curry King! I ran a restaurant in Darlington for many years. I'm 72 years old and I've been here 45 years. In 1972 I came to run a building company, then I did a job for a restaurant and he asked me to come and partner him. When someone first say you should go to Quaker House I say, 'Oh no, I'm not religious,' but then I found out it is a pub. And they soon converted me! I have embraced it well! Now it is my religion!'

Francis' long squealing laugh at this is ridiculously infectious, especially if someone seems to be continually filling your glass of 7.6 strength New World IPA. 'I'm retired now but I always come and hand out onion bhajis all over pub. For free of course! And if they want curry I cook curry. For nothing. Everybody enjoys it! This is a great pub! This is a great town!' And through a warm enveloping, caressing fog of loud music, strong beer and aromatic bhaji, I hear myself agreeing, woozily but heartily, as the evening slips gently away from me.

STAGE FOUR

DARLINGTON TO NORTHALLERTON

8 October, 16 miles

I wake, much later than intended, with a red rubber band emblazoned We Shall Overcome on my wrist and a carefully wrapped but now damply flaccid onion bhaji on the bedside table. Gifts from the previous night; I smile at the foggy memory. It turns out though that smiling hurts my head so I assume an expression of dazed blankness – which isn't hard – as I proceed with my preparations for embarkation on day four.

After about an hour under a shower as volcanic as the clanking pipes of my odd hotel can muster, I am ready to leave. I spread my OS Landranger 34 on the floral duvet. Today will take me into my third county of the walk. Yorkshire, or more specifically North Yorkshire, since despite a shared, uniquely Yorkshire cast of mind – shyness, modesty, a certain easy-going frivolousness – I consider the Ridings of this big county to have subtly different temperaments.

Northallerton is North Yorkshire's county town and it's my destination today. I'll head loosely south following the new A road, crossing the Tees at Croft and then down towards Great Smeaton where the marchers rested a while and Con Shiels Snr and Cuddy Errington rustled up another al fresco Irish Stew. Before my tracing finger gets this far south though, it passes through several villages of North Yorkshire that set me off playing the game that's amused me on many a long car journey; spotting any English villages or hamlets that could believably be the names of English supporting film actors of the 1940s and 50s. I will pass by many today and they are always a delight; Hutton Bonville, Lazonby Grange, Appleton Wiske. ('And now on ITV 4, a Rank Organisation classic from 1948, The Vainglorious Heart, starring Margaret Lockwood, Michael Redgrave and Appleton Fiske as Group Captain 'Sniffer' Daniels).'

This nostalgic reverie of a classier, more courteous age of stiff upper lips and perfect manners is abruptly curtailed by a quick dip into the morning's papers over tea and toast beneath the clock tower. The Republican US Presidential nominee Donald Trump, by his every utterance further revealing himself an odious human cocktail of self-regard and idiocy, has apologised – albeit in a graceless, insincere manner – for some vile and coarse remarks about women. I won't repeat them here, you will surely recall them. With the blustering disdain typical of his kind of man, he's dismissed them as 'locker room' chatter, as some British men seek to excuse their nastiness as 'banter' or, worse, 'bantz'. Many commentators of a liberal bent have sought to sum up Trump's essential nature but none so succinctly as Alan Bennett who has called him 'a lying, bellicose vulgarian'. This has just the right blend I think of elegance and scorn. Watching Darlington go quietly about its Saturday morning business of bakeries and newspapers, it is baffling and more than a little terrifying that Trump could conceivably be the next president of the USA and thus the leader of the free world. Surely not, one's rational self thinks, but then one remembers that alongside the brilliance, vigour, sophistication and dynamism of Americans is a corresponding trait of sometimes behaving like overgrown and wilful children.

America was also about to go to the polls back in October 1936 as the Jarrow men marched south. The Great Depression was entering its eighth year and this giant of a country was still on its knees. But Franklin D Roosevelt's New Deal, a progressive programme of relief and social security, had inspired the country, giving it hope and even a kind of unity that was reflected at the polls. The election, held just as the Jarrow Crusade arrived at the gates of their own political capital in Westminster, proved to be the most one-sided in US history: a landslide in which only Maine and Vermont didn't go with FDR. It's staggering that the American political system can have gone from fostering FDR to Donald Trump in 80 years, but then it's just as difficult to conceive that it's gone from Barack Obama to Trump in a matter of months.

However, as FDR won that pivotal election, Ellen Wilkinson, the Jarrow men and the British political class were looking not to events in America but Europe. Russia's Communist regime and its consolidation of power divided opinion here amongst the intelligentsia. From Spain, stories of fascist outrages committed by Franco and his army against their own people were beginning to emerge. Also on the agenda (literally) was the Middle East. Wilkinson was still in Edinburgh where she spoke to the Labour Conference on the subject of the fraught Arab–Israeli relations. There was a general strike in Palestine which the conference failed even to mention, let alone support. Wilkinson attacked this timidity. She then went on to excoriate the party's line in instructing local Labour Party branches not to support Jarrow and other hunger marches on the grounds that communists were involved. She openly mocked the TUC General Secretary saying, 'When Sir Walter Citrine gets to the Pearly Gates, St Peter will be able to reassure him that there are no communists inside.' In retaliation, Labour apparatchik Lucy Middleton said that Wilkinson had sent 'hungry and ill-clad men on a march to London'. This was a downright lie in every regard that angered the marchers greatly.

As the marchers passed along the lanes between Darlington and Northallerton, locals from the surrounding villages came to meet them with baskets of apples and pears. Brompton is as lovely as I had been told. It's early on a Saturday afternoon and there's just the low murmur of occasional traffic as a van, saloon or country bus pass the big triangular village green overlooked by a couple of attractive pubs, the Crown and the Three Horseshoes. St Thomas' church has stood on this green for a thousand years. Brompton is one of those quietly enduring English villages, like Adam Thorpe's fictional Ulverton, that offers a compacted nugget of the English story in miniature and microcosm through waves of history; Saxons, Vikings, Normans, Civil War, Enclosures, Industrialisation, Mills, Suburbanisation.

A sign erected by the Brompton Heritage Society nearby promises two alluring delights; the Linen Workers Memorial Seat and the Anglo–Danish Hogback Stones. The latter sounds to me like a UK–Scandinavian tribute to Jagger and Richards but are apparently a historic artefact that 'draws visitors from all over the world'. This visitor from Wigan via Jarrow couldn't get in, sadly, as the church was locked but the elusive stones and the Linen Workers Memorial Seat will always remain a brief and tantalising memory of my Sunday sojourn in Brompton. (The stones, by the way, are remarkable examples of Viking settler sculpture that are apparently well worth seeing. But pick the right day.)

On the outskirts of Northallerton, a plum-coloured vintage car passes me sounding – from the spluttering and wheezing of its antique engine – to be in a spot of bother. It's a Vauxhall of Luton (a town which awaits me further down the long road), registration DS89 34 and made in 1928 and so very likely to have been on the road, maybe this road, when the marchers passed by. 'Nice car,' I shout as the driver pulls up aslant the roadside, gets out and disappears under the bonnet. 'Can I have a word with you about it?'

'Now isn't really a good time,' comes a disembodied voice accompanied by a furious percussive burst of hammering, some ominous clanks and the occasional vivid swear word.

'Grand car that,' remarks a stout Yorkshire fellow in a flat cap passing by slowly and regally on a mobility scooter. 'Worth more than these modern ones,' he states solemnly. Not at the moment, I think, as I cross the road into the centre of Northallerton.

By 1936, the car was king of the road. Horse-drawn carriages had practically disappeared from our streets, confined to the odd brewery wagon or coal cart. Trams, once popular and mooted as the transport of the future, had been largely abandoned; a trend that would be successfully if expensively reversed in the 1990s. There was a tragic human cost of the new ubiquity of the motor car though. The powerful road lobby were keen to assert the primacy of the car over pedestrians. Under pressure from the AA and the RAC, the government had abolished the 20 mph speed limit and there was a huge subsequent rise in road deaths (*The Listener* claimed that more people were killed on the roads in the first two years of the 1930s than in the entire Napoleonic wars). In response, Tory MP and 'colourful' character Colonel Moore-Brabazon huffed, 'What is the point of such concern over 7,000 road deaths a year? Over 6,000 people commit suicide a year and no one makes a fuss about that.'

Despite walking down busy roads for the most part, none of the marchers fell foul of a speeding motorist or lumbering lorry, although presumably Colonel Moore-Brabazon would have shed no tears if they had. It seems the spirit of *Top Gear* was already flourishing in Britain in the thirties.

In Northallerton, Rosie, Ruth and John, here on a shopping trip from nearby Stokesley, have been watching the car's erratic progress too and are waiting for me at the pelican crossing. 'Is he having some trouble? Do you think he should get a new one? You can get a Ford Focus as a runabout very reasonable on finance in Northallerton.' None of the trio has ever heard of the Jarrow march but all are warmly enthusiastic about Northallerton. 'It's a lovely place. You'll have a fine time. Plenty of nice pubs up those little streets.'

Those little streets radiate in a series of yards off a grand
central boulevard. In the heyday of coaching and droving, this
street would have thronged with traders coming down from
Northumbria and Scotland. There were four annual fairs a year
where you could sell your mother's prize cattle for magic beans
and get a thick ear when you went home, or celebrate driving
that hard bargain on a crate of cauliflower in one of the four inns
along this main street. They're all still here though the names
might have changed and all are busy on this fine market day.
My room is at the Golden Lion where, under my window as I
go through my unpacking ritual, I hear a broad Yorkshire voice
attempting to lure the ladies of Northallerton to part with their
hard-earned brass. Never an easy task in Yorkshire.

'Eight bunches of bananas, all for a pound, sweet juicy
strawberries, luscious pineapples,' and from further down the
street, 'Chinese spare ribs, lamb chops, twenty pounds for all
them lamb chops, missus, gammon, bacon joints, make a lovely
Sunday dinner, love.'

This is the prime time for bargain hunters as we're
approaching the end of the long market day. The stalls are
packing up, the trestle tables are being folded and the big white
vans loaded and I am watching the clock for a very good reason.
My home town rugby team Wigan Warriors are playing in the
Grand Final of the Rugby Super League, essentially the highlight
of that sport's year. Whoever wins this can rightly claim to be the
best team in the land, or rather lands, since in another modern
development – along with words like 'Warriors' and 'Super
Leagues' and 'Grand Finals' – French and Spanish teams now
take part as well. The match kicks off soon and I know that on
a Saturday in the football season and in the posher 'county' end
of Yorkshire where they hunt, shoot, fish and play a different
(inferior) kind of 'rugger', I will have my work cut out finding a
pub that has the game on. But I have a plan. I will adjourn to a
curry house – with a kindly and obliging maitre d' I hope – and,
in return for a guaranteed hefty spend at a corner table for one,

will hop on to their wifi network. Then, whilst working my way through a lamb dhansak, I'll watch the match on my iPad which will be propped against the first of several pints of lager. It is a plan almost beautiful in its elegance and simplicity.

Unlike so many plans – personal, national, political – this one actually works out. Aroma on Zetland Street is filling up with early night-outers and late market shoppers but they squeeze me in the window (as in, they find me a little table at the front of the restaurant, in case you thought that sounded weird). Happily, the waiter is a rugby league fan too and goes along enthusiastically with my plan. He arrives with the wifi code on a piece of paper on a silver tray and despite it being a lengthy, bamboozling string of random numbers, asterisks and hieroglyphs (always) I get it right first time and a small but crisp image of chunky men in cherry and white hoops on the greensward of Old Trafford, Manchester, appears above the poppadoms.

The next hour passes extremely pleasantly indeed. It's a tight, hard fought encounter but in the second half Wigan gain the upper hand and with it, to mix metaphors horribly, begin to turn the screw. At the bar, a couple waiting for a takeaway sink cocktails and bicker in a brittle way like a couple in a Noël Coward play before leaving with several white plastic bags of food. In the dying seconds (of the match, not the argument), Wigan score a late and conclusive try that clinches it and involuntarily like the oik I am, I half rise from my chair and growl 'Come On Wigan'. As you can imagine, when a solitary strange man does this in a curry house full of locals who know one another, it's quite the conversation starter.

It draws me into a chat with the big cheery group on the middle table. I tell them why I'm here and, this time, all of them have heard of the Jarrow march. They all know at least roughly what it was about and means, and I record our conversation over the increasing hubbub of a Saturday night curry house in a northern town.

'Protest ... desperation ... dignity ... in the face of Conservative bastards – come and have a beer with us!'

I perch at the corner of the table and am given a quick resume of Northallerton and its character, 'It's a market town, livestock market Tuesday and Wednesday. Always been a big agricultural community and there's still that feel to the place. That's why it's such a Tory town. They say round here that in Northallerton they'd vote for a pig if you put it in a tweed jacket. They voted to leave you know [I don't need to ask what]. The farmers think they're going to get more money. One of my students is from a farming family and he keeps saying, "we're going to be rich". Baffling ... he's got a bloody shock coming to him. It's the county town of North Yorkshire too so there's always been that big admin sector, government offices ... that's a big employer. Rural payments agency used to be here but that's gone now.'

What's still here though is the 'Pongo', as all the town calls it. Its proper name these days is Club Amadeus: 'but everyone calls it the "Pongo" and nobody knows why. When we were kids in the seventies and eighties it was Sayers Disco. It was effectively two garages concreted together. Awful but great. Sticky carpets. That sort of thing. But there was nowhere else to go. There still isn't. It's still in two parts. The middle-aged people turn left at the door and the young 'uns turn right.' The gentleman who told me all this can claim a certain authority. He was one of the rumoured and select band of just ten people who were in the audience in the most famous night in Pongo's history, one that fixed Northallerton's premier (and only) night spot as a footnote in the pop history of these islands.

On 16 May 1976 the Sex Pistols played at Sayers Disco in Northallerton. Sending the fledgling band into the lion's den of the northern club scene was part of manager Malcolm McLaren's plan to toughen up the band and presumably provoke outrage. On the fortieth anniversary of their famous show at the Lesser Free Trade Hall in Manchester, I'd spoken to bassist Glen

Matlock about those early sojourns. 'I went into a chip shop and I asked, "What sort of fish have you got?" 'Cos in London you get rock, skate, whatever. The bloke just looked at me and said, "Are you taking the piss? We've got cod".' Drummer Paul Cook said that the furthest north he had been up to this point was Hampstead.

McLaren would give the band just enough money to get to the shows and the band would exist on stolen chocolate bars and chips, then having to badger the clubs themselves to get their money. 'It was vile, horrible, a nightmare. No chance to relax ... nothing ... awful nylon sheets ... utter total boredom,' recalled John Lydon, who would nightly bait the largely unresponsive audiences. Their van couldn't manage hills so Matlock would use the Ordnance Survey map to plot the flattest route possible, even if this involved enormous detours.

In Northallerton they supported the Doctors of Madness 'a real record company band' remembers Pauline Murray of the Ferryhill punk band Penetration, one of the rumoured ten in attendance. 'The Pistols wiped them out, they wiped a lot of bands out ... I saw it happen.' Not everyone was so keen though, as I was about to find out. Declining yet more offers of beer from the wonderful folk at the curry house, I leave them to their poppadoms and head for the Little Tanner pub. 'It's quirky,' they tell me, 'and Brian who runs it put the Pistols on at Sayers.'

The Little Tanner is definitely quirky, one of those strangely likeable new pubs or bars that have sprung up all over Britain in what feels like front rooms or old sweet shops or printers. Now the spaces are occupied, not unhappily, by luxuriantly bearded graphic designers wearing vintage US seed merchant baseball caps and drinking botanical gins and Sri Lankan pale ales. Even if these people had existed in 1976, they would not have been the kind of folk who went to see the Sex Pistols. Their audiences were largely either curious hippies or oikish 15-year-olds like me obsessed with the music press, hormonally restless and for whom liking punk was the cultural equivalent of smashing up a phone box.

The hipsters aren't in tonight but the nice barmaid Louise (or perhaps Lucy, the man with the phlegmy laugh and the large Gordon's at the bar called her both during my brief stay) tells me with an apologetic smile, 'Brian's not in tonight I'm afraid, he's in Thailand. But I know that he didn't put the group on. He was the DJ. I think he said he had to wake them up in the dressing room to come onstage and play. I don't think there was a stage, just the dance floor. And Brian thought they were rubbish ... well, most people did then. It was very new, very different. Certainly for Northallerton ...'

In 1936, the biggest single employer of musicians and the greatest patron and commissioner of music in the land was the BBC. The 'Beeb' would have been the way most of the Jarrow marchers listened to music. Lord Reith believed that light music, along with comedy and quizzes, was 'lowest common denominator' fare and not to be broadcast at all on Sundays. But at other times, thanks to wiser and less snobbish counsels, it vied with classical music as the bulk of the BBC's output. At 10.30pm, every night (except Sunday) there was a broadcast of an hour-and-a-half of music from a West End dancehall with bandleaders such as Henry Hall and Lew Stone and 'crooners' like Al Bowlly. Reith's deputy described crooning as 'a particularly odious kind of singing' but the audience loved it. They deluged the Corporation with bags of fan mail to the surprise of BBC mandarins and musicians alike.

By the mid-1930s, that august, now defunct publication the *Melody Maker* reckoned there were almost 20,000 dance bands in Britain, playing in various palais, lidos, theatres and hotels. The year before the Jarrow march, at a holiday camp in Great Yarmouth, Percy Cohen's band played to 1,500 people a night. British dance bands tended to be either 'sweet' or 'hot', playing music that was essentially romantic and lush or quick and infectious. No British bands ever really 'swung' though in the way that their American jazz counterparts did, like Benny Goodman. Nonetheless, in the UK, dance bands and light music were a phenomenon that cut across all classes and ages, despite the out of touch scorn of men like Reith and his deputy and the ever-reliably wrong-headed conductor Thomas Beecham who declared with all the confidence of the mistaken that 'the performance of music through the wireless cannot be other than a ludicrous caricature'. It seems the public have yet to twig this.

The bar of the Golden Lion ('OK but a bit 70s' was the curry house jury's verdict) is full and raucous as I settle in with a last whisky. There's what looks to be a wedding or at least a hen do; girls in scarlet and cream silks tottering to the toilets laughing. There's a few couples sipping wine and at the bar a cliché made flesh – quite a lot of flesh actually – a group of loud, hearty florid middle-aged men in tweeds, Barbours, a gilet or two and those shirts with the thin-lined patterning that you can only buy in 'country outfitters'. They seem amiable enough but then I can't hear what they're talking about. Maybe if I was a couple of tables closer I wouldn't be so generous. Or maybe I'm just being prejudiced.

I'd definitely felt a slight but perceptible change in landscape and mood as I came south from County Durham into North Yorkshire. No chimneys brood over the landscape of the north east now (or few anyway) but the Durham coalfield still carries the tough, ingrained feel of mining country. Towns like Ferryhill are very different in mood to Northallerton, especially on a busy market Saturday. No official reception met the Jarrow men here in 1936 and no councillor came to shake their hand. The council would not allow them to sleep in any school or council-owned building and so they took cold and uncomfortable shelter in the drill hall, just across from the Little Tanner and a couple of Methodist and Zionist church halls. Drill halls were once a fixture in every town, as meeting places for army reservists. 'Thank God we found decent clergy in Northallerton,' said marcher David Riley. The *Northern Dispatch* for its part said the men had 'groused' and that the welcome was every bit as warm as strange folk from up country could have wished for. The war over Fake News had some of its initial skirmishes in the 1930s maybe, I thought as I drained my Aberlour, negotiated a teetering girl in high heels with a Chardonnay and made my way up the anaglypta-ed and horsebrassed staircase to bed.

STAGE FIVE

NORTHALLERTON TO RIPON

9 October, 19 miles

When I was a teenager, quite an odd one perhaps, I loved the party conference season. Unlike the youthful William Hague I never went to one, but I much enjoyed them vicariously. The telly was on all day providing, for skiving students and dole-ites of which I was from time to time both, a genuine alternative to horse racing or *The Sullivans* in the form of a kind of engrossing live theatre. Several different kinds of theatre actually.

The Conservatives' was always the most tightly scripted, directed and stage managed, with hardly any surprises – except for 1980 of course – and with the only variable being the toadiness of the cabinet, the hair-raising stridency of Mrs T's speeches and the length of the North Korean-style standing ovation that would inevitably follow them. The Liberals or SDP or Liberal Democrats or whatever they were called that year were always homespun and pleasant but mildly disorganised, like a CND jumble sale. Labour generally provided the great box office conference moments of the 1970s and 80s: Dennis Healey in 1976, sweating like a prize fighter, pummelling his way through the boos and catcalls to finally earn a standing ovation; Kinnock taking on Derek Hatton's entryist Militant tendency in 1983 raging, 'You start with far-fetched resolutions.

They are then pickled into a rigid dogma … irrelevant to the real needs, and you end in the grotesque chaos of a Labour council – a Labour council – hiring taxis to scuttle round a city handing out redundancy notices to its own workers.' Militant bayed and sulked. But more cheered; it was clearly the start of the long fight back to power, even I could tell that from a sofa in Wigan. And I could tell that the personable young chap I watched in the late 1980s with the proto-mullet and thin lapels and skinny tie à la Duran Duran, new Shadow Trade Secretary Tony Blair was going places.

By 2005, things had changed in all kinds of ways. My days were no longer my own and thus I could no longer slump all day in front of speeches, motions, resolutions and shows of hands. Tony Blair's days had got busier too. Labour had eventually ousted the Tories, a government that seemed as permanent as the ice caps during my twenties, and now he was giving his third conference speech as Prime Minister to the Labour faithful in Brighton. Looking back now, his words ring hollow with a conviction and sense of rectitude that proved fairly groundless.

I hear people say we have to stop and debate globalisation. You might as well debate whether autumn should follow summer. They're not debating it in China and India. They are seizing its possibilities, in a way that will transform their lives and ours …. The character of this changing world is indifferent to tradition. Unforgiving of frailty. No respecter of past reputations. It has no custom and practice. It is replete with opportunities, but they only go to those swift to adapt, slow to complain, open, willing and able to change.

Around that time I interviewed Digby Jones, the former head of the CBI, on Radio 2 and it proved one of only two occasions that I've ever lost my temper on live radio. Jones's position was essentially the same as Blair's, but expressed with even less sympathy for his countrymen and women. 'The British worker is going to have to change and work harder and be more productive and more flexible. Because otherwise there are thousands of workers in India who are going to steal their lunch.'

Neither the ice caps nor Tony Blair turned out to be permanent, and both Blair and Jones turned out to be wrong – as blithely wrong in fact as Francis Fukuyama was in 1992, in his once-influential book *The End of History* when he confidently predicted that we were entering the final phase of human social development, a serene universal shift to liberal democratic government and an end to geopolitical conflict. Even as he wrote, in Jalalabad or Khartoum or a cave somewhere in the Tora Bora mountains of Afghanistan, Osama Bin Laden was planning the holy war on those same liberal democracies. It is a war that still rages today and has brought murder and mayhem to the cities of the east and the west. As Jon Cruddas now says of the imperious but naive assertions of Fukuyama, Blair and their ilk, 'This sink or swim view of humanity is alright for the winners. Rule from 35,000 feet is fine if you're in the first-class cabin.' Soon even those in that cabin wouldn't be safe, literally or metaphorically.

Similarly aloof, the Labour Conference of 1936 had little cheer to offer the marching men of Jarrow. After a frugal breakfast of bread and jam in the town hall, trudging from Northallerton in the teeming rain, spirits were further dampened by news from the conference that the Labour Party had decided not to support the marchers by protesting the National Assistance Board's decision to stop their benefit. The NAB had come to this decision as the marchers were 'technically not available for work'. David Riley, mayor of Jarrow and the march marshal, broke the news to them saying that it was 'a stab in the back'. A telegram was sent to Edinburgh to the conference delegates saying, 'We, the sons of England's most famous town, resent the unsympathetic attack on our members and the deliberate attempt to pauperise our crusaders.'

Perhaps it was this muted and unhappy start to the day that has led to some confusion about where the actual march went next. According to the official route lodged with the authorities and the BBC, they headed for Thirsk and Boroughbridge, making an overnight stay in each. But this is clearly wrong and no one seems entirely sure why. Did they deviate from the original route? Was the itinerary drawn up incorrectly? Anyway, I know where I'm headed. I'm bound for Ripon and I leave Northallerton on another golden autumn morning in North Yorkshire – an egg yolk sun and a faintly speckled Cadbury's Mini Egg blue sky to the gentle clamour of church bells. The *FT*'s cheery headlines are ringing in my mind too; 'Chill wind blowing through corporate landscape ... the pound in freefall ... protectionism returns ... Jeremy Paxman on writing his memoirs ...' I pop the *FT* in the recycling bin in Northallerton Market Square and head south on the Boroughridge Road.

The miles that stretch between Northallerton and Ripon pass through the most conventionally pretty scenery to date. They offer a peek into Herriot country and a hint of the quintessential Dales. As the road curls gently south west it nuzzles against the River Swale until, at Skipton-on-Swale, it leaps the slow, blue, viscous river at a fine little bridge. Eighty years after the marchers crossed this (breaking step in order not to set up potentially dangerous vibrations, as every schoolboy knows) I leaned here a while, watching the Swale whirl and pool around the reeds and disappear through trees across rolling fields.

At the big, handsome village of Baldersby where the road bends towards Ripon, I stopped for lunch on the village green, my pack beside me on a bench. There was not a soul about and I couldn't tell whether The Smithy was a pub, a garage, a tea shop or a garden centre. In any event it was closed, but this mattered not as I had had the uncommon foresight to bring my own lunch. Everyone I'd met in Northallerton had told me that I simply had to visit the artisanal deli of Lewis and Cooper.

Indeed, everyone I'd met in Northallerton was either headed there or just leaving it when they said this to me. The few that weren't were already in there. But through sharp elbows and enormous patience, I had emerged with some jamon serrano and a chunk of Gouda with cumin. 'Only the best for the working class!' I thought again, as I opened and carved the delicious fare with my Swiss army knife and ate it off the blade, feeling very much the carefree and seasoned man of the road stepping out one mid-autumn afternoon.

It was a very pleasant 20 minutes, watching the occasional light aircraft drone gently overhead and brushing the odd cheesy crumb from the folds of the OS map. It was so unseasonably mild, balmy even, that stretched out with my pack behind my head, I might even have dropped off. But then a thought occurred. Whatever The Smithy was, it was closed because it was Sunday. And if it was Sunday then there was a chance that, even if there wasn't honey still for tea, there was choral evensong at Ripon cathedral soon. A spot of light Googling revealed that it would indeed be happening at 3.30pm in Ripon cathedral, the very place where the town's Bishop welcomed the marchers. Ripon was a comfortable market and agricultural town in the thirties, as it is now, and the Jarrow marchers met a pretty indifferent response here, it's said, except at the cathedral. I thought that the least I could do was symbolically return the favour (I've started to see myself as a marcher) and pop in for choral evensong.

I quickened my pace across the amiable and easy pastures of North Yorkshire. What hills there were were far-off charcoal smudges in the hazy distance and I caught a glimpse of them from the appropriately named nook of Pennine View. Then on again, past Carlton Miniott and Ainderby Quernhow, two more splendid entries for the Villages That Sound Like 1950s Character Actors Game ('... and who can forget Carlton Miniott and Ainderby Quernhow as the two bungling policemen in *Mayhem at the Vicarage*').

Above me and above the rolling dales, the skies had darkened and around 2.30, I felt the first unwelcome splashes of rain since starting off. Soon it came in great, soaking gusts and I was grateful for the shelter of a petrol station awning. Inside in the shop, a gentleman called John Lyndley chatted to me as we both perused the Hula Hoops and Skittles. John told me that Ripon was a lovely old town and he also passed on a cherished family tale that his granddad had known a bloke who'd been on the march who had declared on arrival at Ripon that his 'boots had broke down' and made a new home in that cathedral city. I was hearing many, many stories like this on my travels and whilst they may not all turn out to be quite true, that's really not the point. King Arthur and Robin Hood didn't exist but they are still culturally enduring; potent and vivid ciphers for our country, lenses through which we see ourselves. Jarrow did happen, even if some of the stories are pure and righteous romance.

Remarkably soon, the rain was gone. The clouds became ragged and then dispersed in a stiff wind leaving skies wide, clear and blue as I raced to get to Ripon for evensong. I'd decided at the outset that the book came first, and if in search of a good story or an interesting encounter, I needed to use motorised transport for a short distance, I would, so long as it stuck to the route of the march. But it was Sunday of course and since bus deregulation in the 1980s, rural services in places like this must be long gone. One of Mrs Thatcher's many apocryphal remarks (my favourite is 'happiness is a ticked-off list') was 'a man who, beyond the age of 26, finds himself on a bus can count himself as a failure'. I was happy for Mrs T to think whatever she liked of me from wherever she may be. But she had seen to it that there were no buses for me that Sunday.

Now absurdly keen to see my plan through, I upped the pace to a mild trot, which isn't easy with a rucksack the size of a child's wardrobe. Still, it all felt very 'ecclesiastical race against time', à la *The Da Vinci Code*. I've never seen or read *The Da Vinci Code*, but I have seen the films promoted on the sides of buses (which is where I get most of my movie marketing from) and they generally seem to involve Tom Hanks dashing through a cloister or transept looking quite determined followed by a pretty girl 30 years his junior. Tom presumably makes these films at gunpoint whilst visualising the cheque.

When I was teaching sociology to likeable scallies in Skelmersdale new town in the late eighties, the standard line on 'the sociology of religion' trotted out in the textbooks and syllabi was that we were living in an 'increasingly secularised society'. The theory ran that church attendance was falling, the teachings of religious leaders going unheeded and religion itself, once such a potent force in people's lives, was dwindling to the extent that soon it would be no more influential on society than chamber music or mime. With the supreme confidence of the deluded, no one foresaw the rise of Islamic fundamentalism or that of the Christian right in America, the constant rows over anti-Semitism in the Labour hierarchy or even the brief revival of Catholic churches in England driven by devout young Polish immigrants. The predictions of experts often carry no more weight than the prophecies of oracles.

If anything the church in England was weaker and more beleaguered in the 1930s than it is today. Attendance was low and had been falling generally since the First World War, when the horrors of the battlefields had shattered the faith of many. Those who attended church were largely middle class and female. Mass Observation, the large-scale survey movement, found downright hostility to the church in some towns and cities, with only one in ten people going to church regularly in the mid-1930s. They were building community halls not churches on the new estates and holding whist drives instead of masses. The church was strongest in the affluent south and weakest in the industrial north, outside of the Catholic stronghold of Lancashire. Catholicism generally was still strong, bucking the general trend in the working towns and cities of the north. But Anglicanism and Nonconformism, the great pillars of the

Establishment and the marginalised respectively, were in decline. That *bête noire* of the Jarrow marchers, Bishop Henson, said that the church had become 'an effete establishment ... moving like a rudderless vessel over a rock haunted ocean'. Clearly, those rocks were socialism, feminism and social change, and what was needed was the enduring power of fire and brimstone.

There were no such modern uncertainties when Ripon cathedral was built. Back then, God was a very real presence in people's lives, as indeed was the devil. The flames of hell licked at one's feet at every step of life, for peasant and aristocrat alike, although of course the very rich could buy a Get Out of Hell Free pass in the form of an 'indulgence'. In the seventh century, St Wilfred put a stone roof on the wooden monastery here, thus erecting one of the first stone buildings of the Anglo–Saxon era. Soon, people came to worship here from the many surrounding hamlets and farmsteads dotted across the empty landscape.

That was 1,350 years ago, and St Wilf's place is still looking pretty impressive and certainly welcoming if you've trotted the last few miles to it in intermittent rain while being buzzed by articulated lorries. I slumped into the nearest pew and admired the décor. There's a lot of it to admire. If I were Nikolaus Pevsner I could give you the full chapter and verse on the various naves and misericords and flying buttresses, on gilts and flutings and curlicues. Lacking that kind of critical vocabulary, I'll just say that architecturally, it's a bit of a doozie.

Of course, on this autumn afternoon, what we're all really here for is the singing. Marvellous it is too. The choristers enter to the sound of the organ in full throated, eerie, *Abominable Dr Phibes* mode and proceed to match it note for note with a song that reaches to the very top bits (I told you I was no Pevsner) of the cathedral's soaring interior. Organ fans will already know that the instrument here is one of Harrison and Harrison's, the esteemed Durham family firm who also provided the sonorous beauties in King's College Cambridge, Royal Festival Hall and Westminster Abbey.

Sermons, especially when delivered in a Yorkshire accent, always make me think of Alan Bennett's hilarious 'Take A Pew' in the *Beyond the Fringe* revue. But today the sub-Dean's was very interesting, even faintly political, with a few pointed references to Britain's ongoing national rending of garments over Brexit. 'It's worth remembering at the current time that our patron saint St George is half Greek and half Palestinian ...' There's even a wry dig at David Cameron, the departed and largely discredited former PM. 'You could say that Jesus Christ invented the Big Society, one of David Cameron's favourite ideas. Anyone remember the Big Society? Anyone remember David Cameron?' This may hardly be Lenny Bruce, but in the Tory heartlands of North Yorkshire, it's positively incendiary. (Between Ferryhill and Wakefield, the march never left Conservative-run districts.)

It's over by half four and very lovely it was too. Emboldened by the music and the general vibe of serene, sun-dappled radiance, I try and grab a few words with the Dean, who's present today. A helpful gentleman tells me that he'll go into the vestry and enquire. He disappears off 'backstage', where if the Dean were a touring rock performer he would now be sitting with a white towel around his shoulders wreathed in sweat and drinking from a bottle of Amstel. Ten minutes later, the Dean emerges in full regalia, smiling, and offers me a firm handshake. He is well aware of today's anniversary. Eighty years ago, his predecessor welcomed the Jarrow men here and offered them a tour of the cathedral. Every one of them wanted it, although some of the Catholics – Tyneside was home to a good deal of the country's three million – were worried that they might be excommunicated for even entering an Anglican church. It must have been quite a day.

'Well, of course, cathedrals are used to large numbers. But, yes, it must have been very special. They were here for a particular reason at a particular time in history and the fact that the cathedral was hospitable and welcoming would have been regarded by them as a blessing, an approval of what they were marching for. The link between the church and politics is nothing new. Politics is about how people organise themselves, how they live together and that is the business of the church too. Jesus came to make this world more like heaven. So how do we so structure our society so it more resembles heaven than it does, well, anywhere else,' he chuckles.

In 1936, Ripon was fairly well insulated from the economic downturn that was blighting the rest of the north. This is perhaps why the reception for the marchers here was so distinctly muted. Local paper the *Evening Chronicle* reported that the town had viewed them 'askance' and been 'unsympathetic'. Some youngsters had even 'tittered' at them when they arrived bedraggled and footsore. The Dean though stresses similarities, not divisions: 'Sometimes industrial areas think they have had it hard and that rural society has it easier. That's not always the case. A town like Ripon has all types, all strata of society. Life would not have been easy for everybody, not then, not now.'

The Dean has a big patch, though again I'm sure that's not the right word. 'This Episcopal area encompasses most of North Yorkshire west of the A1, right to the Cumbria and Lancashire borders and up as far as the Tees and Durham. There are lots of small rural communities; remote, isolated, and suffering real issues. There's the difficulty of trying to keep your community and society active and vibrant with small numbers of people. Younger people can't find work and have to move away.' The Dean sounds exactly like William Hague, which is disconcerting, but I concentrate hard.

'And then, also as a diocese we include West Yorkshire which is an industrial, or rather a post-industrial heartland. The north, it's seen some stuff, some changes, but this church is alive, it's full of faith, it's keen to serve the needs of this community. We see the whole breadth of life here. We're a cathedral for everyone and you can come and hear this lovely music at evensong every day. Well, not Mondays … and not all Saturdays. Nearly every day!' and again he ends with a chuckle.

If I was expecting a firebrand revolutionary, I didn't get it. But I think I did get the Dean. He struck me as a canny, slightly guarded Yorkshireman – is there any other kind? – and he was perhaps being a little cautious and circumspect as one would with a rough-looking Lancashire cove with a flat cap and a backpack who gatecrashes your choral evensong and claims to be writing a book. 'Before you go, you must see the crypt by the way. Anglo–Saxon. Marvellous. Nearly 1,400 years old. But watch your step. And hurry up … we're closing.'

Taking this as official blessing, I find my way to the other side of the church, unclip the velvet rope, and make my way gingerly down into a stepped descent and then along a passage of ancient rough-hewn stone. The voices above me grow quieter, and further along by a little alcove where a candle would have once burned but is now in shadow, the passage turns and gets narrower still before opening into the crypt itself. It is a small stone chamber, spectral in the half-light falling from a small window. Around the room in several more recessed alcoves are black oily stains from the candles of Saxon monks that burned more than a thousand years ago. I realise I can hear nothing now from the main church, nothing at all in fact except my own breathing and my pulse in my ears. There is something very old and very eerie about this place and after a minute or so, I turn and go quickly back up the worn, rough stone steps into the huge silent interior of the twilit chapel.

I'm the only person here, and dusk has fallen while I was in the crypt. No matter though. Someone will still be tidying up, putting away the collection box, doing whatever it is you do before locking a cathedral for the night. Except that when I get to the large vaulted front door, having met no one, I find that it is already locked. I turn around and look back down towards the altar. But it's already getting difficult to see it.

If, like me, you're a fan of Robert Aickman's ghost stories, and in particular his story 'The Cicerones' about a hapless tourist who gets lost and trapped in an ancient cathedral at night, you will know why a very real, cold ripple of panic began to run over me. This became colder and stronger when the next door I tried was locked too. And the next. I won't tell you how Aickman's story ends but I will tell you that eventually I found a small narrow wooden door hidden in the west end of the vast church and slipped out into the churchyard now bathed in yellow sodium lights, deserted and gloomy. I didn't care. Relief flooded over me, quickly followed by embarrassment and then a kind of sheepish mirth. Night was coming on over Ripon and somewhere in this lovely old town there was a pint of beer and a whisky waiting for me, and by the time I clasped it gratefully, I'm sure my hand would have stopped shaking.

RIPON TO HARROGATE

12 October, 11 miles

On 9 October 1936, as the Jarrow men enjoyed their Sabbath day of rest in Ripon, the Sunday papers they may have read would have little resembled the enormous overstuffed beasts we stagger back from the supermarket with or burden the paper boy with now. But they would have been full of an early vintage of the fizz and froth of today's news. The 1930s were the decade that pop culture properly got into its stride and what we think of as the mass media began to seed and grow. Hollywood, 'swing' and the doings of sportsmen, musicians, actors and aristocrats were staple fare of the papers, but the big media story of the weekend 80 years ago was the announcement by the BBC that they would be launching a new entertainment platform called 'television' in early November, just as the Jarrow march reached London.

By October 2016, television had grown to be a behemoth that first conquered and shrank the world and then seemed to be beginning to wane and be eclipsed by the revolutionary global power of the Internet. Nevertheless, 70 million Americans would be glued to their small screens – more probably giant screens – tonight for the second presidential debate between Hillary Clinton and Donald Trump. It would be the first encounter since the leaked tape full of lewd misogyny had shown him in his true lurid colours. I didn't think I'd be watching since I was bound for Harrogate where I could find much nicer things to do I was sure. Before I left Ripon I wanted to make a visit that couldn't be described as fun but would be salutary and very relevant to my trip.

For their part, before the Jarrow marchers left Ripon, they held a public meeting as was usual as well as a bizarre mock trial that no one has ever quite got to the bottom of. Marcher Eddie Fitzpatrick dressed as a judge in some borrowed robes and sentenced David Riley to 'bully beef' and fatigues for the rest of his life. Was it just a bit of fun and an excuse to dress up and tease the Mayor? Or a smokescreen designed to hide the real disciplinary hearing of a different marcher who had broken the strict rules by getting drunk and thereby threatened to harm the carefully managed saintly image of the marchers? That image was reinforced and restored however at the meeting. An Alderman of Ripon spoke of how the discipline and self-sacrifice of the marchers had convinced him of the march's worth after initial misgivings. David Riley gave a grim illustration of the real cost of poverty when he stunned the audience by telling them that for every stillborn child in Ripon, there were two born dead in Jarrow. Then, having been declared fit and well (apart from blistered feet and the exhaustion of one older marcher) by Mr Cargill and Miss Blake, the medical students who were part of the march, they were on their way again to the sound of the harmonica band augmented by a drum they had been given in Ripon. They were bound for another affluent Conservative town; Harrogate. Privately, the march leaders worried what kind of welcome or lack of it awaited them there.

Along the way, they were treated warmly, royally even. As they marched through the little agricultural hamlets of Wormald Green, South Stainley, Ripley and Killinghall, one newspaper said that the driver of a passing Rolls-Royce – can there have been many about, one wonders? – wound down his window to hand the men pound notes. I was to pass these villages too, some now dormitories for commuters to Harrogate or even Leeds, but no Rolls-Royces passed my way. I did get a thumbs up from a lorry delivering granary bread and seeded baps though, so this cheered me a little, and that was needed after my detour to Ripon workhouse.

It sits squat and forbidding at a quiet edge of town away from the pretty cobbled streets of bistros and bars. Standing between the pillared gates, under the curved iron arch with its cheerless lantern, one thought comes immediately to mind; what must it have felt like to see this place, to look upon this stained brickwork, those mean windows, that sinister and menacing door, arriving not as a tourist wanting diversion, but desperate and friendless at a place of last resort. 'Workhouse', like 'Means Test', is a word that still haunts working-class life. Its long, dire echo resonates far beyond its era. It's another one of those words that I can remember my nan using when I was a kid in the 1970s. Its era may have gone, but its power to frighten lived on.

The workhouse was a place of shelter and employment for those who could not support themselves, and put that way it may seem welcoming, even kindly. Without doubt, at some level the impulse behind them was to a degree benevolent. But in practice they were grim and unhappy places, frugal and basic, offering only drudgery and discomfort. Partly, this was deliberate. Conditions in the workhouse were purposely harsh to discourage anyone who could possibly avoid them. They were bleak fixtures of civic life for centuries, but by the time of the Jarrow march, they were chiefly the domain of the sick, disabled or elderly. Even so, they were still there; a shadow in every town, the bottom rung on the ladder of degradation. Several of the Jarrow marchers had spent time in them. Jarrow itself had been described as 'a workhouse without walls'.

Ripon's central workhouse, set back by the Jolly Fryer fish bar, dates to the seventeenth century and was one of two in the town. A warden manned the door, vagrants were discouraged, and, on the whim of the gatekeeper, individuals or families were admitted. Once through the entrance hall, the sexes were separated – families were broken up – and admitted to the casual wards. The new inmates were told to strip and bathe, and their clothes were fumigated in the sulphur disinfector room. Then in return for a bed and meagre rations (often stopped altogether if some minor offence were committed), inmates would perform menial, tedious tasks of physical labour such as breaking stones or picking oakum. In Ripon, they chopped wood in the small courtyard. The novelist Barbara Taylor Bradford's grandmother was born in this workhouse; when a birth occurred here the child's birthplace was simply registered as '75 Allhallowgate, Ripon' to prevent prejudice against the child later.

Ripon workhouse is a tourist attraction now, which is odd but very definitely an improvement. You tour around led by a series of information posters and an audio guide. Most of the building is exactly as it was in the Victorian era and, whilst a few effects are recreated, like the permeating odour of carbolic, the overwhelming sense of misery soaked into the walls is very real. Long drab corridors stretch away containing rows of tiny cells each bare but for a narrow, hard bed. At the end of the corridor, there is a restraining seat with leather straps and leashes. Fumigation rooms, pegs for pale, threadbare utility clothes (small versions for the children), cracked baths, bare walls. And everywhere the notices.

RIPON POOR LAW UNION: PAUPERS SHOULD OBSERVE THE FOLLOWING. ON ENTERING THE WORKHOUSE YOU WILL BE CONFINED TO THE DAYROOMS, SLEEPING WARDS AND EXERCISE YARDS OF YOUR CLASS. YOU MUST NOT TALK WITH OR COMMUNICATE TO ANYONE OF A DIFFERENT CLASS.

It is a chilling place. Registration hall, meeting room, kitchen, laundry, dormitories, mortuary; each bleaker than the last. Stern portraits of former governors stare down from bare plaster walls and it is easy and tempting to see these men as villains, when in fact, they were probably more enlightened than many of their peers. At the end of the tour, as is obligatory these days, comments are invited on postcards which can be pinned to the wall. Like the 'below the line' comments on even the most achingly liberal newspaper's websites, they make one despair.

'People on benefits should come here to see what real poverty is.'

'Great Idea. Save us millions in benefits. Stick them in the workhouse.'

'No charging point for my iPad – Lucy, aged 44.'

Hoping that the last was at least some kind of ironic comment on the others, but still in a fairly dismal mood, I find myself back out on Ripon's drizzly and deserted streets, hoping that a late lunch at the Jolly Fryer might conjure a bit more fellow feeling and warmth towards humanity. These hopes are soon realised as I step inside the cosy little café and straight back into the 1950s, maybe the 1940s, maybe even the days of the Jarrow march itself. Wood panelling, low lighting from cute little wall mounted lamps, laminated place mats with coaching scenes; I half expect to see Trevor Howard removing some grit from Celia Johnson's eye at the next table. In fact, it's a middle-aged couple discussing last night's TV.

> HER: I forgot Emmerdale was on at quarter to seven because of the football. I had a bath and nearly missed it. It's so daft though. I'm going to stop watching it.
>
> HIM (shocked): It won top soap again, Helen. Third year running.
>
> HER: Aye, by the *TV Times* ... it's not gospel, is it? Anyway, I'm going to try a small portion of that special today. Bit of an unknown quantity.

Having perused the burgundy leatherette menu with its bewildering array of specials and deals (kiddies, OAPS, early

birds, two-for-ones, etc) I decide to stay classic. Beef burger and
chips, 'with tea and bread and butter please'. The lovely waitress,
a lady of about 70, tells me, 'It comes with tea and bread and
butter love, and free curry sauce as it's Wednesday. I'll give you
some scissors, those packets can be tricky.' I stay here for half an
hour or so, faith in humanity being restored with every friendly,
tasty, happy passing minute.

The marchers needn't have worried about Harrogate, where they
received the warmest welcome of the march so far. Two miles
outside town, a man who had come to meet them unfurled a
banner which read 'Harrogate workers welcome Jarrow workers'
to initial cheers but was apparently asked to take it down when it
was suspected he might be a communist. If this sounds cowardly,
indeed pathetic, it should be said in mitigation that the Jarrow
organisers needed the hospitality or at least support of many of
the Conservative local councils that they'd be passing through.
One of these, of course, was Harrogate.

A journalist from the *Guardian* joined them as they
marched:

> The villagers of Ripley and Killinghall rushed to their
> doors to see the marchers pass; motorists waved as they
> went by; one shouted, 'How are you sticking it? and
> a woman cried, 'Hello, Geordies.' And the 'Geordies'
> themselves were in great form, so that every moment I
> expected the band to change from 'Annie Laurie' and
> 'Swanee River' to 'Cheer, Boys, Cheer.' Contributions
> to the 'kitty' fell in as we went; here it was a pound
> there it was a penny, the penny specifically being the
> offering of an ecstatic little girl who ran across the
> road to meet us as if no one less than Bonnie Prince
> Charlie was at our head … There can be no doubt
> that as a gesture the march is a bounding success. I fell
> in with it this morning on the Ripon road. Under its

two banners ('Jarrow Crusade'), with its harmonicas, its kettledrum, and its four hundred feet, it was going strong. The marchers have with them two doctors, a barber, a group of pressmen, a Labrador dog mascot … It is an example of civic spirit probably without parallel anywhere else in the country.

Once over the River Nidd in Nidderdsale the final three miles to Harrogate are straightforward enough. You enter the town along a lovely wide boulevard, but coming up this last pull of open road must have been tough especially when, at the brow of the hill, the road descends again – always dispiriting. As any fellwalker will tell you, the cardinal rule is 'height once gained should never be conceded easily'.

I visit WH Smith's Harrogate branch for batteries and newspapers and, just alongside the new releases table containing a *Pokemon Go* annual and a Benedict Cumberbatch mindfulness colouring book (no, really), I come across a book entitled *Harrogate in 1000 Dates*. It's a timeline of significant events in the town's history and, whilst it finds room for such landmark dates as the staging here of the 1982 Eurovision Song Contest and the opening of Betty's Tea Room in 1919, the entry for 1936 includes the opening of the town's Odeon cinema but not the arrival of the Jarrow march. This is strange, given that the town apparently embraced them warmly with collections and greetings on the street. Similarly, apart from one awful hour, I have the happiest time yet here, spending a delightful afternoon and evening walking, eating, drinking, exploring – and a long, blissful sojourn in bed.

Harrogate manages the neat trick of being smart without being prissy, and it's a town of contradictions. You can drink gourmet Ecuadorian coffee and eat artisanal cupcakes just feet from where the town drunks shout unhinged abuse at each other and dance to ghetto blasters. Hipster shops are everywhere, and the nice, chatty proprietor of a vintage clothes store tells me she likes the town but is thinking of moving as, however lovely, 'the money from selling my Harrogate place will buy me a lot elsewhere and I need a new project, as I've no pension.' I tell her that with a bit of luck I never intend to retire. I hope there'll always be someone wanting a few hundred words of my deathless prose. She laughs. 'The vintage world is a bit like that. You see these little old couples who've been in it for years, still at all the fairs and stuff.' Still, presumably, selling Jarvis Cocker his polyester peardrop-collared shirts, faded cord jeans and retro specs.

On the corner of the sweetly named Strawberry Dale Avenue, by Bridal Boutique and Commercial Road, stands the Harrogate drill hall where the town's detachment of the Army Cadet Force meet as well as the 58th Harrogate Squadron of the Air Training Corps (motto 'Venture And Adventure'). This is where the Jarrow marchers were put up in Harrogate, and though compared to some of the town's architecture, it's not a particularly impressive building, what it did have was the outrageous luxury of central heating, far from common in 1936. That would have made a world of difference to these weary men.

If any of the marchers had room in their pockets for a paperback book to curl up with on the drill hall floor, it might well have been one of the three Agatha Christie's Poirot novels that were published in the few months before they set off; *The ABC Murders, Murder in Mesopotamia* and *Cards on the Table.* Christie was at the height of her popularity in 1936, having come through a mysterious personal crisis a decade before. On the evening of Friday 3 December 1926, after kissing her sleeping seven-year-old daughter Rosalind goodnight, closing the bedroom door and going downstairs, Christie drove away from her Berkshire home into the night and simply disappeared. Days passed and one of the largest searches ever mounted was undertaken for the celebrity writer. More than a thousand policemen were assigned to the case along with aeroplanes and hundreds of civilian volunteers. Two of her peers in the crime writing fraternity, Sir Arthur Conan Doyle and Dorothy L.

Sayers, were consulted. Her car was soon found abandoned near a lake close to Guildford called Silent Pool. Dark speculation swirled around the press.

Eleven days later she was found staying quietly at the Old Swan Hotel, Harrogate. In a joyous footnote, it was one of the hotel's resident banjo players who spotted her. Whilst all this did make it into that book of Harrogate's most important events, this enigmatic episode has never been fully explained. Did she lose her memory after a car crash? Was she angry or upset about her husband's ongoing affair? Or, as has been recently speculated, might she have been in a 'fugue state' with no real knowledge or control over her actions? Whatever the real story, the Old Swan revels in its Christie connection. It's one of the main venues for the Harrogate Crime Writing Festival. In a nice, if probably entirely coincidental twist, now that Nordic Noir and Scandi Crime writing have become so fashionable and successful, it's fitting that Harrogate should also now boast a Scandinavian restaurant called Norse. I had a wonderful time there and will try to refrain from eulogising the menu and the evening of eel, celeriac and general smoked, soused and pickled gorgeousness.

If your tastes run to classic British fare though, like two chicken curries, rice, naan breads, chips and a couple of pints of lager for under a tenner, head for the town's Wetherspoon which as well as being cheap is probably the most architecturally gorgeous in England. More to our point, this is where the Jarrow marchers came on the evening of 11 October 1936.

It wasn't a Wetherspoon then of course. It was the Winter Gardens Harrogate, adjacent to and part of the world-famous Royal Baths. But happily the Wetherspoon retains the famous old name, and it was here that Harrogate turned out in force to join with the Jarrow marchers at a public meeting. Harrogate loved them. The county set ladies wept openly at Paddy Scullion's tales of midwives putting their own pennies in the gas meter to deliver babies in cold, dark, impoverished Jarrow homes. Marcher Sam

Rowan commented, 'By the time Paddy Scully had finished that night, the women were in tears. They were shedding buckets of tears in their fur coats, I can tell you, down in Harrogate.'

'Red' Ellen gave another witty, blistering oration. 'I know that the authorities are getting very tired of Jarrow. They are going to be even more tired of it by the time we have finished.' The Wednesday gossip column of the *Harrogate Herald* was glowing, if a little patronising. 'A petite figure with a wealth of bronze hair spoke fearlessly from the heart and as she warmed to her subject she fired the audience to frequent bursts of acclamation … As I listened I was reminded of Joan of Arc.'

These days, the only burning steaks in the Winter Gardens are the ones that come sizzling from the grill: '8 or 14 oz Aberdeen Angus steaks from Britain and Ireland matured for 35 days then seasoned by us. With chips (add 597 Cal), peas, tomato, mushroom (add 143 Cal) and a drink.'

The J D Wetherspoon chain was founded by Tim Martin who opened the first in Muswell Hill, London, in 1979, naming it after one of his primary school teachers. It has become a modern British leisure phenomenon. Wetherspoon has been called 'the canteen of Britain', or according to the *Guardian*, 'a chain at the coalface of boozed up Britain'. A writer from webzine *Vice* actually spent a week in various Wetherspoons around the regions and whilst his resultant piece was largely fair, even affectionate, it still roped in the usual clichés: sullen, shaven-headed men getting dourly hammered, couples drinking Guinness at nine in the morning – all of which you can find in the fashionable dives of Soho. But of course if Francis Bacon does it, it's bohemian; if Wayne Rooney, or one of his lookalike spiritual brethren, does it, it's barbarian.

Into this already rich mix of social stereotyping and class mistrust, you can add the fact that Martin, founder of the budget boozer of provincial Blighty, was also one of the biggest donors to the campaign to leave the EU. Bluff and aggressively matey, with a mullet and a penchant for polo shirts, he could have come straight from central casting as the blokeish beer and burgermeister of Brexit Britain. He spent some quarter of a million pounds of his own money on backing the campaign and was rewarded by seeing millions wiped off Wetherspoon's shares in the chaotic markets after the referendum result. This was a delicious irony for many 'remainers'. But the fact certainly remains that while the English commentariat were looking elsewhere in the summer of 2016 – to the Beltway, Baltimore, Aleppo or the Chilcott enquiry – much of Wetherspoon's England was looking closer to home and, rightly or wrongly, echoing the views of Tim Martin.

To the best of my knowledge, the Harrogate Winter Gardens' Wetherspoon was my first. I liked it. As the phrase goes, what's not to like? Some people might find some callow and wearisome irony in the fact that the Winter Gardens is now a Wetherspoon but it makes perfect sense. It fulfils just the same valuable and happy function now as the Winter Gardens did back in 1936 by providing nighttime entertainment for the working folk of Harrogate. Back then it was piano recitals, plays and acrobats. Now it's big screen football and pub quizzes. It was full, and not of slavering beer monsters as I'd been led to expect, but of cheery, civilised working people having a pint and meal after work, many of them watching the World Cup qualifier between England and Slovenia on enormous screens. The match was an arid affair but it was certainly improved by a couple of large Hendrick's gin and tonics in an ice-frosted glass zesty with lemon and costing £3.80 a time. As the game ended around ten, and as I was leaving, several plates full of slathered, smothered, seared and seasoned fare arrived nearby for a table of four. Again, context is all: if you eat late at night in Madrid, you're cosmopolitan and free-spirited; if you do it in Yorkshire, you're a slob. Bon appétit, I thought.

I enjoyed Wetherspoon rather more than my other evening's outing in Harrogate. But then that was probably my fault. Although I seem to be almost alone in this in modern

Britain, stand-up comedy is not really my thing. I know quite a few stand-up comics, and I like them all. But like grand opera, the circus, Formula One and many other popular and respectable diversions, it just doesn't do it for me. Perhaps it's all those panel shows. But as the Harrogate Comedy Festival was on whilst I was in town, and as comedy was certainly a popular entertainment for the average Briton of 2016 and 1936, I thought I should 'take in a show', as the genteel old phrase once went.

What would have made the Jarrow marchers laugh? The answer, by and large, was 'other northerners', chiefly ones making the transition to film fame from careers in music hall. Comedy was the decade's most successful film genre and one of its biggest stars was himself a son of the north east. Will Hay came from County Durham and was in his mid-40s when he made his first film, having been a top draw on the touring comedy circuit. His screen career was brief but glittering, making it all the more surprising that his name is nowhere to be found in the indexes of any of the major social histories of the period – surprising and disappointing since Hay's popularity reflects something in the national character. His speciality was playing a stuffy, bumptious schoolmaster, and how much we laughed at it shows how much British comedy of the time (and for decades to come) would centre around pricking the pomposity of authority figures, from Chaucer's clergymen to Captain Mainwaring. Jarrow's cinemas would have been packed for Hay's mid-1930s hits like *Boys Will Be Boys, Where There's a Will* and *Oh Mr Porter*; cinema being a relatively cheap form of escapist entertainment even in poverty-stricken towns like Jarrow. Some of the comedy films of 1936 now sound like parody; *Cheer Up!, Excuse My Glove!, Keep Your Seats Please!* The last of these was a vehicle for another comic colossus of the period, George Formby. Again, Formby's schtick (if one can use that slick Americanism about a toothy banjo player from Wigan) was the cheeky little guy getting the girl and getting one over on his social betters, usually whilst strumming an upbeat, mildly obscene ditty and winking.

Hay and Formby aside, many of the other 'household names' of the period such as Leslie Fuller, Hal Gordon, Bobby Howes or Gene Gerrard are now only names in the households of real comedy buffs. You can find some of their work on DVD and YouTube and it's not noticeably funny, but then again it's not appreciably any less funny than most British TV comedy today. For the 1936 variety, it helps if you really like men dressing up, men getting into scrapes with 'coppers' or men pretending to be very drunk – or all three, as with Teesside's Jimmy James's classic 'drunk sketch' filmed in 1936 and surviving on YouTube. Though clearly a daft, northern, working-class fellow, he's dressed as impeccably formal as Fred Astaire in *Top Hat* for reasons that are never adequately explained. Perhaps you had to be there.

I was there at the middle Monday of the 2016 Harrogate Comedy Festival and for much of the evening I wished I was pretty much anywhere else, recalling within seconds of taking my seat that I generally would feel more comfortable and relaxed at a public witch trial or the controlled explosion of a suspect package than at stand-up comedy gigs. There are about 30 or 40 of us in an upstairs 'studio' and there are a couple of comics on the bill tonight. I'm not going to name the 'turns' because my grim evening wasn't their fault, not entirely anyway. Hey, stand-up comedy! It's not you, it's me! Although it is a bit you.

It doesn't help that the chap sitting alongside me nearly recognises me. Being recognised is never a problem. It's largely a delight. But 'nearly' being recognised is always a complex and fraught social transaction, involving assuring people that I'm not their postman or Trevor from purchase ledger and culminating in having to explain why my face might be familiar and watching the blank and faintly disappointed look emerge. That's why, unless I'm going to get something particularly useful from it, like a great interview or story, a free curry, or maybe a private tour of an art gallery, haunted castle, gin distillery or secret nuclear installation, I tend to prefer to be 'a bit incognito', the better to observe and eavesdrop. I remembered exactly why when, as I got out my little notebook, my large, voluble neighbour shouted, 'Are you from the *Yorkshire Post*?' Shortly after, a sort of real recognition dawned and we engaged in difficult small talk. 'Shame about Terry Wogan, wasn't it?' he asks. 'Yes,' I reply, this being the only possible answer a person in possession of their senses could give. Nicely awkward now, I'm well set up for an hour of discomfort.

The discomfort wasn't all about the comedy, although some was, like the long, excruciating anecdote from one act about the size of her father's appendage that had not even the merciful relief of a punchline. Then there was the obligatory 'preaching to the choir' about 'issues'. Whilst she doesn't get cross about the underwhelming size of the audience she does mention it. 'I don't have a pension so I'll be doing this when I'm 90,' she said, pausing to look out. 'Playing to 17 people on a Wednesday night in Harrogate.' Then she falters and realises what that sounds like. 'Not that I don't want to. I would love that.' Wise move this; old pros have an adage: 'never have a go at the ones who've turned up.'

But, I repeat, my bad night out was not the comic's fault. No, mainly it stemmed from us, the small audience who were either 'silent smilers' (a perfectly reasonable thing to be, but terrible for a performer, who thinks they're dying) or loudly and persistently trying to get in on the act.

'Anyone in from Canada?'

My neighbour: 'YES! ... YOU!'

'Who was the best Spice Girl, do you think?'

'SCARY BECAUSE SHE'S FROM YORKSHIRE!'

Terrifyingly, the comedian notices us and leans forward into the spotlight, shading her eyes.

'Are you guys on a date?'

'HEE HEE SQUEE! HEE HEE HEE HEE!' comes the worrying, delighted squeal from my new chum.

'NO! NO, WE'RE NOT.' I shout far more quickly and loudly than is strictly necessary for someone not a raging homophobe.

Four women on the front row shriek at pretty much every word, the way that teenagers do in the street, clutching each other, in a desperate attempt to convince the world that they are 'crazy' and having fun. Is this a new thing? Maybe I did it when I was a daft kid but I don't think so. Like selfies and Facebook, it feels part of a new culture of relentless self-assertion and promotion. Eventually, the house lights come on, and before they are up to full, I am away into the night.

Later, brooding in the Bell Tavern over a small, strong craft beer, I conclude again it's no one's fault. I mentioned F1, Billy Smart and Verdi; to that I could add *The Apprentice*, rugby union and taramasalata. Stand-up is just not my thing. I repeat: it's not you, it's me. We should start seeing other people. And starting tomorrow, that could either be Claude Debussy, Jean Michel Jarre or the Chuckle Brothers, which are all possible diversions available in my next destination. Leeds awaits, as it did the Jarrow marchers, and I am going to make a part of the journey to one of my favourite cities in England in proper Yorkshire style.

HARROGATE TO LEEDS

13 October, 15 miles

Harrogate claims to be the happiest place to live in Britain, an assertion often backed up by various surveys. The Jarrow marchers and I had a lovely time here in our different ways, 80 years apart. I would have been sorrier to leave were it not that Leeds was my next stop, and that having walked much of the intervening route previously on my rest day, I was going to treat myself to a ride on the No. 36 from Ripon to Leeds via Harrogate which, from its marketing, was less of a bus, more of a lifechanging experience.

As a Lancastrian, I often say, deliberately provocatively and not entirely seriously, that Yorkshire is wasted on Yorkshiremen. Of course, I don't mean this and for reasons that are many and include Alan Bennett, Jarvis Cocker, Stan Barstow, Richard Hawley, Henry Moore, Ted Hughes, The Human League and Jake Thackray, a fabulously gifted, witty, touching, saucy singer, guitarist and songwriter from Kirkstall who was quite the celebrity in the 1970s. Inspired more by jazz, chansons, beat poetry and musicals than pop, he was the George Brassens of the South Riding, the north country Noël Coward. His song 'The Rain Upon the Mountainside' may well be the best song ever written about the north of England; spare and dark, beautiful but unsentimental. But today it was another of his tunes that I had in my head. 'Country Bus' was his tribute to the rattling antique transport of his youth that ran between the villages of remote Yorkshire and the big market towns and cities. The 'notorious ... amorous ... rumbustious ... malodorous country bus' was a vital network of commerce, adventure and romance.

The 36 provides all those functions certainly but without even a whiff of the malodorous or notorious. In fact, its website seems to promise the most sophisticated, advanced, luxurious bus ever made. Crucially, they run every ten minutes, so I have the leisure to catch up on the news over a cup of tea before embarking. Eighty years ago this morning, still glowing from the public meeting the night before, the marchers breakfasted on ham and beef paste sandwiches and were told by the deputy mayor as they left town, 'I don't think we let you down here. The meeting at the Winter Gardens last night was the finest I have seen in that hall in the past 30 years. It was representative of all sections of Harrogate society. That is saying a great deal as Harrogate people are difficult people to get to turn out at night.' Last night's young comic would agree, if not the staff at Norse or Wetherspoon.

I work through a pile of morning papers. 'Full steam ahead for HS2' says the *Express* on the controversial new high-speed train link. *The Times* T2 section goes with the big stuff too: 'Squeak! The Return of Leather Trousers!' The *Guardian* matches it with its splash, 'Is Spag Bol a Culinary Crime?' The *Mirror*'s 'bombshell' is 'Will Quits Strictly', an item about the fact that former pop singer Will Young has left a TV dancing show. Dark rumours abound with the computer tech genius behind the Amstrad emailer Lord Alan Sugar speculating that 'Will's clash with head judge Len Goodman over the weekend may have prompted him to walk away.' The *Daily Mail* has seen fit to ignore this in favour of a foam-flecked rant about Brexit that takes up most of the front page and reads like a communique from Enver Hoxha's Albania: 'Damn the unpatriotic Bremoaners and their plot to subvert the will of the British people!'

Suppressing a desire to shout 'Parklife!', I expect it to continue, 'The heads of dissidents must be smashed against the

iron walls of party discipline and unity'. But they have gone with
something about Fiona Bruce's shoes instead. More seriously,
on various news websites there's party politics here and abroad.
The BBC website reports on the toxic clashes between Trump
and Clinton last night, 'The tawdriest exchanges in 56 years of
televised presidential debates'. At home, a NEWS ICM *Guardian*
Poll puts Labour at 26 and the Tories at 43, the second highest
Tory lead in the history of polling.

I'm thankful when the next bus turns up, to be honest. I
haven't been on a bus in a long while so I can't tell you whether
the sleek, suave 36 with its free WiFi, USB ports, plug sockets,
reclining leather seats, tray tables and small library of paperback
books is now the industry standard or an extravagant aberration
but it was certainly a surprise to this traveller. My single to Leeds
is £6. 'Do you do contactless?' I ask the driver/conductor. 'Of
course,' he replies, smoothly and somewhat pityingly, as if I had
asked whether the bus had wheels or an exhaust pipe. I take
a front row seat upstairs and am soon joined by a lady sitting
across the aisle from me. 'Hoping for a good view!' she says
excitedly and takes out a tin of travel sweets. Maybe this is her
first time on the 36 too. She offers me a barley sugar. I feel a
little giddy.

The 36 follows the road the marchers would have taken,
the A61 from North into South Yorkshire, through verdant
Harrogate suburbia until it reaches the River Wharfe near
Dunkeswick. This was my cue to tear myself away from the cosy
reclining seats and Spotify and disembark. Just around here,
halfway on the day's itinerary as the marchers crossed the broad
Wharfe, a contingent of policemen led by an inspector appeared
from nowhere to escort them the next few miles into the
outskirts of Leeds. The reason was clear. The march was passing
by Harewood House and its vast estate. Owned by Edwin
Lascelles, first Baron of Harewood, it was built and sustained
with money made from plantations using slave labour in the
West Indies. The Lascelles first came here on a previous wave of

immigration known as the Norman Conquest and by the time the Jarrow marchers passed by it belonged to Henry George Charles Lascelles. He'd gone from the merely aristocratic to the positively regal by marrying the Princess Royal, daughter of King George V and Queen Mary. Princess Mary was a shy soul, active in charity work, who for a time worked two days a week as a nurse and who did not warm to life at court. So perhaps she was in residence in her beloved Harewood when the police steered the marchers away from its grand baronial halls and nearly 30,000 acres of lush parkland.

Today there's only me, so I reckon I could have slipped in under the constables' noses at least as far as Harewood Village. I enter the village in fine rain, breath condensing in the damp air, the first real sign of approaching winter. Like so many huge and opulent homes of the aristocracy, Harewood House has now opened its doors, on its own terms, to the people of England – plantations and the slave trade not being the big earners they once were. Thanks to such generous and democratising advances, you can now get married here, stroll the gardens or peek inside the house and admire the Renaissance masterpieces. 'There are exquisite family portraits by Reynolds, Gainsborough, Lawrence and Richmond as well as a fine collection of Sèvres china, among many other delights. You can even search the servants database and find out whether one of your family members was a footman or scullery maid here, but be warned, it might take you a while; there are several hundred former servants on the list.

I bump into a hearty, friendly group of walkers in the car park of the village hall. They've heard of the Jarrow march ('they were hungry and needed work, didn't they?') but didn't know it passed by the ancestral seat of the Earls of Harewood. They recommend a trip to the house and a circuit of the grounds. 'It's a good three miles but well worth it. It's where they film Emmerdale! A special purpose built set! You can't go in, but you can look at it from afar, like.' The long-running Yorkshire soap does seem to rather preoccupy folks around these parts, and I have visions of couples from Batley hiding in the undergrowth with bootblacked faces and binoculars trained on The Woolpack. I take another of their recommendations though; a mug of tea and a sit down in the village's Muddy Boots café, packed even on a damp and chilly midweek afternoon. I don't stay long. Country houses aren't really my thing and while Harewood is pleasant enough there is far better down the road, through the affluent suburbs of Moortown and Chapel Allerton and into the beating heart of one of the great cities of the north.

Leeds always gives me a heck of a thrill. With all due respect to its peers, to Manchester, Newcastle and Liverpool, and local rivals like Sheffield and Bradford, nowhere buzzes and throbs like Leeds with that feel of a grand industrial city on the make and on the move. It's a big, brash town with money in its pocket, and a ceaseless, restless appetite for enjoyment and culture found in its hundreds of pubs and restaurants, galleries and gig venues. Maybe it's a vestige of my teenage enthusiasm for Don Revie's dark and saturnine anti-heroes of 1970s football, those brooding and malevolent Heathcliffs in Admiral sportswear; Lorimer, Clarke, Giles, Bremner, Cooper. But I love this town.

In Chapel Allerton I decide to hop back onto the 36 for the last mile into Leeds and thus arrive in style. At the bus stop near the library by Gadget Exchange and Tandoori Hut, I meet the first non-white woman I've seen since leaving Jarrow, an Asian mum with little lad in tow, waiting to go shopping in Leeds. Within minutes the bus is here and I take my now regular seat, top deck front, where someone has obligingly left today's free paper. Former pop singer Lily Allen is getting 'trolled' online for apologising to the people in the Calais Jungle refugee camp about their predicament. On the next page though, something that depresses me even more. Art history A Level is being scrapped and I decide to take it personally. This leads directly to me having a brief spat in a hotel bedroom in Leeds with Michael Gove, former Education Secretary and arch Brexiteer.

He wasn't there, I should point out. Our minor contretemps was via social media, via which I angrily and it seems too hastily berated him for being responsible for the scrapping of art history A Level. But I was seething. Seething at the reductive view of education that thinks we plebs don't need to know about the finer things in life – class war conducted by stealth.

At the dawn of the 1980s in my late teens in Wigan, I found myself briefly academically becalmed before beginning my degree, and chose to fill my time with two extra A Levels chosen pretty much on a whim. One was British social and economic history, a subject I would now find fascinating but of which I now remember little except for the pioneering Speenhamland benefits system of rural Berkshire and the six demands of the Chartists. My other choice though was art history, and almost every moment of it – every languorous afternoon in the dark, hot and intimate audio visual room flipping through the slides of Les Demoiselles d'Avignon, Le Déjeuner sur l'Herbe, Munch, Kandinsky, Piet Mondrian – has stayed with me ever since. Those long, absorbing hours taught me that the creation, appreciation and love of art is not just the mark of a civilised society, it is the clearest mirror you can hold up to that society, telling you more of its time than a thousand academic histories or earnest documentaries.

Picasso's Guernica is an astonishing piece of visual art but it's also a bulletin of blazing, angry reportage that awakened the world to the brutality of the Spanish Civil War. British war artists like Nash and Nevinson evoked the horrors of the Western Front with a dreamlike serenity that is at the same time the stuff of nightmares. But even when not reporting the actual, art brings to us vividly and pungently the authentic cultural flavour of its day. In the work of the Italian Futurists, one can see all the dangerous and muscular allure of both Fascism and Communism. Piet Mondrian's geometric grids sing with the pulsating joys of the jazz age whilst Andy Warhol both celebrates and satirises 1960s consumerism within the same gaudy frame.

Sometimes the insights of art history were more personal. Stanley Spencer's work haunted me and shaped my view of a kind of mythic, phantasmagorical England where sex, nature and religion combined in works of beauty and strangeness, like The Resurrection, Cookham and Man Goeth to His Long Home. The Blaue Reiter group from Germany fed my cravings for existential teen darknesses where I could brood moodily (Karl Schmidt-Rottluff's Woman with a Bag is, essentially, The Scream for cool kids; look it up). From Modigliani I learned a lot about sex. Not the act itself but the real nature of the thing. It's not just that his nudes and portraits of women are sexy – they are achingly, breathtakingly so – but they tell you everything about the nature of longing, desire and heartbreak, as well as the myth of the doomed romantic genius. Art history taught me to see the brilliance, bravery and sheer fun in the experimental in every medium, especially music and film; the need for art that challenges the dreary orthodoxies of the day. Without the revolution in the head that the study of art history fired in me, I doubt I would ever have loved or 'got' free jazz, John Cage, Webern, drone, Morton Feldman or Peter Greenaway. This was not a world I was naturally born to in seventies and eighties Wigan. But in their gentle way, my art history classes and teachers helped me storm a citadel I've lived in ever since.

So after I'd checked into my Leeds hotel, I did what any modern person would do with this righteous anger. I tweeted about it. I fired off a raging 100 characters or so condemning Michael Gove's philistinism. Then I thought nothing more of it. Instead, I took to social media again to ask for suggestions of something artistic or cultural I could do in Leeds that evening. I was determined that my Jarrow march, and this book, would show that 'ordinary' working people and their kids do appreciate art and culture and that any healthy nation provides the tools for the enjoyment of it.

The cultural delights on offer in Leeds on that one October night were many and varied. Steve Howe, the guitarist of prog rockers Yes, was playing an intimate acoustic set at the lovely old City Varieties Theatre. French electronic legend Jean Michel Jarre was at the big new arena in the city. At the theatre there was a play about the Brontës and a revival of the classic two-hander *Sleuth*, from which Morrissey pinched some of his best lines like, 'A jumped up pantry boy who never knew his place'.

After some sifting, I narrowed it down to two events which in their different ways seemed unmissable. At the old Yorkshire TV building, there was An Evening with the Chuckle Brothers, Paul and Barry, whilst at the Howard Assembly Room in the Opera House, there was a recital of early twentieth century French piano music. Now, I have a lot of time for the Chuckle Brothers; I've always enjoyed the simple comedic elegance of their 'to me, to you' exchanges. Also, at an awards ceremony 'after show', I once found myself dancing with the moustachioed siblings and the model Sophie Dahl on a podium in a London nightclub, still possibly the most glamorous few minutes of my life. But the Debussy piano preludes, which would form part of the piano recital, have a very special place in my heart. Two scratchy vinyl albums of them in a battered box set from Wigan Library were my introduction into classical music and these haunting, limpid, sensual pieces still make my head swim. I found the invitation tweet from Rowland at Opera North and hit the DM button to message him.

In the meantime, I took to the streets of Leeds to soak up its brisk vibe of brass and bravado. Leeds established itself in the late 1800s as the global capital of the wool trade. Unlike some of their kind though, the civic fathers spent their money on art, learning and fine buildings for the Leodensians as assiduously as they lined their own pockets. Whether you come via Westgate or The Headrow, down Calverley Street or up Park Row, all roads in Leeds lead eventually to its Montmartre, its Buckingham Palace, its Kremlin. The city's fabulously imposing town hall was described by historian Asa Briggs as 'a magnificent case study in Victorian civic pride'. *Architecture Today* called it 'the epitome of northern civic bombast', which sounds altogether more snidey and grudging and perhaps a little jealous.

Bombastic or magnificent, Leeds town hall welcomed the Jarrow marchers with open arms of municipal and architectural splendour. Not till they got to London and the Palace of Westminster would a building this grand open its doors to them again, and the welcome there would be ambivalent, unsatisfying and disingenuous. Leeds had no such qualms. They were treated to a reception and a slap-up feed in the hall's crypt with uniformed staff asking solicitously, 'beer or tea, Sir?' By most accounts, it was the finest night of the whole march, lingering long in the marchers' memories. Bob Maughan had worked for six months in the ten years up to October 1936. Sixty years on, he remembered their night in Leeds as, 'A bit of a holiday, a grand night. Roast beef ... Yorkshire pudding ... a bottle of pale ale ... we were well looked after.' Even Paddy the dog was served his dinner in a silver tureen.

All of this was paid for by a local Tory grandee with the blessing of the Conservative council. They even invited along officials of Leeds Trade Union council to tuck in. Quite why they did this might seem baffling. But I'd guess it was to 'show up' the lily-livered nature of the Labour Party's attitude to the march and, even more importantly, a cussed demonstration of civic pride and independence. Whatever the Tories of Westminster may have thought, the Tories of Leeds were their own men and women (though sadly mainly men).

Flanking the grand doors of the town hall are a pride of stone lions. Designed by sculptor William Day Keyworth, local legend has it that, if the town hall clock should ever strike 13, time will stand still, the people of Leeds will freeze and the lions will come to life and silently stalk the streets of the city. Call me a purist in these matters but as the lions have only been there since 1867 I baulk at that term 'legend', as I do like my folklore to at least predate, say, fridges. But if you do fancy a bit of magic, the lions will talk to you, fairly amiably, if you download the app, scan the code into your mobile phone and put your headphones on. (The voices sounded suspiciously like Brian Blessed to me.)

With only the slightest hankering for the Chuckle Brothers across town, I negotiate Leeds's early-evening throng on New Briggate and arrive at my seat in the beautifully restored Howard Assembly Room, Opera North's chamber space for Steven Osborne's piano recital. Tonight's programme is of piano works by Debussy, Ravel and Poulenc, all of whom had written masterpieces and established their enduring reputations by the time of the Jarrow march. Debussy had died two decades before, Ravel would die the year later, Poulenc in 1963. None of those names would have been known to the Jarrow men, not merely because their class or education would have kept them in ignorance, but simply because of a widespread suspicion against 'modern' music that still persists into our era. Back in the 1930s, even when enlightened ideas like subscription concerts or the Proms sought to bring classical music to the 'masses', it would inevitably be the established repertoire of various long-dead Europeans.

In the year of the Jarrow march several staples of the modern repertoire were being composed or premiered. Prokofiev's *Peter and the Wolf*, Rachmaninov's Symphony No. 3, several early pieces by the young Benjamin Britten. Alban Berg premiered his darkly brilliant Violin Concerto, still the most famous and popular piece from the 'difficult' serialist school. Perhaps most relevant, Paul Hindemith composed his Trauermusik, a plangent requiem for King George written in the single day after his death. The death of the king was a deeply felt personal human sadness that would then usher in a national crisis as the Jarrow men marched toward London.

Hearing the Debussy preludes and short pieces brings back the same thrill that I felt when I played those scratched and much borrowed editions from Wigan Library. The shivery, spectral washes of Footprints in the Snow and The Drowned Cathedral, the kooky wit of Golliwog's Cakewalk, the sheer loveliness of Claire de Lune and The Girl with the Flaxen Hair. My love of classical music was fostered not by my parents or through buying records (I couldn't have afforded them) but through Wigan Library, Radio 3 and the music department of Edge Hill University. Thus, like so many other joys in my life I have the state to thank for it. Or the Nanny State, as its detractors have it. In my experience, however, the people who sneer at the nanny state are usually people who had nannies.

Steven Osborne's performance is brilliant, played from memory with no sheet music and with most pieces prefaced by a little illuminating introduction putting them in context and pointing out things to listen out for. This should be standard procedure at all classical concerts; it's sheer snobbery not to do so. But for all Steven's fabulous playing it is his remarks after the interval when introducing the second half that stick in the mind. (Earlier, I had mentioned to Rowland and my friends at Opera North that I had chosen this event from a range of delights on offer in Leeds that night.)

'Thank you all for coming this evening. I hope you've enjoyed the music so far. In a moment, I'd like to carry on with Ravel's beautiful Menuet Antique but before that, it's come to my knowledge that there's a gentleman in the audience who had to make the difficult decision whether to come to hear me play or watch the Chuckle Brothers. Well, I can only hope you feel you've made the right decision, sir.' The hall breaks into laughter, in which I heartily join, looking around with all the rest pretending to wonder where this bloke can be and what on earth he must be like.

There is odder to come. Back in my hotel room, I scroll through texts, tweets and emails before turning in. There is a message from Michael Gove. In it, he tells me that the scrapping of art history A Level has nothing to do with him. 'I Heart Art History' he tweets, with an actual little emoji heart (rather apt

I think). So I reply to the effect that I stand corrected if he isn't to blame and I apologise. He replies, 'Thank you Stuart – a genuinely fair-minded thinker.'

'A genuinely fair-minded thinker' – Michael Gove. Is that a recommendation for the book jacket I wonder?

I look again at Twitter before turning off my phone. Someone has already seen the exchange and replied, 'Get a room, you two.'

STAGE EIGHT
LEEDS TO WAKEFIELD

14 October, 9 miles

On the morning of 14 October, with some reluctance, I pack up and check out of Leeds. In the lobby of my hotel is one of those giant screens that are permanently and silently tuned to Sky News. The image looming down at me appears to be a reanimated Douglas Fairbanks Junior with a Little Richard Pompadour and dark glasses. This turns out to be Bob Dylan, he of the asthmatic wheezing on the old mouth organ whose words, it transpires, have been considered marvellous enough to impress a group of spoony old fanboys at the Swedish Academy. The scrolling news ticker informs us that Bob Dylan has been given the Nobel Prize for literature by virtue of, as the citation has it, 'having created new poetic expressions within the great American song tradition'.

I roll my eyes and pull my 'what a world we live in today' face. Whilst acknowledging his colossal influence on popular music, I would no more give him the Nobel Prize for Literature than I would the gong for Physics or Economics. Or give Harold Pinter a grammy for *The Caretaker*. Silly old Stockholm. Leeds would never do anything as daft and soft, although they have put up a statue to Billy Bremner and they might give David Batty the Nobel Peace Prize as a black joke.

As is now customary, the day's other news is uniformly 'Brexit', an event which seems to have thrown every conversation and interaction, every normal daily event into an uncomfortable kind of relief and shine a strange, harsh new light that refracts the world differently. Packing and shouldering my rucksack draws the attention of two friendly Polish girls in the lobby, Elenya and Lana. I tell them about the Jarrow march, about how the hungry men went to find work and how (spoiler alert) the Prime Minister refused to see them. 'That is very sad but at least they had a passion, a purpose in life, and are you going to see the Prime Minister?' I tell them I hope to get into the Palace of Westminster. 'Well, we wish you luck.'

Not long after this, making my way up the unattractively named Swinegate, I have a similar conversation by the doorway of Bibi's Italian restaurant, this time with a young Russian woman called Julia who works there. She's been here three-and-a-half years and has heard of the Jarrow march as it's one of the aspects of British history her six-year-old daughter Alexandra has been studying. 'She has learned about Florence Nightingale, all the Victorian people, the *Titanic*. Do you know how many people there are on the *Titanic*? Two thousand two hundred and twenty eight people! Very sad. My daughter is expert on it.'

Julia is originally from St Petersburg, though she hasn't been back there for two years. 'It is very beautiful,' she says wistfully. 'The Hermitage. The Amber room. But very cold in winter. You should go in the summer. Oh yes, go in June. Ah, the White Nights. But –' and she gives my pack a little pat '– it is too far to walk.'

At a coffee stand in Leeds, I find myself wondering if in perhaps a year or two, or maybe ten, when the much talked of Article 50 has been long triggered and we have undergone our slow painful divorce from the rest of the continent, whether I will be having these everyday conversations with lovely people from Krakow and St Petersburg. I hope so. But there seems to be a chill wind abroad even in these happy, busy streets and I don't like the feel of it. The novelist Ian McEwan has recently been even more jittery. 'It's reminiscent of Robespierre and the terror of the French Revolution. The air in my country is very foul.'

I tear myself away from Julia and the lure of Bibi's, which is possibly my favourite restaurant in Leeds along with Tharavadu, the heavenly Keralan opposite the station. But in Leeds, the gourmet, the hedonist, the culture vulture, the epicure are all spoiled for choice. Every time I come back to Leeds it's a little more swaggering, bolder and busier, a touch more glamorous in a blousy, cheeky, 'come and get me' way, and every time I love it a little more. The city's sheer appetite for fun and profit will rock you on your heels. Every grand street is packed shoulder to shoulder these days with 'twisted street food', 'kitchens', 'canteens' or even 'cantinas', and while you may not like the words, who does not the love the thrill of a great city with an almost unseemly dedication to dressing up, getting out and having a good time.

It helps that Leeds has such a thriving student population, a number of whom come for Britain's best and most prestigious modern jazz courses, and consequently Leeds is the world capital of what's known as 'muscle jazz', a wild, technically daunting mix of rock and jazz. Four-hundred-and-eighty-three Leeds Uni students are lodged in the former Montague Burton clothing works. It's student accommodation now, but back in 1936 when its sewing machines hummed with industry, the marchers breakfasted here on porridge, bacon, sausage and tomato on the morning they left Leeds. Before they did, they were given the results of a whip round at the factory that raised over thirty pounds, a sum that would help enormously in the days ahead. Perhaps embarrassed at the party line, some Leeds Labour Party members stitched tattered clothes and brought new boots for the marchers. Leeds RSPCA inspected Paddy the dog and declared him fit to go on (although by this time four marchers had had to be sent home due to ill health). All contemporary coverage mentions this cute canine companion, perhaps to soften any political edge to their reports. But the *Guardian* writer who'd accompanied them since the Ripon road into Harrogate did find time for some other observations too.

This is not a hunger-march, but a protest march … There is no political aspect to this march. It is simply the town of Jarrow saying 'Send us work.' In the ranks of the marchers are Labour men, Liberals, Tories, and one or two Communists, but you cannot tell who's who. With the marchers goes, prominently carried, the Jarrow petition for work, a huge book with about 12,000 signatures, which Miss Ellen Wilkinson, M.P. for Jarrow, is to present at the bar of the House of Commons on November 4 … It was interesting to watch motorists who passed us on the road recognise her and lean out of windows as they went by. Like us all she made friends with Paddy, the Labrador dog who accompanied the procession uninvited for five miles from Jarrow before anyone realised that he intended to go all the way. When the marshal's whistle goes he goes too and there is no holding him. It is interesting, too, to watch men employed on the road rest on their spades to watch men unemployed but also on the road go by. Their eyes spoke their thoughts… At every stopping-place there is such a meeting so that the world shall know of Jarrow.

It would be a wild exaggeration to claim that the world knew of my march but some do, mainly friends or family or through social media. And as I'm crossing the river that bisects the city along the now fashionable Calls district, the 'wide majestic Aire' as the great song by local jazz folk rockers Trembling Bells calls it, I hear the ping of an incoming text. It's a message of good wishes from my friend Gary, a Sikh taxi driver from Manchester, filled with his usual bewildering array of emojis, hashtags and indecipherable acronyms. Gary is pushing 40 but his texts can make you feel very old. I tell him that it's going well, that I'm headed for Wakefield today and that I'll probably stop off around Hunslet or Dewsbury for an early lunch. 'Cool. Don't forget u shd go to a Gurdwara #curry licking lips emoji.'

Of course. The perfect idea. Their own cooks notwithstanding, the Jarrow marchers relied on the hospitality of others for food and shelter and they endeavoured to prove themselves worthy of this by sobriety and self-discipline. One of the central tenets of Sikhism is hospitality to strangers and travellers and the Gurdwara and its kitchens are open 24 hours a day for the sustenance and welcome of travellers, providing they are well behaved and have not taken drink. If the orange flag of the Gurdwara had fluttered over English cities in 1936, the Sikh community would have welcomed and fed the Jarrow men. And what a delicious change it would have made from beef paste sandwiches and porridge.

It would have been theoretically possible too, had their route taken them through Shepherd's Bush, site of England's first Gurdwara established in 1911. This coincided with the first real wave of Sikh immigration to the UK, although Britain's links with the Punjab stretch much further back. From the mid-nineteenth century onwards many Punjabis served in the British army and Sikh soldiers fought in elite regiments seeing active service in both world wars. A memorial in Sussex honours the Sikh dead who fought for the UK in the First World War. Partition of their homeland and labour shortages here encouraged large scale Sikh migration from the Punjab and by the late 1940s, there were substantial Sikh communities settled across the land; Cardiff, Bristol, Ipswich, Peterborough, Doncaster, Birmingham, Aberdeen, Glasgow, Edinburgh, Leeds, Liverpool, Middlesbrough, Southampton, Portsmouth and Manchester. In the Black Country, Sikh men formed a large part of the workforce in the hot and physically demanding forges and foundries. Elsewhere they went into medicine, IT and commerce. There are currently around half a million Sikhs in the UK and they have become the leading ethnic minority in business.

After a quick consultation with Google maps, I turned south-west, through the rugby league heartland of once-proud

Hunslet who still play at the South Leeds Stadium. I've never been to that sporting crucible but as a kid I'd made several trips to Elland Road because of my perverse obsession with Don Revie's maligned ubermensch. This provided a heady change from the rough and guileless non-league football on offer at Wigan Athletic's Springfield Park, or the Cowshed as it was known, where muddied oafs would hack at each other in the winter twilight. It was towards Elland Road that I turned now, headed for the industrial suburb of Beeston where a small detour would take me to one of Leeds' three Sikh temples, the Guru Nanak Nishkam Sewak Jatha Gurdwara on Lady Pit Lane.

The morning was grey and damp and the walk through Leeds southern urban sprawl not the prettiest. Along the way I checked by text with Gary about the etiquette of my visit. I should simply open the door and enter, no appointment needed. I should wear long trousers and long sleeves (as if I would wear any other kind in Leeds in October), should not be drunk (he knows me so well) and should cover my head (yes, my flat cap would be fine). Around 1pm, I turned into Lady Pit Lane, a drab terrace with one dominant building – a squat Victorian structure that looked like it might have once been a mill or an old school, carrying as it did that air of old, cold hard times and unyielding officialdom and authority. 'Security cameras monitor this building twenty four hours a day' read a stern black-and-white notice. But above the door was a bold sign of eggshell blue and above that the weakly fluttering orange flag that bids welcome from miles around to Sikh and non-Sikh alike.

I stand for a long time in the street. I feel self-conscious and uncomfortable, unsure of etiquette and protocol and aware that the odd kid passing on a bike or taxi driver is wondering what I'm up to. I push the door. It won't open and I feel a mild swell of relief. Pull yourself together I think, and I push again. This time it opens and I'm in an unprepossessing vestibule strewn with a few boxes of clothes, household goods and tins of paint. On the wall is a mirror in which I can see myself looking shifty

and awkward and a welcome sign which spells out the protocol
for visiting the Gurdwara. I should 'wear modest attire and
remove shoes when entering the congregation hall. This is a
sign of respect to the sovereignty of the Guru Granth Sahib. All
gurdwaras have shoe racks. You will see Sikhs bow in front of
the Guru Granth Sahib upon joining the congregation. Non-
Sikhs are not required to bow, but should enter and quietly join
the congregation.' And I am asked to keep my head covered at
all times, 'as a sign of respect to the Guru Granth Sahib. Flat
caps and baseball caps are not suitable, but there are headscarves
provided in the box below.'

Thanks Gary. Realising what the mirror is for, and
remembering how useless I am with a bow tie, I spend the next
six or seven minutes trying and failing to tie the orange scarf
successfully around my head in a way that does not make me
look like a bad Keith Richards impersonator or a 1940s charlady
in an Arthur Askey film. This proves impossible. I try simply
placing the scarf on top of my head but this makes me look like
a granddad on the beach in the same 1940s Arthur Askey film
or Michael Palin in his D P Gumby guise from Monty Python.

Whilst doing all this I become aware that I am being watched
by a small Indian lady on my left who has peered around the
partition. I start to speak but she disappears into the interior of
the Gurdwara again. I wonder if there is any kind of bell I can
ring or ding in the manner of a hotel reception. I'm sure there
isn't, and I'm sure even thinking there is is mildly objectionable,
but I'm not really sure where to go from here. Just as I am
starting to think about removing the headscarf (which wouldn't
take long) putting my shoes back on and sloping sheepishly back
onto Lady Pit Lane, admitting failure in my adventure in multiculturalism, a tall, young Indian with a superbly knotted turban
that makes me feel distinctly inadequate comes through the
door behind me carrying a bag of tools. He eyes me with mild
curiosity, and my headscarf with what I think is pity. 'Can I help
you?' I explain as best as I can in a couple of sentences about the

march, the anniversary, the marchers' reliance on hospitality, my curiosity about the temple. He pauses, thinks for a second and then with a puzzled smile says, 'Well, you'd better come in then. Have you had any lunch?'

Inderpal turns out to be the most thorough and amiable guide to Sikhism and the Gurdwara that any traveller could have. Devout but not stuffy, he is charming and easy going, and clearly proud of his faith, his community and his temple. He indicates his bag of spanners and wrenches. 'You'll have to excuse us, we're not quite at our best. We're having work done, as you can tell.' For the first time I become aware of hammering and sawing from somewhere deep within the temple. We take a seat at one of the long benches in the kitchen area. There is one other diner, a beaming, leathery old boy missing a few teeth. He sits by the door in a long cream robe, chewing on a fresh green chilli. 'I've had ten of these today!' he says, grinning.

The Sikh kitchen or 'langar' was introduced in the sixteenth century by the founder of Sikhism, Guru Nanak. It was intended as a place where all can eat together in equality, regardless of creed, class, race or social standing. It has come to embody much of the Sikh faith's philosophy and a Sikh prayer goes 'Loh langar tapde rahin', or 'May the hot plates of the langars remain ever in service.' Today's langars are run along almost industrial catering lines. The benches we sit at are alongside several large ranges on which sit huge pots and tureens stirred by four or five Sikh ladies. Behind them, the woman who observed me struggling with my headscarf (which is proving remarkably stable if hardly stylish) is chopping bags of onions and green beans whilst chattering gaily in Punjabi to a companion. The kitchen runs 24 hours a day, its doors never close and the food is 100 per cent vegetarian.

One of the ladies comes from behind the cookers to speak to me. 'You like curry? You know Indian food?' Oh yes, I reply, and seemingly delighted with this answer, she scurries away returning with two metal trays divided into sections containing vegetable curry, chana dahl, rice and chapati. She hands one each to me and Inderpal. It's predictably delicious and as we eat Inderpal explains more about the Gurdwara.

'It is not just a kitchen and not just a temple. It is partly a school and partly a community centre. We have classes upstairs in music and dance. There is a nursery and a library and we have rooms. At the moment we have a student from the Punjab staying with us while he studies in Leeds for his degree. He will be with us for a few years. And we have the main hall of worship which is called the Dahar Sahib. In there is our holy book, the Guru Granth Sahib, which is the last of our gurus and the only one that is not a human man. We'll go there when we've eaten,' he says, scooping another mouthful of rich, aromatic yellow dahl with his folded chapatti.

'You should try one of these. Try it raw,' says the genial man at the next table, holding up a transparent plastic bag in which I would say there were 500 green chillies, gleaming as if painted and radiating latent heat and pain like mini hand grenades. 'Hand them over,' I hear myself saying and I take the bag. I grab a fistful and pass a couple to Inderpal. 'I love chillies,' I say bullishly and take a few big bites as a horse might into an apple proffered over a fence. Inderpal looks at me in a kind of horror, which turns to amusement and finally, I'd like to think, admiration. I'd like to think that but I can't really think of anything right now, much less say anything, because after a few seconds in which the mild burning sensation on my tongue was faintly pleasurable in an odd way, twin geysers of electric heat are pulsing upwards from the area of my (long gone) adenoids and threatening to burst my eardrums and eyeballs simultaneously. As a student, using some knock-off madras powder a mate's dad had got from Liverpool docks, I once made a curry so hot my flatmate Nigel went blind in one eye for several hours. That was a korma by comparison.

It's said that beer is a much better coolant after a hot curry than water, which is why Cobra, Lal Toofan and Kingfisher are so popular on the subcontinent. But clearly none of these are to hand so I content myself with drinking, in three or four draughts, the entire contents of one of those metal water jugs you used to get at school dinners. By now, I am crying a little which amuses and delights the small crowd of Sikh ladies who have gathered around me. One of them actually claps. Another pats me on the head, dislodging my headscarf. She pops it back on, as you would a bonnet back on a baby in a buggy. 'That will keep the doctor away,' says the small fellow who gave me the chillies as he takes back the bag grinning, helping himself to another couple which he proceeds to crunch his way through as blithely as if they were mini carrot batons or mint-flavour Matchmakers at Abigail's Party.

When I think I can stand unaided, I get up and Inderpal takes me up to the next floor and the main hall. Women of various ages are grouped along the walls of the room and one is seated at its head under a canopy. She is reading into a microphone in a low monotone from the holy book. Inderpal and I lurk at the entrance to the room and he whispers in my ear, 'She's reading from the Granth Sahib, our holy book. Someone is here reading from it all day and all night. Twenty-four hours a day.' The women in the room listen intently, eyes closed, some gently nodding to the recitation. 'Come on, come with me,' says Inderpal, beckoning me into the Dharbar. We pad quietly right up to the reader and the holy book. Inderpal drops to his knees, bends forward and lowers his head to the floor to kiss it. I follow suit. Then we rise and gently exit backwards. I am worried about doing something wrong, but Inderpal and the ladies smile indulgently and I get the feeling that unless I behave badly, my ignorance of Sikhism and its etiquette is no problem. I am their guest, and they are happy to have me here.

If you are used to the traditions of Christian churches, possibly synagogues too though I'm not qualified to say, a Sikh temple is almost disconcerting in its informality. No gilt, no statuary, no reliquary, no icons, no religious pictures. The most holy part of it, where the most 'sacred' things are happening, is just above what resembles at most a very basic works canteen with vats of dahl and sambar on the go. How different it feels from my altar boy days spent in a fug of perfumed incense swinging a thurible around my head in front of a burnished gold tabernacle. Although to be honest, here too the sacred and profane sat side by side. Just on the other side of the wall from the altar, they were pulling pints of Guinness and playing snooker in the Catholic Club.

We ascend another flight. There is a large room for teaching, kids' paintings adorning the walls, and there's a handwritten message of thanks for their service to local life from the local police. Inderpal opens a side door and we emerge onto a wide section of flat roof high above the cramped terraced houses of Beeston. 'This,' he says indicating a tall flagpole with its bright triangular pennant of silk, 'is the Nishan Sahib. It is the flag of the Gurdwara intended to be seen from miles around and saying that this is a place of safety, originally in time of war but now just for any who wishes to come, Sikh or otherwise.' We stand under it for a while as it flaps damply. In the distance I can see the stand at Elland Road.

I have the feeling that, just as the recitation of the holy book will continue around the clock, Inderpal would be happy, keen and capable of talking passionately about his community all day. There is something sweet and winning about this, whatever your faith or lack of it. But I have my own pilgrimage to continue with, not to Amritsar's Golden Temple, which many Sikhs aspire to one day visit, but to Wakefield, the next stage on the march's itinerary. Inderpal wants to show me one last thing though, the rehearsal rooms where one can study the classical music traditions of India. 'I don't know if there are classes there today. But I hope you can hear some.' We arrive at the door a floor below though just as a class is breaking up. Two older Sikh gentlemen are leaving, behind them a young ginger-haired British guy. His headscarf is as poorly knotted as mine and seeing each other's, we tacitly acknowledge our shared incompetence with a wan smile.

Inderpal asks one of the older gentlemen to tell me about the instrument he plays. 'It is an Indian instrument,' smiles the man, fingering a fine wiry grey beard, 'that you may never have heard of it.' Keen not to be thought a fool, but in fact being an idiot, I randomly name some Indian instruments I have heard of, such as the tabla and the sitar. Still smiling, the man shakes his head patiently. 'No, I play the santoor. It is a trapezoid instrument with 72 strings. 'Wow,' I say, establishing my idiot credentials even more decisively. 'Is that difficult to play?' He turns to the young Western man. 'John, is it difficult?' 'Well, I've been coming here to learn for ten years and I'm still a beginner,' he says, pushing his headdress back up out of his eyes, where it has slipped down like an outsized party hat on a toddler.

We descend the stairs together, me just about persuading Inderpal that it was really not necessary for the musicians to go and get their instruments out again and play. As the Sikh men fall into conversation in Punjabi (I imagine something along the lines of, 'Who's the doofus who can't tie a headdress?'), John tugs at my sleeve to pull me back a little behind the group. 'I'm a music teacher in Bradford. I fell in love with Indian music and when I found out that he was here,' his voice drops to an awestruck sotto voce as he points at the older musician walking ahead, 'and would give me lessons ... well, I come here every week, have been doing for ten years. His name is Ustad Harjinderpal Singh, and he's one of the great virtuosi of Indian music. Look him up.'

I jot a decent approximation of this name in my black moleskin notebook for later research. John and Ustad leave and I say my goodbyes to Inderpal. It has been a fascinating couple of hours. I've been wonderfully fed, I've learned a great deal and I'm very grateful to my young host. Gauche to the end, I fumble in my pocket and pull out a fiver, wondering aloud if there's a collection plate or a community charity or, who knows, a fund for a new flag like they have for new roofs on old churches in the Cotswolds. 'No, no, no,' he waves it and me away. 'It has been a pleasure. Where are you going now? Wakefield? Well, when you have seen Wakefield, come back here. There's a wedding on tonight. We'll be here from 6.30 to 9. You must come. No drink here. But people will have drink later. You can have more food. More chillies!'

It was tempting then, and even more so after an afternoon spent trudging along the anonymous drizzly main roads of Yorkshire. I walked through quaintly named Robin Hood, past the Old Halfway House Pub (To Let), outside which a young lad in a Wakefield Trinity Wildcats replica shirt mends a puncture, past the Wakefield Diesel Centre and down Meadowgate Drive (where I sang a variant of an old Suzi Quatro hit some of you might remember) and eventually past a sign that welcomed me to Wakefield. Here the marchers enjoyed a quieter reception than in Leeds. But then that night in the grand town hall would prove the most splendid of the whole three-week trip. In Wakefield, they were given potted meat 'butties' and tea and then taken to their lodging at a disused chapel on Salem Street.

I have treated myself to accommodation that's a little nicer and lying on the bed after checking my blisters (hardly any: I was hoping for at least a few battlescars) I tap the musician's name that John gave me into Google, hoping I've got it roughly right. Hits galore pop up; links, YouTube clips, recordings. Thus it become apparent that the older, bearded gentlemen I met earlier is one of the greatest exponents in the world of the santoor, 'the hundred stringed instrument of the valleys', which I assume is poetic licence. His CV is dense with achievements and accolades. 'Born in Jabalpur, India in 1953 ... age 14 years his father sent him to learn Tabla ... made him the disciple of the santoor maestro Pandit Shiv Kumar Sharma ... toured extensively for SPICMACAY (Society for the Promotion of Indian Classical Music and Culture Amongst Youth) and gave concerts, lectures and demonstration programmes in schools and colleges ... He has toured abroad and performed in various cities around the UK.' There is a clip of him playing the santoor in Manchester's glitzy and prestigious Bridgewater Hall, home of the Halle Orchestra, and in chamber concert at Opera North's Howard Assembly Rooms, the very room where I had heard Steven Osborne play Debussy and Ravel and discuss the Chuckle Brothers.

So it was rather as if, earlier that day, I had bumped into Yo-Yo Ma in a back street near Hunslet and had him explain to me patiently and sweetly, as if to a stupid child, what a cello was. And then almost asked him to get his instrument out again and play a few of the Bach Solo Cello suites for me, there amongst the chickpeas and the bags of gram flour and the okra. It was a real shame that the Gurdwara wasn't here in 1936. The Jarrow marchers would have been welcomed with open arms, and 200 orange headscarves and a handful of glossy green chillis to make that welcome even warmer.

WAKEFIELD TO BARNSLEY

15 October, 10 miles

'Jarrow Marchers R.I.P in Ancient Wakefield City.'

It may not be quite as striking as 'Freddie Starr Ate My Hamster' or as infamous as 'Gotcha!' but the above headline in Wakefield's *Evening Chronicle* for 14 October 1936 shows how even then the British press was confidently finding its unique voice reporting gleefully and punningly how the marchers had bedded down next to a cemetery.

Even then though, independent local papers were beginning to be swallowed up by the giant national groups and chains. Circulation of newspapers boomed among the working classes in the interwar years and differences of style began to develop between low sale, upmarket publications like *The Times* and popular sensationalist dailies like the *Express*. Competitions and promotions were a major part of these papers' sales drives, some of which seem quite bizarre now. The *Daily Mail* offered certain types of free insurance to subscribers such as a hundred pounds in school fees to any child whose parent had suffered 'a fatal accident' and ten pounds to any Girl Guide who broke an arm. The popular titles would sometimes employ five times as many canvassers as editorial staff and these would tour the country offering inducements such as clothes and gifts to subscribe. One report said 'it was rumoured that a whole Welsh family could be clothed from head to toe for the price of eight weeks' reading of the *Daily Express*'. Quite why they had to be a Welsh family is not clear, but it gives an idea of the promo budgets of the new mass market press.

I could find no trace of exactly where the Jarrow marchers stayed in Wakefield, neither street nor chapel nor cemetery, and this despite the best efforts of some generous and enthusiastic help on social media from Christine Wood, Richard Earnshaw, Chris Treece, Stuart Watson and 'Kevin'. Stephen Garside even sent pictures of what we think is the now disused site with both chapel and graveyard gone. We do have a record of their stay though in the diary entry of one of the marchers, David Ramshaw. 'Wakefield. Civic reception. Menu, sandwiches and tea. Slept in pulpit of condemned church.' On waking at 6am, he then woke the other marchers with a mock sermon from the pulpit. John McNulty wouldn't have heard this. He was outside sleeping on a gravestone.

The marchers didn't stay long in Wakefield and neither did I. Not through any dislike of the city I should say, simply because I had written quite a lot about 'Wakey' in a previous book and didn't want to go over old ground. Some things are worth repeating though. Wakefield is now a national centre for modern art. The Hepworth, named for sculptor Barbara Hepworth, the town's most famous daughter and the greatest female British artist of the twentieth century, is a stylish and striking multi-million-pound venue. It had 100,000 visitors in the month following its opening in May 2011, and half a million within six. The Art House in the centre of town provides dozens of working artists with studio space and its associated venture, the Artwalk, sees those studios, as well as the shops, offices and bars of the town throw open their doors every first Wednesday of the month to become a city-wide living gallery, filled with painting, sculpture, lithographs, etchings, gouache and any other imaginable kind of art. I encourage you to make the trip one month.

When the Jarrow march passed through Wakefield, British art was in a febrile state. Hepworth, along with husband-to-be Ben Nicholson, Henry Moore, and critic Herbert Read were having a public argument with senior artistic figures like Paul Nash over whether more modern art should be allowed into the shows of the Royal Academy. Eric Gill and Jacob Epstein's sculptures were appalling the Establishment with their eroticism and modernism. Three months before the Jarrow march, the International Surrealist Exhibition opened in London, bringing Britain its first sight of Breton, Magritte and Dali.

Most intriguingly, a small but significant part of British art history was blossoming both as the Jarrow march set off and not very far away from them. The then-current *Shell Guide to Northumberland and Durham* described Ashington as a 'mining town built in the early part of this century ... dreary rows a mile long with ash pits down the middle of the streets', which makes it sound like an unlikely place for a new art movement, but that was exactly what was happening here. In 1936, the Ashington Group – 'the Pitmen Painters' as they became known – held their first exhibition in Newcastle. The group of 24 arose from a Workers Education Authority class in art in which the men had started to express themselves in striking and individual paintings. The exhibition was a huge success and the painters were acclaimed. British artists Clive Bell and Julian Trevelyan championed them and art historian Sir Anthony Blunt (later to be Keeper of the Queen's Pictures and later still exposed as a Soviet spy) said that the exhibition was 'the most important event of the year from the point of view of English art'.

So while Jarrow marched, Ashington painted, but while audiences and critics from outside the manual working class generally applauded, some within were suspicious. Wal Hannington, leader of the National Unemployed Workers Movement, grizzled that art clubs, like the BBC's morning talks for the unemployed, and occupational and recreation centres were a crafty tactic of the ruling class to 'dope' the workers.

Orwell, who was touring the north at the time for what would become *The Road to Wigan Pier*, thought such initiatives were 'simply a device to keep the unemployed quiet and give them an illusion that something is being done for them'. Whether capitalist sop or genuine liberation of the spirit, the story of Ashington's artistic movement is told in *The Pitmen Painters*, a play by Lee Hall of *Billy Elliot* fame, which addresses these conflicts and questions; after attending a modern art exhibition at the Royal Academy one painter says he realises that art teaches you 'not to put up with what you're given'.

There are some, and they may have a point, who say such proletarian defiance is as much what motivated the Brexit vote as bigotry. Wakefield is as good a place to dwell on such matters as any, and perhaps better. Put simply and factually, Wakefield voted overwhelmingly to leave the EU; 66.3 per cent on a turn-out of almost 80 per cent.

The *Guardian*'s Northern Editor Helen Pidd visited the town the morning after the vote and reported finding a nervous bafflement among many, not least the town's large Eastern European community. Aneta Duchniak opened Duchniak's, the first Polish restaurant in Wakefield, two years before the vote. According to Helen's article, 'Many of her regulars are Yorkshire folk who have taken a shine to her delicate pierogi dumplings and hearty borscht soups. Lots of them wanted Britain to leave Europe, she says, and yet they made a special effort to come in afterwards to tell her it wasn't personal. "They said, 'We want to support you, it's nothing against you, it's against Brussels controlling us'."'

Some see this kind of thinking as specious and self-deluding, a mask for ingrained racism. I'm not so sure. Whilst I wouldn't claim that it's an intellectually sound position, or to be defended necessarily, I can well believe, from my conversations in towns like Wakefield or Dewsbury or Rochdale or Oldham or Wigan, that some who voted to leave bore no personal animosity to immigrants but harboured some vague and misguided grudge against the EU. This grudge was fed by the falsehoods of UKIP and the right-wing tabloids and acted on out of impotent anger.

Also, these towns have good reason to doubt the word of those infamous experts in Westminster. As Pidd points out, 'When Poland joined the EU in May 2004 – along with Cyprus, the Czech Republic, Estonia, Hungary, Latvia, Lithuania, Malta, Slovakia and Slovenia – there was little fear or fanfare about what their membership could mean for Britain. The government certainly wasn't worried. Tony Blair's administration estimated that no more than 13,000 of these new Europeans would seek a new life in Britain each year from 2004. These figures were largely based on predictions made by the academic Christian Dustmann of University College London, and worked on the (incorrect) assumption that other large countries in the EU, in particular Germany, would also open up their labour markets. It soon became clear that Dustmann's estimate was hilariously – or catastrophically, depending on your view – wrong. Between May 2004 and June 2007, 430,000 Poles applied to the Home Office worker registration scheme, joining the 69,000 Poles already in Britain, pre-EU enlargement. As the scheme was voluntary, the true figure was thought to be much higher. In July 2006, the respected Polish newspaper *Polityka* estimated that one million Poles had moved to the UK.'

That will almost certainly now change. Indeed, it is already changing. More Poles head for Germany now than the UK and that will surely increase as we slowly, wearily, raise our drawbridge against Europe. In addition, the Polish government wants its workers to come home and is luring them with a very generous child benefit system. The Polish economy suffered from the mass exodus to England by losing its youngest and brightest and experienced shortages of qualified workers in key industries. But many academics believe that some Poles will never leave, just as their forefathers came and stayed during the Second World War. Dustmann, he of the original massive underestimate, told Pidd,

'Overall migrants from Poland are very well educated, young, and have a high labour-force attachment. They easily assimilate and will be indistinguishable in the next generation.'

For now, there are still many visible signs of our new Polish communities. I pass several Polski skleps on my way out of Wakefield headed for the A61 and the route to Barnsley. I stop into one and buy a kielbasa from Milena which I munch on like a lolly as I stomp past the Hepworth and the Wildcats Belle Vue stadium. My day was very much like the marchers' was 80 years before; uneventful and benign, weak sun and cloud enlivened by the odd blustery shower. But my walk fell on a Saturday and so there was a reason to quicken my step to my next destination, the grand old South Yorkshire town of Barnsley.

Berneslai gets its first official mention in the Domesday Book, though the Saxons had a foothold here long before. Before that even, 2,000 years ago and for reasons that are unclear, the embalmed bodies of several North Africans were buried beneath the town, a discovery made by Barnsley-born Egyptologist Joann Fletcher. 'You don't think 2,000 years ago that Ancient Egyptians came to Yorkshire – but they did … in some ways it blows your mind,' she said, mind blown.

But the big significant date in the town's popular history (along with their FA Cup Triumph of 1912) occurs in 1249 when the town opened its first market. Nearly a thousand years of street marketing have not even begun to dull the locals' appetite for the notion. The market is 700 years old and has some 400 stalls indoors and outdoors, and whether coming on foot, by bus or by train, you cannot miss it; it is a huge structure, as big as the Cardington Airship Hangars in the Fens, looming over the bus station and the rail interchange. On a Saturday, from certain angles, Barnsley can feel like a vast market with a town clinging on for dear life. Once, the outdoor stalls of Barnsley were known for their wool and fish, and you can still find balls and shoals of both here. But these days, in the gigantic covered

unfussy uber market, big enough to house a 747 and maybe a
Saturn Five, you can also find those essentials of modern life, a
discount Iron Man Duvet or a bumper economy rack of vials of
Black Cherry E Cig Vape. You can find handmade Loake loafers
for a couple of hundred quid, a gallon of hair conditioner for
coppers, plus flavours of Polish crisps that even Polish people
think niche. At Vinyl Junction 42, I noticed a couple of seventies
albums by John Miles; a nice coincidence in that his granddad
was the cook on the Jarrow march. Flicking through I see a
whole rack of second-hand albums by the dreadful right-wing
rock guitarist Ted Nugent. I wonder if someone has found out
about his support for Trump and flogged them all in a fit of
rock pique?

The day turned bright and warm by the time I leave the
market to take in the town. Just by the stalls selling discount
leather belts is the Alhambra, a blue and white building that
is now a bingo hall but in 1936 was one of the town's many
picture palaces along with the Cudworth, the Empire, the
Pavilion or the Theatre Royal. A year later, the Ritz opened its
doors with William Powell in *My Man Godfrey* (and closed on
16 March 1974 with Reg Varney in *Holiday on the Buses*). It
was subsequently demolished, perhaps to avoid giving the town
painful memories of the latter. After a meeting in the miners'
hall, the men were treated to free seats by the various cinema
managements. Still proudly independent at that time, the
Alhambra was taken over by the Odeon chain two years later
(the fate of many independent cinemas), but only on condition
that it could keep its own name. This it did to the end and
still does as a shopping centre, though it closed as a cinema on
26 November 1960 with the *The Entertainer* starring Laurence
Olivier, a classy but draining movie. Back in 1936, several
marchers fell asleep in the Alhambra's comfy one and nines after
the exertions of the day.

What did they snooze through, those weary men of Jarrow?
No records were kept but it may well have been one of the

British comedies we discussed earlier. This, though, was the period when Hollywood began to establish itself as the global powerhouse of mass entertainment. In 1936 alone it produced a tranche of films that still make cineastes drool. There was Chaplin's brilliant satire on mechanisation and alienation *Modern Times* and Gary Cooper in Frank Capra's charming *Mr Deeds Goes to Town*. Ginger Rogers and Fred Astaire were paired in the delightful *Follow the Fleet*, whilst Spencer Tracy starred in a darkly intense drama about the mob titled *Fury*, the American debut of the great German expressionist Fritz Lang. He had successfully made the move to Hollywood as Europe fell under the growing shadow of Nazism and the threat of war. From Britain in this prevalent mood of futuristic paranoia, came Alexander Korda's classic *Things to Come*. This version of H G Wells's dystopian novel brought to the screen seemed even more prophetic than it did on publication three years before when the author had predicted the Second World War and the coming of a world super state.

The fact that Barnsley could host the men in four or five picture houses is testament to what a boom time this was for the cinema. Between 1934 and 1937, the cinema-going audience grew from 18 to 20 million per week on average. New cinemas were opening all the time and, like Barnsley's Ritz, were often elegant and stylish art deco entertainment temples in gilt and neon. Their appeal cut across class boundaries too. Whilst workers could enjoy Fields's and Formby's homespun cheeriness, middle-class filmgoers preferred comedies of manners and tremulous tearjerkers. Going to the cinema had none of the slightly seedy and downmarket associations of going to the pub, which would generally be a drably functional 'boozer'. This made cinema-going especially attractive to middle-class women, as well as to couples of all classes for whom it provided a warm, dark, convenient venue for 'courting'. The cinema was a profoundly democratising force at this time, offering a new range of 'celebrities' to admire for their talent, grace or beauty rather than the aloof and remote aristocracy who had been admired from afar for so long.

'Tarn' is quieting now as the market packs and folds itself back once more into the back of vans and trucks; a late bargain here, a quick sale there. The wide civic square is sunlit and almost empty, feeling like a planner's model of an imagined cityscape, a South Yorkshire Brasilia or Canberra. I stride purposefully past the Old No 7, a terrific boozer with labyrinthine depths I once spent far too much time in after a gig in Barnsley, in order to fully take in one of Barnsley's most famous and controversial sights. It's a grand thing but it very much annoyed a visitor to Barnsley called George Orwell back in the thirties.

In 1936, as plans for the Jarrow march were taking shape, Eric Blair AKA George Orwell, Old Etonian and former colonial policeman turned journalist and writer, was sent north by his publisher Victor Gollancz to research a book on the conditions of life in the depressed industrial north. Orwell thought of his trip initially as 'venturing among savages' but that didn't prevent him producing a sympathetic but unsentimental account of life in towns like Wigan, Sheffield and Barnsley that became the searing and enduring classic polemic *The Road to Wigan Pier*. For his researches he kept rough notes and a diary that you can now find in his collected works. Here is his account of his trip below ground in Barnsley's Grimethorpe Colliery:

> The place where the fillers were working was fearful beyond description … the seam of coal is only a yard high or a bit more, the men can only kneel or crawl to their work, never stand up. The effort of constantly shovelling coal over your left shoulder and flinging it a yard or two beyond, while in a kneeling position, must be very great even to men who are used to it. Added to this there are the clouds of coal dust which are

flying down your throat all the time and which make
it difficult to see any distance. The men were all naked
except for trousers and knee-pads.

Orwell came away from his time in the mines of the north with
enormous respect and admiration for colliers. He later wrote, 'If
there is one man I feel inferior to, it is a coal miner.' I once met
someone whose family Orwell had lodged with while he was in
Wigan and it had become part of that family's lore that he was
a 'lovely young man'; thin, unfailingly polite, never snobbish,
always willing to help. In *The Road to Wigan Pier*, Orwell never
patronises the people he meets, though occasionally you can
sense a mild innate disgust at their manners, eating habits and
such. But he was on their side and they came to respect each
other. 'When I sit typing, the family, especially Mrs G. and the
kids, all gather round to watch absorbedly, and appear to admire
my prowess almost as much as I admire that of the miners.'

Perhaps this is why in the book's notorious conclusion,
Orwell excoriates the intellectual left such as George Bernard
Shaw as 'cranks' and mocks 'every fruit-juice drinker, nudist,
sandal-wearer, sex-maniac, Quaker, "Nature Cure" quack,
pacifist and feminist in England'. While this is overheated to the
point of silliness, it arises from an anger with the 'crank's' lack
of genuine empathy or solidarity with the industrial working
class Orwell had lived among and come to know. Orwell was a
socialist. But he was also a patriot and a traditionalist; he would
have loathed identity politics and Corbyn's regime I think,
seeing it as a distraction from the proper business of socialism
– the improvement of the lot of the worker, the poor and the
disadvantaged.

It was in this savage mood that Orwell turned his
considerable scorn on Barnsley town hall. The foundation stone
was laid on 21 April 1932 and it was opened by the Prince of
Wales (soon to be notorious himself) on 14 December 1933.

The cost was £188,037 12/10d. George Orwell in his book was highly critical of this expenditure, claiming that the council should have spent the money on improving the housing and living conditions of the local miners. Nonetheless, the huge, dazzling edifice, more akin to the seat of parliament of a Baltic capital than a provincial town hall, has become perhaps the town's most iconic feature – and the clichéd adjective is justified here. Built from Portland stone and designed by the architect responsible for the Northern Ireland parliament at Stormont (which it resembles), it's visible from the adjoining motorway and receives extravagant praise on TripAdvisor – 'Absolutely amazing building, a Barnsley landmark ... This is a place you step in and just think wow' – as well as the obligatory churl – 'impoverished ... a step back in time ... grubbiness of public spaces'. But as this last was posted by Toby and Bunty, perhaps we shouldn't be surprised.

The building that so irked Orwell has had a makeover in recent years. A plume of glittering spray arcs from a chic new water feature and at night the town hall glows a pale and eerie blue, turning Barnsley into the Gotham of South Yorkshire. In a tiny room high in the spire, a pale fluorescent light burns through the night, prompting local speculation that it's where the mayor keeps his sunbed. In June 2013, part of the town hall became Experience Barnsley, a museum dedicated to the history of the town and its people from the twelfth to twenty-first centuries. Outside a poster proclaims it 'a proud Yorkshire story told by the people of Barnsley'. The endless exhortations to take pride in this county can become tedious. But I liked the cut of Experience Barnsley's jib. As well as the quite proper nod to antiquity, there's much on the town's social history, coal mining and other industries, and the approach to this was robust and refreshing with no puff or blather.

That October week in 1936, the Jarrow marchers, feted at the town's new and advanced Steam Baths and fed on meat and potato pie, were not the only celebrated visitors to Barnsley.

A Wigan compatriot of mine came here too. George Formby, banjoleleist, Apartheid rebel and recipient of the Order of Lenin, came to Barnsley to support the mining community. It had suffered a terrible tragedy, the Wharncliffe mine disaster, in which 58 men were killed in an underground explosion just two months previously. Every pit village and town knew and feared these frequent reminders of the human price of coal. But King Coal itself would surely never be unseated or deposed. Surely. In fact, coal mining was one of those rooted certainties of British life that would turn out to be as evanescent as the spray from Barnsley's proud new fountain.

STAGE TEN

BARNSLEY TO SHEFFIELD

16 October, 13 miles

By day ten, the morning's packing has assumed a brisk, almost militaristic routine. There is the folding and rolling of shirts, the thrusting into spare corners of socks and unmentionables, the stowing of the 'good shoes', the meticulous stashing of the travel tooth brush, the painkillers and the plasters. Always too, when the sign has just been flipped to 'Please Make Up This Room', the trudge back along the corridor to the room for something left behind: a washbag, a contact lens case, an iPad. This last though is crucial since, thanks to this modern miracle, I'm carrying with me several volumes of literature from or about the 1930s. I have with me academic histories, memoirs, reportage. I have Orwell's first novel too, *Keep the Aspidistra Flying* as well as the collected works of the curious English Catholic writer Charles Williams and the rather less curious but equally Catholic Graham Greene. I have A J Cronin's *The Stars Look Down* – a bleak and apposite tale of a family's struggle for survival amidst a strike that the local Labour Party and Trade Union don't support in a depressed north-eastern mining town. It was written the year before the march and the echoes of Jarrow are deafening.

As well as this, I have a collection of short stories by the Welsh writer Kate Roberts that chime perfectly with my march.

Coal dust hangs thick and heavy in Roberts's writing as the ghost of it still does in the streets and pubs of Barnsley. At its peak, Barnsley district had ten deep mines and the last to go was Grimethorpe. That huge colliery was famed for its brass band and then as the setting for the film *Brassed Off*. Grimethorpe's last shift came up in 1993, having limped on for almost a decade after the defining mid-1980s strike. It's all an age ago now, but for some those days feel like yesterday.

I hop into a minicab for a short distance to pick up my route again and the driver tells me that one taxi firm, Black and White cabs (by far the most numerous on the rank) was set up by sacked miners who pooled their redundancy money after the strike. 'Some of them, they're like those Japanese soldiers who don't know the war's over. They're still fighting the fight. We wind 'em up about it. "'Ere we go, the battle of Orgreave again! Give it a rest!" Something comes over 'em when owt to do w'it strike comes up. Thatcher, Scargill, picketing ... you can feel 'em tighten up, see their expressions change. Mind you, they saw some stuff I suppose.'

Memories are long here. A friend who grew up locally told me about the working man's club in Mapplewell, the Tin Hat as it was known, where above the door was the name of one man who crossed the picket line during the miners' strike and who was never to be let in. I run this past my driver and he laughs bitterly – 'Sounds about reet'. As we drive, he points vaguely in the directions of the various pits, once employing thousands, now silent caverns brimming with dark, oily water 'Dodworth were that way ... Cortonwood ... that were a decent size ... Grimethorpe obviously. A lot of my family worked at Goldthorpe. They burned a dummy of Thatcher there on the day of her funeral. Bloody hundreds of 'em turned out. Right carry on it were.' He laughs at the grotesque memory. Later I check this story and find that at this mock funeral, where a fake coffin and effigy were burned in an atmosphere of grim celebration, the number present was actually about two thousand.

He drops me at a roadside café where I have my first cup of tea of the day and carry on with Kate Roberts's story. It's called 'Protest March' and accords completely with my Jarrow project. In it, Blodwen, living with her husband in poverty in a subterranean hovel, joins a protest march against the Means Test, that sinister, invasive scourge of towns like Jarrow. But even as she marches, she becomes disillusioned and begins to doubt that these gestures will ever change anything or that anything can be changed. 'The crowd itself was looking like something absurd to Blodwen now and depressing in its absurdity. She thought, if the government were to see them now, what they'd do was laugh at them. After all, what were they marching for?'

Marching rather than disobedience, the banner rather than the flung brick of the suffragettes, was the dominant protest mode of the 1930s. John Tanner at the Experience Barnsley Museum told me that eight Barnsley women walked to London as part of a 1930s hunger march. In 2016, whether you viewed it as energising or pointless, some of that mood seemed to be back. Just a few weeks before I began my march, supporters of Jeremy Corbyn rallied in Liverpool to show support for their leader and against Owen Smith, his rival in the Labour leadership elections. The difference in opinions even on the left about such events showed up the great open wound in the current British Labour movement. From Corbyn's camp, an enthusiastic tweet from @cameronsporkies was typical:

So Owen Smith, this is what unelectable looks like. Banking on another MSM cover up? #KeepCorbyn!

Attached was a photograph showing an enormous throng outside Liverpool's famous St George's Hall. Even to the relatively impartial, it looked an awful lot of people; it transpired that the picture actually showed the crowd for Liverpool FC's triumphant homecoming parade after winning the 2005 Champions League trophy. (Obfuscation has always been rife around 'demos' with police and activists making inflated or shrunken assessments of the numbers involved; in the 1980s, the constabulary's often spectacular underestimations of crowd size became a comic staple of satire shows like *Not the Nine O' Clock News*.) The *Guardian* reported 5,000 people at the Corbyn Liverpool rally whilst police officers estimated attendance at between 3,500 and 5,000. Organisers suggested 10,000. This size obsession has become such a contentious issue that there are now competing crowd size estimation techniques, such as the Jacobs method using grids over pictures. Gordon Arnold, a retired architect from Dallas, has created a crowd-counting app named CrowdSize which put Corbyn's rally at around 4,000 people. A team from Warwick University is working on a system that will soon be able to accurately estimate the number of people at mass gatherings by the number of mobile phones present in an area.

Quibbles about size miss the real point, however. To equate the turn-out at a rally, whether for Jeremy Corbyn or Nigel Farage, with general support in the wider population is to fundamentally misunderstand the nature of electability and indeed democracy in general. This kind of wonky thinking is a modern malaise made endemic by the internet and in particular social media, what psychologists call 'false-consensus bias'. Or as some have it, living in the 'Twitter Bubble'.

Living like this, and I've been as guilty as anyone, is to wrongly assume that everyone thinks like you do, and furthermore, that anyone who doesn't is a member of an aberrant minority. It is the tyranny of the timeline. False consensus bias is what fuelled the spluttering rage of many Remain supporters after the Brexit vote. Swapping opinions with only those people who agree with us has given us a distorted picture of what the wider world is really like. This has always been the way of things to an extent of course. We tend to gravitate to people who share our world view; we seek them out, we drink with them, eat with them, marry them. There was always an element of this in our consumption of the traditional media too. People by and large bought the newspapers that shared (or maybe shaped) their beliefs. (Interestingly, when I taught sociology, students were often shocked that newspapers were politically partisan or identified these allegiances utterly wrongly. They thought, for instance, that the *Guardian* was Tory because it was 'posh' and the *Sun* Labour because working-class men read it.) But there was always the chance still that you would see on TV news or hear on the radio a voice that challenged yours or an opinion you didn't share. As the old media gives way to the power of the new, such moments become rare. By only 'following' and 'friending' people like oneself, other, dissenting voices can almost be avoided altogether. For me, this is what undermines much of the new radical left's critique of the Mainstream Media (MSM as they would have it) and we'll come back to it.

We make Facebook friends of those who agree, we follow them on Twitter, we chat with them, and anyone who doesn't share our opinions is a troll. After Brexit, some people were forced to concede that living in the Twitter Bubble might be warm, congenial and supportive but means you have some nasty shocks in store. This is not simply an inconvenience or an interesting sociological quirk – it may well be destroying proper political discourse and debate. John West, a US journalist who's studied the phenomenon, put it powerfully if somewhat technically in a *Vice* piece about the use of Twitter in the run-up to the US election: 'All of this paints a bleak picture of online political discourse … It is one balkanized by ideology and issue-interest, with little potential for information flow between the online cocoons.' Trump versus Liberal Hollywood, Remain versus Leave; Corbyn versus the centre left, the Balkanisation, as West puts it, is ongoing and about as healthy as it was for the real Balkans. Corbyn even acknowledged it a day so after the rally when he said, not entirely convincingly, 'The idea I live in some remote bubble of adulation is frankly ridiculous.'

I finish Kate Roberts' story 'Protest March' over my lunch on the road somewhere around Tankersley. Its political message is fairly hopeless but it does at least end on a note of human consolation when the disillusioned Blodwen is welcomed home by her previously cynical husband. Roberts wrote this story during a previous 'fad' for marching as a form of political discourse, just before the Jarrow Crusade and at the height of the popular wave of protest and hunger marches. Two other marches passed through Sheffield in the same month as the Jarrow Crusade. There was the National Hunger March, a more avowedly political enterprise entirely, and the National League of the Blind March, which was supported by Sheffield's Trades and Labour council. To give an idea of the diversity and sometimes woeful disorganisation of such ventures – something the Jarrow march organisers were desperate to avoid – on the night the Crusade arrived in Jarrow, a straggling and desperate group arrived at Pomona Street School in Sheffield. They were ex-servicemen who were marching from Inverness to London to protest their meagre war pensions. Fifty had set off, but only 16 arrived in Sheffield at 3am, gaunt, exhausted 'ghost like figures' according to a local paper report, who'd badly lost their way on the moors above Sheffield.

There was no such hapless waywardness for Red Ellen, David Riley, Paddy Scullion and the Jarrow men, and hopefully none for me. Sheffield wouldn't welcome me as it had done them of course with cigarettes, tea and sandwiches and I didn't expect it to of course. I know Sheffield a little and I knew that it is not hard to find your own welcome there and make yourself at home in this compact and vibrant city. Built on seven hills (like Rome, as they will quickly tell you), and with something of the air of a mountain stronghold about it. It is its own domain, utterly unlike Bradford or Leeds or its suspicious cousins in South Yorkshire; different, individual, a unique mixture of unyielding grit and romantic softness, a city where the hardest-looking bloke in the pub is likely to call you 'love' and give you a different smacker from the one you were expecting.

Geology, topography, sociology; all contribute to the sense of a strapping, over-vigorous city bursting its banks and spilling over the hillsides. Then there's the industry. Sheffield has never had any business in wool or textiles, carding or knitting. Sheffield makes steel, and is proud of it. Some of this gets into the local character. As Graham Turner said in his splendid 1960s book *The North Country* (now sadly out of print), 'Neither [Leeds nor Bradford] can claim the virility which Sheffield's basic raw material, steel, confers; making natty gents suitings hardly compares with fashioning 300-ton ingots.'

Milling and making steel is harder work for less profit than carding wool. Sheffield likes to think itself a macho cut above Leeds for this and other reasons, even if some Sheffielders will concede that Leeds and Bradford are prettier cities because of it. In truth, despite the much-vaunted Yorkshire pride, there may even still be those who resent being lumped in with Yorkshire at all. Local industrialist Allan John Grant welcomed the Jarrow march in a speech that began, 'There is no time to discuss the principle of these marches now that the deputation from Jarrow has reached Derbyshire ...' putting Sheffield in a different county altogether.

Orwell came to Sheffield just before the Jarrow march and no one could have accused him of pandering to the locals or sentimentalising their city. 'Sheffield, I suppose, could justifiably claim to be the ugliest town in the world ... it has a population of half a million and it contains fewer decent buildings than the average East Anglian village of five hundred. And the stench.' This is the snobbery of the old Etonian to a degree, but even J B Priestley, a comradely rival from Bradford, described entry into Sheffield as descending through a 'murky canopy' into 'the steaming bowels of the earth'. Modern Sheffield would surely have nothing so sulphurous to show me. But on my way into the city, something terrible, suffused with misery and wickedness both pulled and repelled me.

It's an ordinary enough road, heading anonymously south from the main A61 Penistone Road in from the outer suburbs of High Green, Burncross and Grenoside. Narrowing and cutting through working class suburbia, after the brash American uberstores, the Domino Pizzas and PC Worlds, the road gathers around itself smaller, more homely, sometimes dowdier enterprises; Hing Fan's Fish and Chips and Chinese Meals To Takeaway, the Mirage E Cigarette Shop, Sybs Roofing Services, Tracey's Sandwich Bar. Next door a shop selling vintage football programmes gives a hint of where you are near. And then a small, cold feeling as you take in the street corner and wonder what it was like on that summer day in 1988. Here a tiny road leads to the West Stand of Sheffield Wednesday's famous old football ground; the B6079, better known as Leppings Lane.

Hillsborough stadium hosted five FA Cup semi-finals during the 1980s and at several there were frightening scenes and near chaos. In 1981 during the tie between Spurs and Wolves, far more spectators were crammed onto the terrace than was safe and there were 38 injuries, several involving broken limbs. Sheffield Wednesday chairman Bert McGee was sanguine, snorting at police officers who feared fatalities. 'Bollocks – no one would have been killed.' Cage-like pens were then introduced which invalidated the safety certificate and there were no more cup semi-finals at this once-regular home for such big clashes until 1987. Again there was confusion and overcrowding at the 1987 cup quarter and semi-finals. At the latter, some people were pulled up out of the crowd by fellow fans from above for their own safety. In 1988, Liverpool and Nottingham Forest met in the semi-final at Hillsborough and again there was severe overcrowding and dangerous crushes. No action was taken. The following year, the teams were drawn to meet each other again at Hillsborough. Huge crowds built up outside before kick-off with Liverpool supporters being allocated the smaller West Stand at the Leppings Lane end. With 5,000 supporters still outside minutes before kick-off (and a request to delay the start turned down), Chief Superintendent David Duckenfield ordered gate C to be opened and fans surged into the central pens on the terrace.

If you want a detailed account of the horrifying result of this decision, of what happened that afternoon, of the obscene deaths of 96 men, women and children; of the incompetence, wickedness, abuse and lies that followed from police, government and sections of the media over the next two-and-a-half decades, I urge you to read *And the Sun Shines Now* by Adrian Tempany. It is the definitive account of the disaster and its sordid aftermath by someone who was there. Tempany nearly died at Hillsborough and like many other heroic individuals, fought for justice and truth through the long decades ahead. Looking back over those last sentences, I hear a tone that could not be described as impartial. But how can one be impartial over Hillsborough? Tempany's book will make you rage and weep.

Feeling suddenly awkward and not wanting to be thought ghoulish, I walk briskly past C gate and the other blue gates of Leppings Lane with just a quick glance. I pause properly at the Hillsborough memorial at the main stand just a little further on and read the inscriptions and the dedications. It's a simple stone tablet, usually decorated with scarves and pictures, reading, 'In memory of the 96 men, women and children who tragically died and the countless lives that were changed forever… You'll Never Walk Alone'. I have no personal connection to the Hillsborough tragedy. I can't claim to be one of those countless lives directly affected by it – some who've tried this shabby trick have been rightly savaged for it, like UKIP's Paul Nuttall – and so I don't expect to find myself crying until I realise I am.

Perhaps it is because Tempany's book and Kevin Sampson's *Hillsborough Voices* are still fresh in my mind. They are hard to shake, these awful, vivid accounts of the day and the barely believable details. Police prevented fans from climbing the fence to safety, stopped friends helping other friends and allowed only one of the 44 ambulances on hand to enter the ground and so only 14 of the fatally injured ever made it to hospital. The authorities then spent the next 27 years lying or obscuring the truth about what happened and blaming the fans themselves.

This beggars belief. But there were some prepared to sink even lower. Bernard Ingham, former press chief to Mrs Thatcher, said in a letter to a victim's parent that the fault was with 'tanked up yobs' and later that people 'should shut up about Hillsborough'. Similarly, former *Sun* editor Kelvin MacKenzie lied and smeared the dead in the most vile manner in his paper for years to come, only eventually apologising partially and under duress, just before I began my walk.

That was because in April, a few months before I set off from Jarrow, a kind of victory occurred for the victims of Hillsborough and their families. Thanks to tireless and often thankless efforts, the Justice for the 96 campaign won. At the end of the longest judicial hearing in British history, a jury ruled that every single death that day was an unlawful killing. As I walked down Leppings Lane that October day, the newspapers were humming with talk that prosecutions might finally begin.

Calling Hillsborough a tragedy feels wrong. It suggests a freak occurrence such as the sinking of the *Titanic* or the downfall of Othello caused by his own flaws. Hillsborough is actually more akin to what happened at Aberfan in 1966, when negligence meant that a dangerous slag heap collapsed onto a primary school killing 116 children and 28 adults. Later, the National Coal Board was found 'wholly responsible' for those deaths. Aberfan and Hillsborough did not simply happen to working-class people; they happened to those people because they were working class. They died because richer and more powerful people than themselves did not care what became of them.

Hillsborough though has a more sinister dimension than the horror of Aberfan. Though it is little consolation, Aberfan was at least not a wilful act of enmity. It is not too lurid or sensational to see Hillsborough as the final and most terrible battle in a decade of class war, with police used as a tool of government in oppressing those it saw as the 'enemy within'. That meant essentially the left, the Labour movement and the working classes generally. As the Hillsborough enquiry ended and as I entered Sheffield, a similar event, the police actions and the violence at Orgreave coking plant in 1984, was exercising many and creating calls for an enquiry into that too. Some of the officers on duty at Hillsborough had also been at Orgreave.

There'd be more to hear about Orgreave as I neared London. For today, after Hillsborough and Leppings Lane, I loosely follow the River Don's course into the city, passing the new and fashionable Kelham Island Quarter where industrial heritage rubs shoulders with craft beer emporia and the like. If the Jarrow march passed by they'd have found it a buzzing tightly packed district of riverside mills. I say 'if' since there's some confusion about the actual route they took into the city centre. Getting slightly lost, they wrongfooted the small welcoming committee. There was a welcome but a curious one in the form of a single woman who thought they were a fascist march and hurled abuse at them.

Given the headlines of the day, this doughty lady could be forgiven for being jumpy. Mosley's Blackshirts might have been given short shrift in the East End and elsewhere but he had enough friends in high places to ensure he couldn't be discounted just yet. One such ally may well have been King Edward VIII whose close personal friendship with an American woman called Wallis Simpson was becoming very interesting to the press, Westminster and the man in the street. In Germany, the Nazis passed a law forbidding Jews from using parks or public swimming pools and from owning electrical equipment, typewriters or bicycles. Dark clouds were forming across the skies of the world as 1936 moved to a close.

In other news, as they wouldn't have said then, there was major civil unrest in India. Britain's imperial phase was ending and its relationship with the subcontinent had been volatile and problematic throughout the decade. In 1931, when the

Lancashire cotton trade was at its lowest ebb, India restricted
its imports of cotton goods, hitting the north west of England
hard. Gandhi himself came to Bolton to meet the workers and,
while sympathetic to their plight, he reminded them that his
own people were never very far from starvation. They took him
for a night out to the Swan Hotel in Bolton but the ascetic
Indian took only bread and water, which unsurprisingly rather
dampened any party mood.

Stanley Baldwin was all for continuing the policy of
liberalisation towards India, not wanting another chronic
running sore like Ireland to deal with. But the UK's rule in
India was still harsh and draconian. On the weekend the Jarrow
march reached Sheffield, 35 people were killed in riots involving
Hindus and Muslims in Bombay. All of this weighed heavy on
the mind of Ellen Wilkinson who had visited India many times
and was a passionate advocate of emancipation and self-rule for
India and a fervent Internationalist. 'To me, the mill girls of
Shanghai are as important as the mill girls of Manchester,' she
said in 1936. How would that have been received in Sheffield 80
years later I wondered?

The Indian question bedevilling Stanley Baldwin in 1936
was long settled by 2016 but that night I had my own Indian
question, namely at which one to eat in Sheffield. I'd not
even considered other cuisine as Sheffield will always mean
to me my first gleeful adventures into Indian food during
friends' student days here in the early 1980s, when David
Blunkett's 'People's Republic of South Yorkshire' rang to the
sound of ABC and the Human League, bhajis were 10p and a
'suicide' phaal curry came free if you could manage to eat it.
Happy days.

I put the question to the hive mind of Twitter naturally.
Marc Webster said, 'Get yourself to Shapla for a curry. Crappy
end of town, but underrated and never had a bad meal yet,' and
many other correspondents agreed. Nadia Shireen suggested
the Thali Café and Ian Howie told me, 'the Mogul Room on

Sharrow Vale Road is excellent. You can also have a good drink in the brilliant Lescar as well'. Shabir's gets several good reviews but in the event I choose a restaurant on Leopold Square which comes to my timeline garlanded with recommendations and testimonials, many sounding almost tearful with jealousy that I find myself nearby on Aagrah buffet night. Purists will baulk at that word 'buffet', and I take their point. Unfairly or not, the ubiquitous city-centre Chinese variety always conjures images of glutinous sweet and sours congealing under hot lamps, with pale and flaccid chips lolling unappealing nearby and, 34 times an hour, the bringing out of a small cake to a tuneless chorus of 'Happy Birthday'. Useful when strapped for cash or pushed for time perhaps, and I have often been both, but happily being neither on this Sunday evening, I make my way briskly to the £12.50 buffet at the Aagrah, the money burning a hole in my rucksack.

It has been said that I bang on a bit too much about food on my travels, so I will gloss over the gorgeousness of everything to do with the meal; the people, the staff, the tenderness and insinuating warmth of the gobhi gosht or the sweet and pungent murgh sindhi korma or even the gosht Punjabi masala, its succulent lamb steeped in a sauce bright with cardamom and sleepy with aromatic methi. Suffice to say that the whole night comes back to me often. But one comment on Twitter the next day about another Sheffield curry favourite makes me think. 'Ah … and to think that once upon a time Mr Shabbir just had one small business in Westgate, Shipley. Corporate isn't always better.' That tells you a lot about the strangely proprietorial relationship we have with this cuisine of Empire and the people who cook it. The Indian restaurant business in Britain started with a handful of esoteric outlets and grew, in a nice reversal, to colonise us until, according to Robin Cook's famous speech on chicken tikka masala, it became our national dish. But now, some say unthinkably, it may be declining again in this new uncertain Britain.

The Jarrow marchers could have eaten Indian food if they'd really wanted to but it would have taken as much of an effort as their crusade. E. P Veeraswamy published his seminal work 'Indian Cookery' in 1936, but to get it cooked home-style in anything like a restaurant setting here, one would have had to visit one of the handful of curry cafés set up by Indian sailors who'd jumped ship or were dumped at major ports like Cardiff and London. Most of these renegade seamen came from Sylhet – now a mountainous area of Bangladesh – and the 'Indian' curry house we know is really usually Bangladeshi. After the Second World War, many of these early Asian entrepreneurs bought up defunct cafés or bombed-out pubs and were the only establishments to open late. The British love of the 'after pub' curry was born.

The brilliant food writer Bee Wilson points out that the naming of British curry houses reflects their vintage:

> If you see one that is called Taj Mahal, Passage to India or Koh-i-Noor (after the famous Indian diamond), it probably dates back to the first wave of curry houses in the 1960s. These eateries appealed to retired Old India Hands, who wanted to eat hot chutney and be treated like 'sahibs' again. The names of 1970s curry houses began to shrug off the colonial past and evoke, instead, a vague sense of eastern exoticism: Lily Tandoori, Aladdin, Sheba – glamorous names to counteract longstanding British prejudices that south Asian food was malodorous and unclean.

I didn't know it, as I scooped chana and sambar on Leopold Square, but behind the scenes and the kitchen doors, the curry is in crisis. Two or three Indian restaurants are closing every week in Britain. Like the public house, it is a cherished mainstay of our social life that we are in danger of losing. A real shame this, and not just gastronomically, as for years curry houses have been rare islands of independent family enterprise in high

streets dominated by chains. They played a vital role in the
regeneration of many local economies in the 1980s and 1990s.
Now those chains, from the cheap and carby pizza big boys to
the ersatz, unconvincing curries offered by the Harvesters and,
yes, Wetherspoon are forcing them out.

The price of our beloved curry has barely changed in 20
years outside of a minor trend for fine dining establishments.
But costs are rising fast. The weakness of the pound has doubled
the price of spices imported from India. Staples like cooking
oil and rice have become more expensive and hiring costs are
rising. Staffing generally is a major issue. Thousands of Indian
restaurants are critically short of staff and facing a number of
problems. Since the Brexit vote, economic uncertainties have
hit curry houses (in fact, most independent restaurants) hard in
terms of rent and overheads. Young Asians are being lured away
from family curry house business into more lucrative jobs, such
as in IT, medicine and finance. And of course, the climate with
regard to immigration has cooled and hardened.

In April 2016, a few months before I set out, a new law
was passed prohibiting Bangladeshi chefs from coming to work
here unless they can earn £35,000 or more a year after living
expenses. In effect, this is a ban since few Indian restaurant
chefs earn that and everyone knows it. Lord Bilimoria, the
Indian peer and entrepreneur behind Cobra beer, called the law
'ridiculous' and 'discriminatory' adding, 'I sometimes think we
are a very ungrateful nation. You are damaging an industry that
provided food your country loves.'

It's estimated that one in three British Asians voted for
Brexit. Many Indian restaurateurs have told reporters that they
cast their vote this way hoping that leaving Europe would bring
more favourable terms for south Asian immigrants. The president
of the Bangladesh Caterers Association Pasha Khandaker urged
his 4,000 members to vote 'leave', sentiments echoed by rallying
voices like then employment minister Priti Patel, who told
British Asians that by voting leave, they could 'save our curry

houses and join the rest of the world'. So far, it isn't working. You can see this for yourself tonight. Walk down your high street and look in the chain pub, look in the pizza franchise, look in the chippy even and then compare this busyness to the two occupied tables in the little independent curry house.

Happily Aagrah was still full to bursting when I left; smiling waiters weaving through tables groaning with vast, fluffy naans, chilled Indian beer, bottles of red and their laughing, ruddy drinkers. Sizzling tikkas trailed smoke through the bright and noisy room and the air was heavy with fenugreek and methi and cardamom and pleasure, for now at least.

SHEFFIELD TO CHESTERFIELD

18 October, 12 miles

According to media lore, the former TV sports host Des Lynam was so comfortable on air that his heart rate actually fell when the camera was on him. He was certainly in a relaxed frame of mind with regard to geography when he once announced on *Grandstand's Final Score*, 'Chester nil, Chesterfield nil. No goals there in the local derby.'

As I prepared to leave Sheffield on the calm, bright October morning of 17 October, I couldn't be too judgmental towards suave Des though. I too was heading out of my geographical comfort zone, away from the England I know reasonably well and headed for towns and places that are really merely names to me, if famous ones. I know the north east a little; I have travelled in Yorkshire extensively, often making nocturnal incursions over the Pennine passes of Oldham and Halifax, crawling through the moor grass by night, face daubed with mud, a dagger between my teeth and with false papers in my rucksack that claim I'm from Heckmondwike. But where exactly is Chesterfield. North? Midlands? East Midlands? All I know for sure is that from there I will head to Mansfield, through the East Midlands and into the home counties. For both the men of 1936 and for me the second half of the Jarrow march will be as much as it can be in a small, crowded island, terra incognito of a very mild kind.

Before leaving 'Sheff', I take a stroll down to Norfolk Street or at least as good an approximation of strolling as I could manage fully laden. On one side of the road is the Crucible, Sheffield's famous theatre and sports venue and home of the World Snooker Championships. The two weeks of this baize jamboree are a mainstay of BBC TV's sporting output, and moreover one of the few major sporting draws the public corporation has managed to cling onto, and it is thus guarded and boasted of fiercely. Ideologically opposed governments and commercial satellite giants like Sky and BT have steadily eroded the BBC's position as the nation's most trusted and watched sporting broadcaster, a position it held through most of the twentieth century.

Back in 1936, the World Snooker Championship was still being held in Thurston's Hall, Leicester Square, London, and was a far smaller affair than today's truly global contest of professional skill, but many of the Jarrow marchers would have followed the contest eagerly. This year proved a turning point for the sport seen previously as a more complex yet less skilful variant of billiards, and also the sign of a misspent youth. There were double the number of entrants to the world championships – which was admittedly only a rise from five to 13, but it felt a significant breakthrough. The final between the legendary Joe Davis and Horace Lindrum was the greatest yet seen and signalled snooker's arrival as a major sport. The *Daily Mail* Gold Cup switched codes from billiards to snooker and the august *Billiard Player* magazine changed its name to *Billiards and Snooker*. For many working-class men, Davis was a folk hero akin to Fred Perry or Stanley Matthews. His home town, whose Billiards Championship he won at age 13, turning pro soon after, was coincidentally where I was headed; even if I still didn't know whether Chesterfield is north, south or Midlands. All I was sure of was that it is nowhere near Chester.

Before departure though, my real reason for popping down to Norfolk Street was to visit the building across the road from the Crucible. The Victoria Hall is Sheffield's major Methodist place of worship; a Grade Two listed building that styles itself as 'the church in the middle of the city with the city at its heart'. It opens to the public every morning for coffee and I sipped mine as I wandered around the spacious commanding interior trying to visualise the events of last night, 80 years ago, when the marchers held yet another famous public meeting. Great swathes of Sheffield's citizenry came to see them, as well as the Mayor of Jarrow who'd travelled down by train, the Bishop of Sheffield and 20 other clergymen of various denominations. The Bishop of Sheffield's presence infuriated the men's own local bishop, the unsympathetic cleric Henson who had denounced the Jarrow march as 'revolutionary mob pressure'. He would have been very uncomfortable at the rhetoric warming the Victoria Hall that night. The chairman of the Sheffield branch of the Transport and General Workers Union took to the stage and was cheered mightily when he hailed his 'comrades from Jarrow' adding, 'You represent to me a tremendous tragedy, the tragedy of unemployment ... There is a certain section of people who regard the unemployment problem as something to be forgotten. They do not want to think about it. But there are also those who do think of you.'

I finish my coffee and browse the second-hand books, hoping to start a conversation to divine whether anyone still thinks of them now. Affecting interest in a battered James Herriot, I ask the two older women dividing the Georgette Heyers from the Catherine Cooksons whether the Jarrow march means anything to them. Helen frowns and initially confuses it with the General Strike (understandably) but then finds her thread and knows her stuff. 'They'd closed the shipyard hadn't they and then promised them help that never came. So they marched down to tell them what for. Did they meet here? Well, that must have been something. And that's something to be proud of, isn't it? Are you a Methodist, love? No? Well, here in this church, we work with refugee families. We support them, we try and find them homes and jobs. Well, not always jobs as there are funny rules about that. They're not allowed to work some of them. But that's what we should be about. That's what the Church should do. Help the needy, help the vulnerable. I can't abide those folk who think the Church should be just clapping and holy water and—' and at this she clasps her hands and makes a wounded pious face tilted heavenward. I laugh and wonder what Hensley Henson, Bishop of Durham would have made of Nonconformist Helen of Sheffield.

The Barnsley taxi driver who'd told me about the legacy of the miners' strike also furnished me with a choice nugget of information about my destination today, namely that Chesterfield was, and I quote, 'a real ballache to get to'. For cabbies maybe. But there's a very quick and convenient train, or there's the typically luxurious, futuristic X17 bus, or if you're on Shanks's pony like me, there's the irredeemably dull waymarker of the A61 and the Chesterfield Road. I began my walk in a blaze of autumn sunshine, which made for a far more pleasant morning than the original marchers had, whipped and soaked by the worst weather of their trip so far. Robert Winship had to be left behind in the hospital with malaria which brought the total of men having to drop out to six. Slightly less than 200 men then departed the city in icy rain and buffeting winds; although morale was still high after porridge, ham, tea, toast and butter. Ellen Wilkinson left for some Labour Party business in Glasgow and the men set off on the 12 wet miles to Chesterfield.

I stride past Hallam University and along by one of the great railway pubs of England, one of my very favourites, along with the ones at Stalybridge and Huddersfield. This splendid place is the Sheffield Tap. If it were the end not the beginning of the day, I would certainly slip through the arches of the fine Grecian architecture of Sheffield Midland Railway Station for a pint or two of citrusy Jaipur IPA, or Cask Ruin from Bakewell, or most apt, Yorkshire Blackout, brewed to the 1930s recipe of a soldier who never returned from the Second World War and described as 'deliciously smooth and dark with chocolate and vanilla flavours'. But I have promises to keep and miles to go before I sleep, as the great Robert Frost once wrote. Twelve in my case.

My way leaves the city and wends down Bramall Lane. Sheffield United's home ground has none of the dark connotations that Hillsborough now sadly has, just a very distinguished past. Bramall Lane, named after an important manufacturing family, has a good claim to be the first ever football stadium. It had the first floodlights and the first sizeable capacity terraces and stands for spectators to watch in relative comfort. It hosted the final of the first ever football tournament (four years before the FA Cup). It is the oldest major stadium in the world still hosting professional football and the biggest outside the top two tiers of English football. Its proud history rather throws into awkward relief 'The Blades' current lowly status but their fans are still loyal and vocal. It's quiet though this morning after a very lively Saturday, which two lads in garish polyester leisurewear are discussing whilst wobbling on their bikes like circus performers on the pavement by Munchies Café, Smoketastic Vaping Shop and the tattoo parlour. Appropriately, one is vaping, the other eating a pasty. Both are copiously tattooed.

'Four nil … and we had four disallowed. Mental.'

'We never had four disallowed, tha daft bastard.'

'We did and all. Did you not watch it on Sky? What kind of fan are thee? Part timer …'

'So it could have been eight nil. Is that what tha's saying?'

'Well done, mastermind. Part timer. Glory hunter. Tit.'

Those 'thees' and 'thous' and 'thas', which somewhere else would smack of affected archaisms, are still common in Yorkshire and Lancashire. They are an echo of the Norsemen we once were; part of the daily natural living speech of South Yorkshire and even when it comes, as these did, amid a shower of casual obscenities that I have removed, it's still charming in a robust kind of way.

Up the road now and along one of Sheffield's many edges where after a faceless row of bookies and garages, a sudden, sublime view slides open, revealing the city cradled in a bowl of hills foregrounded before the sunlit Pennines. Sheffield's unique topography is always liable to gift you a moment like this. Step around the corner of the Washeteria or, more likely, the E Cig shop and the land will sweep away before you in a wash of green and brown, a carpet of mossy valleys and sketchy trees. After a couple of hours, I reach Dronfield, 'the place where the male bees swarm', and a hotly contested patch. Dronfield lies halfway between Sheffield and Chesterfield and a tug of love was fought over it not that long ago. Amorous, avaricious Sheffield wanted it for her own and Dronfield was almost merged into that city and hence South Yorkshire. But the local community preferred to stay true to Derbyshire and through concerted effort of will they got their way.

Around here, on the route of the old eighteenth century turnpike, maybe at Dronfield or Old Whittington something curious happens to the vowels. But working out exactly where and what is the stuff that keeps linguists up at night. Yorkshire is a huge county and there's a corresponding variation in the way people speak. If sufficiently skilled, we could guess, even if we hadn't passed by Harewood House, that *Emmerdale* is set in North Yorkshire from the gritty prettiness of its rural setting and the yellowy stone of its cottages, but also from the way they sound their 'a's in the bar of the Woolpack. It's said that the best way to tell if someone comes from Leeds or Bradford is to get them to say Bradford; a true Bradfordian says 'Bratford'.

But there's no easy way to differentiate a north Derbyshire accent from a South Yorkshire one, or to spot that you've crossed the border. You're just suddenly aware that it's happened, the change as swift and surprising as the fall of dark in early winter.

Even the people around here can't really explain the linguistic subtleties beyond a few vague generalities about 'broader vowels beyond the Trent'. Browse the local websites and you will find considerable joshing disagreement about whether Chesterfielders – Cestrefeldians if you will – are northerners or Midlanders. No consensus seems to be reached, although being annexed into the Yorkshire TV region seems to have annoyed a few. Here's a typical response: 'Probably northern I think, otherwise we would all sound like Brummies! Having said that, I would rather watch Central/Midlands TV than Yorkshire. I find it really irritating listening to *Look North* & *Calendar*, banging on about how brilliant Yorkshire is supposed to be. I think they have forgot that we are supposed to be in their TV region.'

When the marchers reached the handsome market square in Chesterfield, they were greeted by a party of communists from the nearby pit village of Normanton who were holding a public rally and offered them 20 pounds (well over a thousand now) from the sale of flags and pamphlets. Under pressure from the Conservative councillor on the march, march marshal David Riley turned this down saying, 'This is the fourth time the communists have tried to gatecrash. They are not going to get in as easily as they think.' This seems ungrateful, even a little craven, but it does show again how desperate the Jarrow organisers were to preserve the saintly odour of being non-political. The dubiousness of this stance was underlined by the fact that the march did accept a substantial donation from a local Conservative association.

It's market day in Chesterfield and, true, the lady in the fleece and headscarf hawking mushrooms and plums sounds very different from her South Yorkshire counterparts, like the 'dee-dars' of Sheffield. But I half expected her to sound like Gina Lollabrigida and be singing out about her *zucchini e asparagi* in a lovely *bel canto*. On this warm and gentle afternoon, with stalls and tables spread across the broad piazza of the square, there is an implausibly Italianate feel to Chesterfield; appropriate since Chesterfield is home to what is, according to the council, 'The most famous architectural distortion in the world, after the leaning tower of Pisa'. You could, I think, confidently substitute the words 'most famous' with 'only' in that sentence. But then again, I may have overlooked the Tilted Chapel of Bratislava or similar. In any event, I couldn't dream of a sojourn in Chesterfield that didn't take in its most famous feature, and it shouldn't be hard to spot.

First though, I took a promenade in the square. Perhaps it's a trait of this eastern flank of the country but England seems as much a nation of market towns today as it did in 1936. Chesterfield holds one on three out of five weekdays and then again on Saturday. It looks bustling to me but one stall holder selling fruit and veg mutters about how council interference, high rates, poor parking and other strictures have made it a pale shadow of what it was. It has a friendly, unfussy, hardworking feel though, like Chesterfield itself.

Eighty years ago, Chesterfield proved admirably hospitable to the Jarrow men. The Victoria café laid on free hot food and the stall holders and townsfolk raised £19 13s (almost as generous as the Normanton commies) as well as donating clothes and bedding. Both major established churches in the town held services for the men; the Catholics were made welcome at Spencer Street's Church of the Annunciation whilst the Anglicans were taken to the parish church in the town centre, where presumably they raised their collective eyes in amusement to its spire as they doffed their caps and found a pew.

Just as the bewigged head of little Mozart brands everything in Salzburg, and that prim shot of Shakespeare with the terrible haircut can't be avoided in Stratford, so a particular example of dodgy medieval cowboy construction defines Chesterfield. It adorns everything from IT consultants to tanning salons. There's Spire Beauty Academy and Spire Insurance Brokers in a building called North Midland House (which is a clue I suppose to where Chesterfield sees itself). As for the infamous object itself, I didn't have to ask directions. I just scanned the skyline and there it was. The Church of Saint Mary and All Saints, Chesterfield has a spire which twists through 45 degrees and leans nine-and-a-half feet from plumb. That's all fairly meaningless though until you see it up close (you can glimpse it from the trains to Newcastle from the Midlands) and the only sensible reaction on seeing the spire, twisted as a Mr Whippy ice cream cone, is 'how the hell did that happen?'

Naturally, there's some unfeasible if entertaining old guff/ revered legend about just how this has occurred. According to one tale, a blacksmith from Bolsover did such a botched job of shoeing the devil's hoof that Satan jumped up enraged and kicked the spire bandy. Another explanation questions the virtue of the town's womenfolk, the spire being said to have craned its neck to look down on the rare occasion a virgin was married in the church. The truth is that they simply used crappy unseasoned wood which warped pretty quickly in Middle England's rainy climate. Also, the Black Death had made it even harder to get a decent tradesman out of Ye Olde Thomfons Local Directory than it is now. But it's the actual engineering facts of how the spire was built that proves the old adage that the truth is invariably stranger and more interesting than fiction. In a town as bristling with signage as Chesterfield, it wasn't hard to find my way down to the old mechanics' institute, now home to the museum, to get the straight dope.

Veda, Peter and Amanda at the museum are so helpful, enthusiastic and skilled at what they do that I imagine even now someone behind a desk several hundred miles away is planning to put them out of a job. They exude a quiet, firm civic pride in their town as well as provide you with lots of accurate, useful information. When I arrived just before lunch, an elderly lady was just leaving, thanking them warmly with a handshake each, whilst in the back room a party of small children was being gently corralled around some old Roman artefacts. Chesterfield has its roots in an Iron Age market town but was really founded by the Romans, whose stay here was brief but productive. When they abandoned the town to head north and subdue the ruffians up there, it grew steadily through the Saxon period, is mentioned in the Domesday Book and under the Normans developed quickly into a market town with a thriving wool and leather industry. Then in the fourteenth century, they decided to build a church.

While I am having this explained to me, there has been an elephant in the room, or more specifically a windlass. Peter notices that I've been eyeing it with some interest and so, with the same air that you might relent and let a small dog get up on the furniture, takes me over to explain exactly what a windlass is. Essentially, it's a huge, old, wooden version of those things hamsters run around on in their cage. This one is as tall as a house and would have been placed as high up as it could be during the construction of a tower. Men (and sometimes donkeys) would clamber in and walk inside it, exactly hamster-in-wheel style, and this motion would be used to pull building materials up to those constructing the tower. They have also been used to pull water from wells and in gold mines. If you were thinking of asking me how the medieval windlass differed from the Chinese or differential windlass at this point, don't.

It took 60 years to build St Mary's and thus the windlass must have been dismantled and re-assembled many times, being raised storey by storey as the tower grew higher – you can see the carved instructions on the wheel, Ikea flatpack style – until eventually it was completed. After that, the huge wheel lay forgotten on the top storey for 700 years until re-discovered after the Second World War. The wood used was a thousand years old and probably came from Sherwood Forest. I'm not an engineering buff by any means, but just standing by this tremendous and aged object was a thrilling experience. You can almost feel the hands that have run along it, the labour inside it, hear the voices raised in laughter and curses as the hard working day went on. It tells a powerful human story.

My hour in the Chesterfield museum brought home to me again that history is not just a parade of kings and queens, royal intrigues and stately homes. It's also about work, workers and engineering. Inspired by the mood, I walked just five minutes up the Newbold Road to the Holy Trinity Church. The rector here put the Jarrow men up back in 1936 and the caretaker was so thoroughly decent to them that they bought him a pipe in gratitude. I went into the churchyard in the chilly dusk, half hoping to find some kind of plaque to the march. Instead though, and just as worthwhile, I found the grave of one George Stephenson. Like the Jarrow marchers, he came down here for work from the north east, in his case to build the railway to London. He liked Chesterfield so much that he never left. He died here and his body lies in the vault of the church. 'Yes, it's not a bad old place,' said Peter at the museum and George seems to have agreed. I liked it too, but it was getting dark, and I had no kindly caretaker to help me out, so it was time to find somewhere to stay.

STAGE TWELVE

CHESTERFIELD TO MANSFIELD

19 October, 12 miles

As the Jarrow men walked south through County Durham, Yorkshire and Derbyshire, General Franco's Fascists were on the march, marching northwards and eastwards across Spain from their military basses in cities like Zaragoza, Valladolid, Cadiz and Cordoba. Though it was far away and in a different country, along with the Battle of Cable Street and the Jarrow Crusade itself the Spanish Civil War has become part of the doomed romantic mythology of the 1930s for the left. A democratically elected people's movement, a broad church of progressives of all kinds, helped by poets, painters and young working-class idealists and destroyed by Fascist bullies in uniform aided by Nazi bombs while the rest of their world turned their backs.

That may be the romantic view, but it is also essentially the truth. In February 1936, a Popular Front coalition won a narrow victory at the Spanish general election. Instability followed, and General Francisco Franco returned from exile on the Canary Islands to wage an appalling war against the legitimate government which, after two years of bloodshed, he won. Franco said he would 'save Spain from Marxism whatever the price' and when a journalist replied that that meant he would have to shoot half of Spain, Franco said, smiling, 'I repeat, at whatever the cost.'

In September 1936, 27 nations met in London to debate the Spanish question. They decided on a policy of non-intervention, a policy they shamefully stuck by even when Hitler began to aid Franco. The USSR was the only country to help the Republicans, along with thousands of civilian volunteers from all over the world for whom this was a defining moment of the age – one in which they were prepared to take arms for freedom against the forces of oppression. 'I suppose it's a fever in the blood of the younger generation that we can't possibly understand,' fretted Virginia Woolf in a letter to her sister. But for the younger literary generation it was really very simple. Spain and its new democracy had to be saved. It was a cause worth fighting and – if need be – dying for.

Most went to join other likeminded young people in the International Brigades. W H Auden drove an ambulance across the battlefields along with Julian Bell – Virginia Woolf's nephew – who lost his life on one. Orwell went with a gun as did Laurie Lee. Poets like Stephen Spender and David Gascoyne were supporters of this 'poets war'. But it would be wrong to think that all the artistic community were on the Republican side. T S Eliot felt 'a few men of letters should remain isolated'. And South African poet Roy Campbell was aggressively pro-fascist. Evelyn Waugh said he knew Spain 'only as a tourist … but if I were a Spaniard I should be fighting for Franco'. Graham Greene and George Bernard Shaw dithered.

Some of the Jarrow Crusaders went to fight in Spain the year after the march. They were amongst 60 men from the north east stationed at Albacete as members of the English Battalion of the International Brigade. It would not be surprising if their experience on the Jarrow march hadn't galvanised some into more direct action, especially after the march had met with such lily-livered support from the official British left.

Ellen Wilkinson made several trips to Spain in the run up to the war, being deported to France at one point. After Jarrow, as

Franco's forces tightened their grip on the benighted country, she went again at the head of an all-woman delegation visiting hospitals and schools and meeting POWs and political leaders in Barcelona and Madrid. On her return to Britain, she appealed to the British people to support the Republican cause as a 'fight between right and wrong' and an international struggle against fascism. She set up the Milk for Spain scheme to help civilians – people bought cardboard tokens at their local co-op to fund essential supplies – and helped transport stricken Spanish families to Britain.

Just as it did when the marchers left Chesterfield, a foreign conflict rages and preoccupies the commentariat as I set out for Mansfield. The headlines I'd scanned on the newsstands of WH Smith all talked of the start of 'the Battle of Mosul' with Iraqi state forces hoping to soon retake the stronghold of the ISIS Islamic State army. Not long after, the same headlines would be largely repeated, this time referring to the Syrian government's attempt to retake Aleppo from rebel and Islamic State troops. What was once Syria's second city was now a ruined husk of shattered buildings and lives over which the West watched in impotence, largely. But there was also clamorous contradiction and confusion. As in 1936, emotional appeals and accusations could be heard on every side. Then, some on the left like Frank Graham, active in the Newcastle branch of the National Unemployed Workers' Movement, went to fight in Spain having been scathing and dismissive of the purpose or efficacy of Jarrow's 'non-political march'.

Intractable, impenetrable, bloody. Reading the various papers of different political stripes that morning in Chesterfield brought me to only one sure conclusion, namely that the Syrian conflict is one that makes reasonable people despair and leads one to regard with suspicion anyone who claims to know right from wrong. This war appears to be one between (at least) two sets of horribly bad guys with a great many innocent people caught between their competing murky ideologies. This

is my very limited understanding of it of course, but at least
I acknowledge that it is limited. This puts me ahead of some I
felt, as I binned the papers and set off.

There is little to say about the road from Chesterfield to Mansfield
other than that the Jarrow marchers took it on 19 October 1936
and now so have I. The weather was foul as they crossed from
north Derbyshire into Nottinghamshire, from agricultural land
into the Nottinghamshire coalfield. Several soaked marchers
became sick. This is D H Lawrence country, mining country,
or at least it was. It was once a living if ravaged landscape, man
intruding violently into the peace of nature, scarring it like
pockmarks on a pretty face. Now that mining is gone, the land is
slowly healing which is a kind of consolation. It is a green but not
a pleasant land – dirty bedraggled cow parsley, unkempt hedges,
tilled fields shaped and formed from slag heaps.

As with Barnsley, as with Ferryhill, even though the pits
are silent and flooded and the daily routines and processes of
mining are a fading memory, something of mining's hard and
resilient culture still lives on. These towns and villages will never
exude the same quiet contentment as a Cotswolds hamlet;
the gentle hubbub of a Gloucestershire agricultural town or a
Dorset port. It is not that those places haven't known hard work
or hardship, but it is a different kind of work. Mining villages
and towns always carried themselves differently. In their heyday,
they wore a sense of hard-won self-righteousness and shared a
proud collectivity. Hundreds of feet below ground, camaraderie
is not merely a pleasing bonus. It may be the difference between
life and death. I spent an afternoon not long ago with a group
of miners from the former Bold Colliery in St Helens as they
returned to the site of their old pit, now a nature park. The sense
of intimacy, even physical, between them was extraordinary and
quite unabashed. One of them had run the stores where the
men got changed at the start of shift and picked up their safety

equipment. Thirty years on, he could still remember every one of his fellow miners' pit number.

As I walk on in Nottinghamshire, past a roundabout with an angry, prescient little placard proclaiming 'Vote Leave, Sack Cameron' and over the brow of the hill, I am met by a sudden, unexpected sight, like an image from an old black and white film or flickering newsreel: a chimney and winding gear stark and proud against scattering clouds. Pleasley Colliery would have belched, roared and clanked to high heaven when the Jarrow marchers passed it in October 1936. Perhaps its winding gear and trucks would have reminded them of home.

The colliery stands above the River Meden and sits on the Top Hard seam. The first lease to mine that seam was given to William Edward Nightingale, who married into a mining fortune and was father to the famous Victorian nursing pioneer, Florence Nightingale who is said to have 'turned the first sod' when the shafts of Pleasley were sunk. For over a hundred years it produced coal in enormous tonnage and supported the local economy of the village that grew up around it. That's still here, a quiet place with neat rows of bungalows, languid cats in their windows and a pub on the river; a commuter village for Chesterfield and Mansfield I assume. Up the rise towards the country park, the houses thin out on the hillside. A woman walks her boisterous Labrador, and a man in baggy, multi-pocketed shorts leans awkwardly to mow his steeply sloping lawn.

There are two clear reminders of Pleasley's working past. The tall winding tower standing sentinel, and also the Pleasley Miners Welfare. The latter dominates the small village centre, shoulders set back on its own broad swathe of lawn. I go up the path, past the perspex shelters for the smokers, and try the door. Closed and quiet, but a few signs computer-printed on A4 sheets and taped to the window mention future concerts, a couple of talks and meetings or request members to 'please respect others when leaving the club and do so quietly'. Once the Miners Welfare and the Miners Institute were at the very heart of the community. Paid for by deductions from the men's wages, they combined library, dance hall, theatre, pub and university. Tredegar Workmen's Hall in South Wales had an 800-seat cinema and hosted celebrity concerts. None of that today in Pleasley though. There is a wildlife quiz in the bar tonight, admission one pound, and I'd have been there had Mansfield not beckoned. I retreat back down the path and find a short cut behind the Welfare, through the car park and the scrubby woods to where the mine workings crown the little hill, bold and clear against the blue sky of the fine early afternoon.

Whilst aware that I just did this very thing, it doesn't really make sense to talk about 'mining country' as a homogenous whole, even in a small nation like England. There are subtle differences in culture and attitude between fields as seen during the two big gruelling strikes of the 1970s and 80s. It might be thought, for instance, that the miners of a small Kent coalfield, far from the industry's hegemonic heartlands in the north, would be less radical and militant than those northern miners. In fact, they were amongst the most hardline. This was, in part, because some miners sacked during the General Strike could only get work in Kent, and thus a bitter radicalism was handed down father to son. Also, Kent pits like Shakespeare, Snowdown, Tilmanstone and Chislet had some of Britain's harshest working conditions. Snowdown, deepest, hottest and most humid, was known as 'Dante's Inferno' and regarded as the worst pit to work at in Britain.

By contrast, the Nottinghamshire miners appeared the least intransigent and most biddable during the 1984 strike. Sociologists and Labour historians have offered as many explanations as there were pits for this. Nottinghamshire had big underground reserves of coal, making the men feel secure. They were well-paid and without major grievance. Nottinghamshire collieries, said the NUM's David John Douglass, were often worked by miners displaced from Scotland and the north east in the 1960s. The lack of support when those mines had closed made them less concerned to stop closures of other pits in the 1980s. Nottinghamshire's large Polish mining community resented Arthur Scargill's support of the Communist government in Poland against the Solidarity union. Marxist historians like Alex Callinicos think that Nottinghamshire miners never had the case for striking adequately made to them by a complacent NUM and were alienated by the uncompromising aggression of the Yorkshire miners' stance.

I suppose I could have asked the men of Pleasley Colliery about all this since they were very much in evidence that lunchtime. But I thought better of it. Pleasley is no longer a working pit but former miners are keeping it alive as a mining museum on a nature reserve. But if that sounds twee or contrived, it is anything but. My feeling on arrival was of wandering into a working pit at change of shift. Apart from a brisk nod from a man on the gate in a sheepskin jacket, there was little in the way of welcome. No 'Is this your first time at the Pleasley Colliery experience?' or directions to the gift shop. Awkward maybe, but at least no one can accuse Pleasley of having gone soft.

Hard work has carried on here since the pit closed in the early 1980s. Sludge has been bucketed out, engines restored, shale swept away, shafts reinforced. Only this time it has all been voluntary. The men who once worked seams here are now engaged in preserving it as a piece of industrial history for their grandkids in Mansfield and Bolsover. Unsure whether it's acceptable to just wander around but doing it all the same, I take a few pictures looking up at the towering winding wheel, explore the cavernous engine house with its gleaming brass of indeterminate but virile function, all thrusting pistons and columns, and then venture into the west shaft and the workings of the pit. Three men in hard hats and dirt-streaked overalls are maintaining some kind of track and checking the glistening innards of wire along the passage walls. Noticing me ambling about, I get the now customary brisk nod and then am left with

the same dilemma vis-à-vis introductions as I would be at the
Finnish ambassador's cocktail reception. Eventually we fall into
desultory conversation. 'Pleasley really closed as a working pit
in 1983 but they kept it open as an escape hatch for Shireoaks
Colliery, which were my first pit, and then of course that went too
after the strike. We're here keeping it going, showing folk what
it were like.' With that, he turns to his mate and they continue
to prod at a junction box. The exchange wasn't unfriendly, and
they weren't unhelpful, but I came away with the impression
that I was keeping men from proper and more important work,
which I probably was.

'Café' is far too refined and continental a term for the eating
and drinking experience at Pleasley. The walls of the green
corrugated-iron shed are lined with old signage from the pit,
chiefly warnings and admonitions:

TREATMENT ROOM. INCIDENT ROOM.
CONTROL NOTICE. ANY PERSON FOUND
CAUSING A NUISANCE IN THE PIT HEAD
BATHS WILL BE STOPPED FROM USING THEM.

Amongst the shift lists and the old promotional materials,
framed under glass are fraying, cracked black and white pictures
of men in helmets, shirtless, skin creased and grained with black,
all with the dark-eyed Arabian glamour that surely contributed
to the collier's status as an aristocratic prince of the working
class. About a dozen of them, older now in Lonsdale hoodies,
Berghaus fleeces, zip-up cardies and kagoules, are crammed
into the steaming kitchen where four volunteer ladies in pinnies
pirouette between microwave, griddle and toaster, bringing forth
mugs of dense whirling Birds instant and bacon and egg baps.
They forget mine, but I might have done that too, distracted by
the constant chat, teasing and reminiscence. Dennis seemed to
be holding court that morning and I wish I could have broken
into the inner rank of slurping courtiers to hear him. Happily,

there's an interview with him on YouTube, which for lovers of industrial history is as exotic and mesmerising as any whaler's tale or explorer's yarn. Dennis talks of the 'bright, hard coal' of the Waterloo seam hiding in the low water and, chillingly, of rationing drinking water when 'entombed in 23 seam ... that were difficult'. We should guard against romanticism though. At the time of the Jarrow march, mining was a foul, hard job that made young men old; stone dust setting like cement in the bronchia, or silica slicing the delicate tissues, or the gurgling hell of wet lung and the air heavy with methane which might ignite and bring the roof down on you, aflame.

Escape hatches. Incident Rooms. Accident Reports. The phrases and the tone speak of a working world that was once my own family's but is as alien to me now as it is to those grandkids in Mansfield. It is a world disappeared, a world apart from water coolers, hot desking and shredding. Not necessarily a better or more noble world, just one so ancient and obscure that it reminds you how much Britain has changed – and how quickly – from a country that welds and delves and builds to one that sells and advises and speculates. At the time of the Jarrow march, the national government under Baldwin were themselves puppy dog-devoted to the primacy of private enterprise and limited state interference in the economy. But that was very soon about to change, and change faster still after the convulsion of a world war. Two years after Jarrow, coal royalties would be nationalised. Immediately after the war, in a deeply symbolic act, the entire British coal industry would be taken into public ownership. Forty years after that, in what looks like belated revenge, it would be annihilated.

The three miles down the main road into Mansfield pass quickly as I have one eye on the clock, or more accurately the phone. Earlier I'd picked up a tweet from Jodie, the development officer at Mansfield museum telling me they have a present and some tea and cake for me. 'You'll always find a warm welcome in

Mansfield. We may not have much but we'll share what we have. Come any time before 4.' Jodie might not have known it but in this she echoed how Mansfield had behaved to the Jarrow men. Even the local branch of the Labour Party, perhaps ashamed of their colleagues in Chesterfield, defied the national leadership and turned out in force to greet them outside the town hall and thence to some downtime at the municipal baths and the parochial hall before giving them free cinema tickets.

I arrive with a little time to spare and so make my own little tour of the town. As I arrive, yet another market day is ending in a clatter of tubular steel and laughter. Across the emptying square and arrowing its way through Mansfield is the town's most visibly curious feature, or 'notable landmark' as the publicity blurb rather wanly describes it. This is a colossal brick railway viaduct that bisects Mansfield Berlin-wall style, although unlike that cheerless edifice this has 15 roomy arches under which carpet warehouses and kebab shops thrive, and where surely nighttime assignations occur over White Lightning and Blue WKD. Cutting up Leeming Street in the direction of the museum, I'm pulled up by the gorgeous window display of the Vinyl Lounge emporium; 12-inch albums of mod classics, Motown and psychedelic rock hung with the care of a gallery of Titians or Warhols. Inside, 'Suspect Device' by Stiff Little Fingers gives way to 'My Smile Is Just a Frown Turned Upside Down' by Carolyn Crawford. I can smell coffee. Naturally I enter.

Vinyl albums, like coal, were deemed a product consigned to the ash heap of history, an archaic irrelevance. In much the same way that we were told we need never dirty our hands with nutty slack and firelighters again (or handle another printed page in the paperless office), experts enjoined us to welcome the bright ephemeral world of digital music. But not only are market forces cold and cruel, they are often simply wrong, for they reckon without love, obsession and sheer human oddness. No one ever fell in love with CDs – those horrid little plastic coasters spilling plastic teeth everywhere. No one bought minidiscs or compact cassettes outside of a few broadcast professionals who now keep them at the backs of drawers with the Chinagraph pencils. The market simply never saw the bearded hipster coming on his sit-up-and-beg bike, or the middle-aged mod with the mid-life crisis on the new Vespa, or the teenage girl wanting the new 'old skool' fashion accessory. All these groups and more have contributed to the much-vaunted vinyl revival, and all are good news for Richard of Mansfield.

Richard looks a lot like his customers I'll bet. A rugged and genial, smart, middle-aged guy with a good crop, salt and pepper sidies and crisp white Ben Sherman. He'd worked variously around the music industry in London before coming back to Mansfield and setting up here. He's done a nice job. Moody lighting, red and black leather seating, racked vinyl, a display of rare Smiths and Bowie, a retro black and white pegboard advertising pancakes and maple syrup and espresso. 'You don't get this in HMV, do you?' he says waving a proud hand, and in truth that is exactly why shops like Richard's are thriving. They treat the customer less like a zombie consumer than an informed member of a stylish and discerning club, although without the terrifying elitism that blighted the northern soul shops of my early teenage years. Here, asking for the wrong version of Sliced Tomatoes could see you cast into the outer darkness of 'uncool' for months.

'Mansfield's a big northern soul town,' says Richard, which I could have guessed. Towns like Mansfield often are; formerly built on textiles, coal or engineering with hedonistic, intense, obsessive working-class sub-cultures centred around grafting, playing hard, looking good, dancing and understated machismo. I could have spent a lot of money on northern soul 'sevens' here, but in truth I'm not the vinyl fetishist that's often supposed; my northern soul collection is now mainly zeros and ones on a hard drive the size of a pack of cards. In 1975, I could have bought a small flat with it on collectable vinyl. Also there's the matter of my rucksack. Though ample of litreage, it is no DJ bag. I wish Richard well and carry on up to the museum as dusk comes gently on.

As 80 years ago, the good people of Mansfield have turned out in force to meet me. Jodie and her team show me around 'the Tin Tabernacle', as the museum was once known. It now houses a terrific arcade exhibition called 'Made In Macclesfield' that reflects the manufacturing powerhouse the town once was. The exhibition concentrates on eight famous industries that built Mansfield's reputation for manufacturing: Metal Box, Shoe Co, Mansfield Brewery, Barrs Soft Drinks and others in hosiery, precision engineering, mining and quarrying. There are artefacts, photos, film and audio featuring past and present employers of the town. Jodie is quick (understandably) to point out that modern Mansfield still has a manufacturing base, mainly light engineering and IT companies, but these are often 'hidden' in anonymous units on the outskirts of town. Made in Mansfield recalls the halcyon days of very visible commercial might when 40,000 people would have crowded these streets every morning and evening going and coming from work making shoes, speakers, metal boxes, textiles, and beer sold around the world. Even the sand from the quarry was prized for the bunkers of elite golf courses.

I'm interviewed for local radio by a young lad called Matt who asks very intelligent questions about the nature and efficacy of protest marching as a political tactic, in the news since Corbyn's re-election, whilst later Jeff and Liz the curator tell me all about Mansfield's musical pedigree which is small but fascinating. Mansfield's most famed musical son was perhaps Alvin Stardust. Born Bernard Jewry, he renamed himself Shane Fenton when he took over as lead vocalist with the Fentones from the original Shane Fenton who had recently died. If this seems a little creepy, then bear in mind that much about Alvin's seventies' image was exactly that to be honest. Even as a child I found the leather glove, the queer praying mantis stance and the line about going back to his flat to 'lay down and groove on the mat' deeply upsetting. Looking back, he was a sort of Gene Vincent for Arthur Scargill supporters I suppose, had I but known it; the Elvis Comeback Special restaged at Orgreave. He was also by all accounts a 'gentleman' who did much to support the museum.

'Oh, and we've got something for you,' says Jodie as I'm about to leave. 'Gosh, have you?' I say, pretending to have forgotten. And it's a lovely thing. Amanda, an archivist at the museum, has put together a framed front page of the local paper the *Mansfield, Sutton and Kirkby Chronicle* of 23 October 1936 (price: three halfpence) carrying a contemporary report on the march passing through.

> The Jarrow marchers, many of them drenched to the skin, who marched through here at tea time on Monday, found Mansfield's liberal hospitality a welcome contrast to pitiless rain and wind through which they had tramped from Chesterfield. True, the men were bronzed and weather-beaten, and most of them looked fit enough but then, as Miss Wilkinson, the Jarrow MP put it – no doubt with perfect truth – 'these men have been better fed during the last fortnight than they have been for years!'

This excellent present under my arm, I stop off to sip a pint in the warm, dozing snug of the Brown Cow. Mansfield Brewery closed its doors in 2002 and its remaining operations moved to Wolverhampton so I make do with a nice drop of Everard's Ascalon, a 'traditional chestnut ale brewed with British-grown Challenger and Admiral hops. Orange, zesty flavours are complemented with chocolate, earthy flavours, leaving a perfectly rounded finish,' according to the beermat. I prop up the framed front page on the bar in front of me and study that.

'There must be easier ways to read paper, lad,' says a plaster-splattered man at the other end of the bar with his folded tabloid in front of him, and, ice broken, I tell him about my day. 'Aye, we made some stuff here, beer, shoes, knickers, hats ... did they tell you they even made sand for golf bunkers here? Perhaps he buys it for his Scottish ones,' he says and points to a familiar brutish orange face on the front of the *Mirror*. It is of course Donald Trump. It's the third and final presidential debate tonight and while some are still saying 'too close to call', most reasoned analysis says that Trump will lose even despite a deep-seated antipathy towards Clinton that is hard for us Brits to really fathom. Can any reasonable, sane human being, however much they distrust the shifty and dynastic Clintons, really consider voting for a man like Trump? Surely not. Common sense and humanity will prevail, I conclude, as I take another long pull on those zesty chocolatey depths and wait for the perfect rounded finish.

STAGE THIRTEEN

MANSFIELD TO NOTTINGHAM

20 October, 14 miles

From the BBC News Website, March 2016:

> The closure of the DH Lawrence Heritage Centre
> in Eastwood has been described as 'tragic'... Durban
> House, which explored the writer's life, was closed
> to save £80,000 a year. The authority said the service
> had not stopped and would merge with Lawrence's
> birthplace museum in the same town. Malcolm Gray,
> chairman of the DH Lawrence Society, said it was
> a 'frustrating' decision. But Alex Khan, cultural
> services manager at the Conservative-led council,
> said: 'I actually find it quite exciting – it puts the
> focus of the DH Lawrence Heritage service back
> somewhere it has a very strong link ...' Mr Khan
> denied the closure was 'a slap in the face' following
> Nottingham's status as a Unesco City of Literature,
> awarded in December.

Walking the miles of the dreary Nottingham Road from
Mansfield in the squalid, damp, overgrown margin of grass

where there should really be something to stop foot travellers being knocked into the ditch by the backdraft of passing tankers, ankle-deep in Red Bull cans and fag packets and lord knows what unspeakable detritus flung from some passing window by a git, I remembered some words of D H Lawrence's quoted by Matt Perry that I'd read the night before:

'The real tragedy of England, as I see it, is the tragedy of ugliness. The country is so lovely, the man-made England is so vile. I know that the ordinary collier when I was a boy had a peculiar sense of beauty coming from his intuitive and instinctive consciousness which was awakened ... the human soul needs actual beauty more than it needs bread.'

In many ways, D H Lawrence was a pillock and there's a hint of that here. But his heart was in the right place. Whether the demise of the 'ugly' pits of Nottingham at its great human cost in community and livelihoods would have cheered the comfortably-off novelist or not is moot, since both are with us no more. But Lawrence was the first British novelist of the industrial age to have what we might call ecological consciousness, condemning mechanisation for what it did both to the human spirit and the British landscape. It did, however, help to pay the young Lawrence's family's rent as it exploited. It's a thorny one, and I'm not sure either DH or myself have any, let alone all the answers.

Until the lorries and the unnavigable undergrowth made it too risky, I had in my ears as I walked the churning road the beginning of the Second Movement of Alan Bush's *Nottingham Symphony*. Its limpid but subtly astringent loveliness turned even this dismal trudge into something vaguely meaningful and uplifting. But then my spirits were already high with the thought of an evening in Nottingham. I don't know it as well as I might but I've always liked its independent cast of mind.

From D H Lawrence to Alan Sillitoe to Ned Ludd (possibly) to Samuel Fox the philanthropic abolitionist Quaker to Games Workshop to Ray Gosling to Lord Byron to his daughter the computer pioneer Ada Lovelace to Brian Clough (adopted) to the hardcore metal label Earache Records, Nottingham produces people who do things their own way.

Alan Bush wasn't from Nottingham, but it was just like the city to ask Britain's most outspokenly Marxist composer and Communist Party stalwart to write them a symphony for the week of celebrations commemorating the quincentenary of its Royal Charter in 1949. Bush was held in real suspicion by the powers that be. When the BBC placed a ban on Bush and composers of his political persuasion, Vaughan Williams refused broadcast rights for his new work in protest. He didn't share Bush's views but he loathed such high-handed treatment, telling the BBC in a telegram 'Well, you're not having my stuff either', at which they relented. Commissioned by the Nottingham Co-operative Society, Bush's *Nottingham Symphony* was first performed on 27 June in the city's Albert Hall by the London Philharmonic Orchestra. It's a fabulous piece if, like me, you're partial to tuneful but interesting twentieth-century English music. Bush himself says the piece 'ends in a mood of purposeful optimism' and it put me in very much the same as finally, after several dreary hours, the A60, Nottingham Road, at last lived up to its name and reached Nottingham.

The day started well too. Once again, an interesting invite had pinged into my phone via social media. Whilst its undoubted popularity as a platform amongst world-class morons has made it the object of some scorn, Twitter has thus far proved an invaluable tool on my journey, which I should stress is an actual journey, and not the ones described on reality TV. I have found that social media, like the old Yellow Pages ad used to have it, is not just there for the nasty things in life. Nasty things like trolling women from behind the anonymity of your little egg avatar or perpetuating badly spelt feuds over football. It has also, in my case this trip, been about learning interesting things from interesting people; history, tips, steers – the kind of ninja knowledge that only locals have. Michael is a lecturer at West Nottinghamshire College who's been following my progress. Noting that I'm going to be stomping past his door, a mile or so out of Mansfield, he tells me he'll have the kettle on if I fancy dropping in for a cup of tea and to meet some students.

He meets me outside the bustling bright red campus which even I couldn't miss. It looks a terrific place to work. As we negotiate the throngs of students, Michael tells me that it's just had a lengthy, extensive £5 million refit. (Having spent a few happy years teaching further education in my early twenties, I always keep abreast of nice places to work that might give me a job in the future.)

'That new Health and Beauty Centre stands on the site of an old Mining and Technical College, the place where once you did day release from the pit.' He catches my smile and returns it. 'I know. It sounds ironic but it's not as strange a transition as you might think. A lot of our students, their dads used to be miners and they came to colleges like this and retrained in everything from hairdressing to IT when the mines closed.'

When I get to the refectory (or NutraStation or cantina or whatever they call them these heady days) they've made a big backdrop Image Me, with me photoshopped into the Jarrow march, which is sweet and funny. And though I suspect the students don't have the first idea who I am or what I'm up to or what the Jarrow march was, they sit behind their gleaming big screen Apple Macs and listen attentively as I tell them about the march. After listening thoughtfully, one lad asks, 'Why didn't they just get the train?' There's a lot of laughter and I join in, but it's a rather good question, given that lobbying the government for their town was the purpose of the trip to London rather than a sponsored walk. But of course that's from the pragmatic context of today. Part of the point of the long trek was the romantic endeavour of it all, the heroic endurance that was meant to convince the Establishment that these men were not idle or feckless but determined and disciplined.

Afterwards I take some questions and as usual these wander entertainingly off topic. A petite Indian girl asks me whether I'm going via Birmingham where she's originally from and I wonder for a second whether she's about to ask me to drop a parcel off at her mum's. But no, she just wants to chat about the new-ish Bull Ring and Symphony Hall. By some route that I can't recall, we establish that one young man is the nephew of the colourful late Welsh actor Victor Spinetti and we have a diverting chat about his friendship with the Beatles. Afterwards, another staff member called Liam, knowing of my interest in esoteric sounds, tells me about his PhD in children's music and we bemoan the unavailability of the crazy, educational jazz-rock numbers from Sesame Street on CD. More usefully perhaps, Liam thinks that there's something on in town that night that might interest me. It's an event at Rough Trade Nottingham called 'Wanted: A Real Media', which will attempt to offer alternatives from voices of the new left. Now, we donkeys live a long time, as Orwell's Benjamin said in *Animal Farm*, so I'm old and wise enough to know that this title probably translates as, 'Wanted: A Media That Agrees With Me'. But it sounds like it might chime with some of the things I've been thinking about in relation to Jarrow and now.

Of late there have arisen several websites and left-wing media pressure groups who are 'critiquing' (as the Americans say) what they call the mainstream media or 'MSM'. Since Glasgow University Media Group's groundbreaking 1976 study 'Bad News', radical sociologists have been ploughing this furrow, looking at how the structure and language of press, radio and TV news especially serves to reinforce the status quo and the

Establishment. While indisputably leftist in stance, these types of early surveys were analytical and sociological in approach. But over the last decade, the media seems to have grown, on its fringes at least, far more fissile and partisan: from Breitbart to Wikileaks to Anonymous to The Canary, from alt-right to new left.

Anyway, I agree to go, as it sounds like fun (of a sort) and the matter of media ownership relates very much to both today and 1936. The interwar years and especially the thirties saw a rapid growth in the mass media and a corresponding concentration of that media in only a few well-connected hands, and the subsequent creation of press empires and barons (to mix my honorifics). This was crucial, since while radio and TV were still very much in their infancy, the British press was, as historian Nick Shepley puts it, 'how the country talked to itself, its nervous system, it's arteries of discourse.'

This system, these arteries, were largely and solely in the control of a handful of wealthy and titled men. Lord Northcliffe owned *The Times*, the *Daily Mail*, the *Weekly Despatch* and the *London Evening News*. His brother Lord Rothermere owned the *Daily Mirror*, the *Sunday Pictorial*, the *Daily Record*, the *Glasgow Evening News* and the *Sunday Mail*. Another brother, Lord Harmsworth, was also a major player. Between them, they had the ear of six million readers.

Lord Beaverbrook made the *Daily Express* the most successful mass circulation newspaper in the world and used it as a mouthpiece for his personal opinions, from appeasement of Hitler (whom he greatly admired) to free trade. These few men wielded extraordinary and unprecedented political power over a mass audience of readers. They advanced their political agendas from the far right of the political spectrum in an age of uncertainty and crisis. They also did it cannily, through a diet of entertainment and a daily concentration on what would now be called celebrity culture, gossip and chat about film stars, comedians and musicians.

That said, press coverage of the Jarrow march was uniformly warm (especially in the then vigorous regional press) if bland and patronising. Put simply, the Jarrow marchers were celebrities and the march was covered as such; as a cheery human interest story involving plucky chaps, adorable dogs and that 'fistful of dynamite' Ellen Wilkinson. For her part, she was scornful of both Lord Rothermere's empire of puppet titles and the newly formed BBC. Many on the left still are 80 years later, as I was to find out.

I check in and unpack in my modern business hotel on Maid Marian Way. I like chain hotels because I know what I'm going to get with none of that unpredictable 'family run' or worrying 'funky and individual' business, where you might be expected to eat with Tiddles the cat on your lap or have a shower from a watering can. Comfortingly for us busy misanthropes on the move, my hotel is the sort of place where Phil and Jeff from head office meet Mike from the Uttoxeter branch for firm handshakes in the lobby before grabbing a beer and thrashing out rotas.

I strolled down into the town centre which is dominated by the busy, spacious Old Market Square, over which the town hall looks down in a paternalistic, aldermanly way. Here, there's the ubiquitous street food, a rasta busker playing the sax to a tinny version of 'Red, Red Wine' from a beat box and a few entertainingly incompetent skateboarders. Down an alley, I find further evidence of the city's subversive bent in the form of a properly old-school left-wing bookshop, the sort that you thought had become extinct in the nineties, where you could pick from Guy Debord's *The Society of the Spectacle, Women's Voice*, the Trotskyist *Spare Rib* and anarchist pamphlets which always smelt faintly of that unpleasant arrowroot herbal toothpaste.

Nottingham's Five Leaves is still thriving. Several earnest-looking students of different genders and races leaf through forbidding-looking texts and inspirational postcards expressing solidarity with various South American rebel groups. Or maybe that was my memory playing tricks on me. It was a fascinating place anyway with tons to agree and disagree with. The left has always been a place where passion and sanctimoniousness rub vigorously along together and it always will be. I'm more Bevan and Attlee these days than Corbyn or Brand. But I come out with a recycled tote bag full of stuff old and new; some miners' strike posters for dewy-eyed nostalgia, a great postcard that says 'To Make The Rich Work Harder You Pay Them More, To Make The Poor Work Harder You Pay Them Less' (which I may wave like a ref's yellow card in future arguments with free marketeers) and a cracking reprint of a 1964 Nottingham samizdat magazine called *Anarchy 38*, 'A Journal of Anarchist Ideas', which seems to be nothing of the sort but bristles with energy and brio from the young Ray Gosling on Nottingham and Alan Sillitoe on poverty. It is exactly the kind of thing the teenaged Maconie would have ensured was visible from his Oxfam overcoat pocket, chiefly to impress thoughtful girls.

I leaf through *Anarchy 38* in a big lively pub in town called the Major Oak, named after the tree where committed wealth distributor Robin Hood (who would certainly have shopped at Five Leaves) used to hang out with Maid Marian and the Merry Men. I make a few notes on a tremendous piece detailing the sundry riots that took place in Nottingham between 1754 and 1854 which confirms my impression of the city. I don't impress any girls but an Irish man comes over to me and says, 'Don't I know you? Aren't you in education?' No, I answer truthfully. 'Oh,' he replies, 'well, who'd have thought it. There's another fellow alive in the world who's as good looking as you.' I nearly bought him a pint but I have a date elsewhere.

I meet Liam along with Gordon, the college's union rep, outside Rough Trade Nottingham, one of only three branches of the successful indie in the UK, the other being in New York. Downstairs, men with waxed moustaches and girls in black hoodies with magenta hair are leafing through racked vinyl by Laura Marling, Gil Scott-Heron and the Sleaford Mods. Upstairs, there's a large room with a spit and sawdust feel, a bar stocked from microbreweries around the world and cupcakes under glass. Beers bought, we make our way to the other end of the room where a small stage faces about 30 plastic chairs. After a short while, a man and woman appear along with a ponytailed roadie. There then ensues some mildly hilarious faffing with microphones that intermittently either do not work at all or emit earsplitting shrieks of feedback, all such as you might get in an Alan Ayckbourn portrayal of a fringe leftwing meeting. When this has been sorted to some reasonably bearable degree, Nancy Mendoza of *The Canary* tells us about the ethos of her website, which she hopes is part of a drive towards 'greater plurality within the news. Today's media has become an echo chamber to mainstream ideas and practices, which are not speaking to, or for, the range of groups in society.'

If you've looked at *The Canary*, you'll know that what this translates to is pretty straightforward left-wing agitprop but with a garish modern vibe. It's somewhere between the *Socialist Worker* and *Heat* magazine online with the clenched rectitude of the former and the relaxed chattiness of the latter ('Trump just dropped his stupidest tweet yet ... and the Internet is in stitches!') This is a neat trick if you can pull it off and should you want to. Writers give up the certainty of payment and are paid according to the traffic they generate, which seems to me about as nakedly capitalistic as you can get and might even make Rupert Murdoch let out a low whistle of admiration. It also means the quality of the writing is wildly variable and generally partisan. But it is an alternative certainly. And there are adverts for skiing holidays.

Tom from Real Media is next and starts with a few colourful anecdotes about how he used to go drinking as a youth in Nottingham city centre, this presumably to soften us up a little for the fairly indigestible stuff to come. Indigestible to me anyway. The small audience lapped it up but then I wouldn't exactly call them a 'tough crowd', as comics say. Tom makes one or two good points, such as that conspiracy websites are 'disempowering' and that the structures of the modern media concentrate power amongst the rich and the middle classes. This is certainly true, but you came all this way to tell me that? It's in paragraph one, page one of every GCSE textbook on the sociology of the media. Then there is some stuff about 'horizontalism' that I simply do not follow whatsoever, so I have to acknowledge that it might have been searing stuff.

A few phrases brought out the worst in me, it has to be said. Firstly, there's a mention of Karl Marx followed quickly by a snort of 'I'm not a Marxist of course' as if only a prize chump would have any time for the most influential and insightful economic analyst of the last 200 years. (Well, that about wraps it up for poor old Karl, I thought, now that he's been dissed above a record shop in Nottingham.) Tom also mentioned those of his kind working at 'the coal face'. Perhaps it was having spent some time around pits and miners recently but I doubted very much if anyone here with their zesty IPAs and cupcakes had ever been within a postcode of a coal face, least of all Tom, or for that matter me.

Then, in the midst of some diagnosis of the ills of the modern media, he says ' ... as much as I hate the BBC ...' Until relatively recently, I had rather innocently assumed that hatred of the BBC was the preserve of the swivel-eyed, foaming demagogues of the right. This then brings home to me how little I have in common with their rabid counterparts within the modern left. Tom is every bit as driven an ideologue as

Paul Dacre. I would say that in the end, the best, if not most passionate defence of the BBC is that it is viewed by the right and left alike as supporting the other side. I would say that such flak from both flanks means the corporation is doing a fairly decent job of being impartial, but then both Russell Brand and Guido Fawkes would probably snigger at that. Also, given my time in the BBC's employ, they may respond, 'Well, he would, wouldn't he?'

In much the same way that woolly old geezers and fresh-faced youths are forever telling me that Jeremy Corbyn is a saintly man with his heart in the right place, I will assume, if not entirely convinced, that Tom and Nancy are similarly good eggs. But I found their vision of a new, better media no great improvement on the one we have; certainly every bit as partial philosophically and theoretically. Feeble initiatives like giving a quarter of the licence fee to independent creatives (like Tom) to make their own news and documentaries are fine, as long as you acknowledge that that dosh and platform must also be given to UKIP and maybe even the EDL. Freedom is indivisible. If you don't think that, at least have the honesty to say that it isn't actually free speech you want, but your speech and paid for by people who don't agree with you.

It may seem mean but it also needs to be pointed out that there were 18 people in that room, at least one of whom was very much not in agreement. The rest definitely were but I felt this isn't a launching pad, it's an echo chamber. Like the reception at Corbyn's rallies, it may feel awfully nice to be part of, but it tells you nothing about support in the cold, wider world, where real people have to be housed, real kids have to be fed and educated, the really sick have to be cared for and sometimes real wars have to be won against some real bad guys. I don't think the people at *The Canary* or Real Media or Jeremy Corbyn or any of their ilk are bad guys themselves but I think they might be making it easier for the ones who are.

We left during the Q&As. (It's always a bad omen when you hear 'it's not so much a question, more a statement really'.) Nottingham had some venerable and famed boozers that I was keen to try and two enthusiastic guides. The people's struggle is thirsty work after all. We made our way through streets awash with students running politely riot through the streets. I couldn't work out why. It was a bit late for freshers' week, and there seemed no logic to any of the costumes but a definite lunatic gaiety about the various smurfs, zombies and cowboys; togas, bear outfits and onesies. They swarm over Brian Clough's statue and by the time I get there, only a few girls remain snapping themselves with the bronzed figure in a tracksuit arms aloft. 'Who is this bloke?' asks a girl in a baby's bonnet to her friend taking a selfie. 'No idea,' comes the reply. To the side of them, a supremely posh ginger kid in a sombrero is explaining to his upset girlfriend that, 'Look, he just bumped into you because he' s swaying because he's very, very drunk and you are just so, like so, over-reacting Daisy'.

According to the article I was reading earlier ('Riotous Times in Nottingham'), the people of Nottingham – and these are very much edited highlights – rioted in 1754 over an election, in 1755 over bread and in 1756 over the price of cheese, during which they started lobbing huge Cheddars and Stiltons about at the Goose Fair. In 1779, 1783 and 1787 they rioted over wages for knitters and in 1795 over the price of butter. It was the cost of meat that incited them in 1788 and 1792. In 1793, keen to liven up a quiet patch, Nottingham's supporters of rival sides in the French Revolution rioted. Next it was a rigged election, then bread and meat again. In 1831 they rioted over the Reform Act, and then in 1839 it was the Chartists. In between and along the way, there was generally a riot every couple of years over meat, bread, butter, cheese or knitting. Had you had a watch, you could have set it by the impressive regularity of Nottingham's riotous townsfolks appetite for disorder.

I missed out 1811, a very serious disturbance, when the Luddites smashed and burned through the city culminating in the razing of the castle itself. Their leader was Ned Ludd and in some cities, his name would be blackened and shamed forever more. In Nottingham, they named a pub after him. Since I was passing, I went in and raised a quick glass of whisky to the old troublemaker and then was on my way.

STAGE FOURTEEN

NOTTINGHAM TO LOUGHBOROUGH

21 October, 5 miles

Above the mirror in my Nottingham hotel, stylishly painted, rendered as if in the writer's flowing hand, is a quotation.

'Don't let the bastards get you down!' – Alan Sillitoe

This variant on the old wartime witticism, *Illegitimi Non Carborundum*, is one of many quotable lines uttered by Arthur Seaton in Sillitoe's brilliant *Saturday Night and Sunday Morning*, played equally brilliantly by Albert Finney in the film: Elvis-Presley-as-lathe-turner, all feral proletarian glamour. This morning, toothbrush in hand, wrapped in towel, I'm amused and irritated to see Seaton/Finney's growl of plebeian defiance turned into a motivational quote for the ambitious Midlands middle-manager.

Thursday night has become Friday morning, and a very Nottingham-style riot is sweeping through the streets of my head. We had moved on after the 'Real Media' meeting from the Ned Ludd to the Malt Cross, an old Victorian music hall still with stage and balcony, now a fashionable bar selling botanical gins, cakes and swanky porters. There we had gone over the meeting, Liam, Gordon and I, and found that we were largely of one mind. Yes, there was much wrong with the modern media, an issue that seemed to preoccupy the new left, but a little more attention paid to the future of Liam and Gordon's students, their parents' jobs and homes and the traditional working-class communities of the post-industrial north and Midlands would be nice too. A trend toward this within the Labour Party, christened 'Blue Labour' by Jon Cruddas, was influential a few years back, but this realignment seems to have been overlooked once more in favour of more theoretical concerns, such as identity politics and endless handwringing and internal wrangling, post Corbyn. Anyway, as soon as this pub closes, the revolution starts.

In truth, by closing time we were in Ye Olde Trip to Jerusalem. Many pubs in England, even several in Nottingham, lay claim to be the oldest in the land. The Porch House in Stow-on-the-Wold claims to have had the towels off since the end of the first millennium BC. Ye Olde Salutation, which we'd passed on our way here, also makes the claim as does Ye Olde Fighting Cocks in St Albans which still awaited me down what G K Chesterton called the rolling English road, made by the rolling English drunkard. But Ye Olde Trip to Jerusalem has as strong a case as any, established in AD 1189, the year Richard the Lionheart became king and responded to Pope Gregory VIII's call for a new, third crusade to the Holy Land. This is how the pub got its name. At least, that's one theory.

The pub is literally built into Castle Rock on which Nottingham castle stands and, unsurprisingly for a pub this old, it has accrued legend and rumour like a battleship gathers a crust of barnacles. In the upstairs lounge is 'the cursed galleon' a little wooden ship that must never be dusted. All who ever made this mistake died soon after and now it is kept in a glass case, thick with inches of grime. There is a very old chair that it's claimed any woman who sits in will become pregnant and has been so well used that it is now very fragile.

The pub's queerest and best feature though is its network of caves carved out of soft sandstone, creating strange and secret chambers perfect for conspiracies, assignations, trysts, secret meetings and plotting the overthrow of the government. In one of these caverns, a young man approaches who tells me that his best friend is Matt, the radio reporter who interviewed me in Mansfield. At this stage in the evening, this astonishing coincidence is certainly reason enough to call for another round of drinks.

Attempting to leave some time later, we get sucked into a group of drinkers at the bar playing some kind of game. A chain hangs from the ceiling with a small hoop at the end and on the opposing wall a small brass spike, curved like a mini rhino horn, is fixed at about head height. The game consists simply of swinging the chain like a pendulum and attempting to hook the horn. One old boy is undisputed pub champion at this, even doing his own versions of trick shots such as swinging the chain over his shoulder. (When not thus occupied, he goes table to table doing close magic with cards and matches.) No red-blooded games fan from out of town could refuse the challenge of course, and certainly not one as deep in his cups as I am. Thus it seems important that we join in the game for another couple of halves and single malt chasers. Eventually, I succeed and it is then of course necessary for an extended analysis of my successful shot at the bar over another round. (The game by the way, I later find out, is called Ringing the Bull and has been successfully exported from Ye Olde Trip to pubs all over Britain and the Caribbean.)

A gregarious chap at the bar with a braided ponytail says that buildings like Ye Olde Trip containing labyrinthine innards are common in the city. 'Nottingham's like a piece of cheese – full of holes. They run from here straight into the castle, these tunnels, and that's how the castle was burned to the ground by Ned Ludd.' We move on to the forthcoming US election and I wonder aloud, probably waving my pint about for emphasis, how any sane person could genuinely vote for Trump instead of Hillary Clinton and why she is so mistrusted. A chap from Crewe at the bar interjects, 'Ah, well, that's because she's a mass murderer.' He then goes on to describe the international cocaine smuggling ring the Clintons were helping to run out of Mena Airport, Arkansas and the dozens of people they have personally killed in order to keep the evildoing quiet. At this, we all fall silent, look at our shoes and shift our weight awkwardly. 'My, is that the time?' I hear myself saying, and Liam, Gordon and I head out into the night where, after some frankly ill-advised explorations of the castle's battlements, we say our farewells, and I head unsteadily up Maid Marian Way.

Next morning, a little bleary, I looked up Mena Airport online. There's quite a bit on there about the drug ring that was apparently based there, some of it exhaustive and plausible, but most of the Clinton murders stuff is on sites which also carry stories on how the moon landings were faked and the Illuminati are embarking on a mass world depopulation programme. Most of these carry a lot of scorn about 'the mainstream media', and have mottos like 'THE REAL NEWS YOU WERE NEVER SUPPOSED TO SEE'. Well, it certainly is an antidote to the mainstream media I suppose. One of the wisest things I ever read about conspiracy theorists was that they never believe just one conspiracy theory. They believe them all.

Hapless stooge and dupe that I am, I took an armful of MSM and a pack of Nurofen down to Old Market Square for a coffee and a browse of the papers. Hillary Clinton still has a slender lead in the polls, presumably amongst people who don't believe yet that she's a shape-shifting lizard. Or maybe people who do think that, but still believe her to be preferable to Donald Trump. Trump himself says that if he loses he may contest the election result.

The big 'celebrity' news story of October 1936 was certainly the subject of a cover-up. A major one too involving all of the press, the government and the royal family. But even with the best efforts at subterfuge by the most powerful in the land, a scandalous royal love affair was rapidly becoming the worst-kept secret in Britain amongst the high and mighty if not the hoi polloi. As the Jarrow marchers left Nottingham, Stanley Baldwin was meeting the new king to try to talk some sense into him about an American woman called Wallis Simpson.

Today we have a picture of King Edward VIII formed largely by his indulgent lifestyle, dandyish dress, vanity, admiration for Hitler, dereliction of duty and long, indolent, luxurious seclusion in Paris with the woman he abandoned his country for. But for most of 1936, between accession and abdication, he was regarded as a man of the people, a friend of the working class, and by government as a potential troublemaker. Throughout 1936, it was rumoured that he would soon be visiting Jarrow and though this never happened, he did take a tour of the depressed Welsh steel town of Dowlais. Here he was met by malnourished kids, unemployed men, ruined factories and a sense of desolation and misery which seemed to genuinely affect him. Some in the crowd held up banners reading 'Hunger Marchers Ask The King To Abolish The Means Test'. Edward was heard to turn to an official accompanying him and say 'something must be done'. It was an innocuous aside. But to some in government, it sounded as incendiary a revolutionary sentiment as anything being cried from a barricade in Barcelona or committee room in Moscow. Prime Minister Baldwin was not best pleased with Edward's habit of making visits to coalfields and steel towns or his sympathetic noises towards the poor and the unemployed. Perhaps this might explain why Baldwin showed little sympathy to Edward when his romantic entanglements started to become a complication for the state.

Edward Windsor had met Wallis Simpson in 1930 and soon became infatuated, calling on her for cocktails at her Bryanston Court home most evenings, whether her husband was at home or not. By May 1936, the affair between them was causing serious concern in official circles, especially when it became clear that Wallis Simpson and her husband intended to divorce. Edward wanted to charter a yacht and take her to Venice but was persuaded that this would appear to be tacit approval of the Mussolini regime. Instead, he contented himself by pootling around the Mediterranean in what fellow sailor and socialite Duff Cooper described as 'spick and span little shorts, straw sandals and two crucifixes on a chain around his neck'. On his return, he declined to open a new hospital in Aberdeen on the grounds that he was still in mourning for his father, which is a difficult look to pull off in tiny shorts, and especially when the same day he was seen collecting Mrs Simpson at Balmoral in an open-topped sports car. Tory MP Chips Channon wrote in his infamous diaries, 'Aberdeen will never forgive him'.

While the affair was common knowledge amongst Channon's circle (bafflingly so, as most agreed with Channon, that Mrs Simpson was 'jolly, plain and unprepossessing'), the ordinary Briton knew nothing, kept in the dark by closed ranks and the deferential, sycophantic nature of the press. American magazines carrying the story were censored, leading the indefatigable Ellen Wilkinson to ask in the Commons, 'What is this thing the British public is not allowed to know?' Even the Archbishop of Canterbury's secretary complained, 'So far our English press has been effectively muzzled by a gentleman's agreement secured by Lord Beaverbrook.'

As the marchers neared Nottingham, Prime Minister Baldwin went to see the King in order to try to get Simpson's divorce at least postponed if not abandoned. Edward insisted that the matter was 'the lady's private business'. Baldwin then suggested that Simpson be packed off abroad for six months to take the heat out of the current situation (and it was fervently hoped that, as historian Juliet Gardiner put it, 'in her absence his puppy dog passion would cool somewhat'). Edward was unmoved. He informed Baldwin of his intention to marry Simpson but was prepared to enter into a 'morganatic' marriage under which the couple could wed but Simpson would not become queen. This

had some support among the Establishment, not least Oswald
Mosley who thought the young and unorthodox Edward would
be 'Fascism's ideal king', but most thought it a bad idea and
an admission effectively that Simpson was not fit to be queen.
Edward replied that if he could not marry Simpson and be king,
he would abdicate.

When they learned of this a month later, in November
1936, what did the ordinary man and woman think?
Chips Channon felt that the issue had divided the nation
into Cavaliers and Roundheads again, into romantics and
puritans. Letters to national newspapers seemed to show
huge popular support for the King, but on the other hand the
singing of the national anthem at public events was markedly
less enthusiastic than normal. A women's demonstration at
Buckingham Palace carried placards reading 'God Save the
King from Baldwin', whilst at Marble Arch, a banner read,
'After South Wales You Can't Let Him Down'. The notion of
Edward being 'a people's King' with a feel for the common
man still held firm. Writer Harold Nicolson summed it up
thus: 'The upper-class mind her being American more than
they mind her being divorced. The lower class do not mind
her being American but loathe the idea that she has had two
husbands already.' Small children in the streets sang a new
version of an old carol: 'Hark, the herald angels sing/Mrs
Simpson's pinched our king!'

Back in Nottingham in October 1936, the marchers stayed
at Sneinton House, euphemistically described as a 'municipal
hostel' but in effect a workhouse. Two more men dropped out
here. One had to have all his teeth removed, a common drastic
solution to dental problems for many working-class people in the
era before the NHS. Boots the Chemists, based in Nottingham,
donated some essential medical supplies. The Co-Op gave them
32 pairs of socks and boots and 12 pairs of trousers. Two local
textile firms provided 200 pairs of fresh underwear, and thus
refreshed and emboldened, the Crusaders left the city and set

out across the flat agricultural fields of Nottinghamshire bound
for Loughborough.

Even if I had not been intending to replicate their route
exactly, I would certainly have been drawn to Bunny just
from seeing the name on the map. The village, named by the
Saxons after their word for reed ('Bune'), lies halfway between
the two and here the marchers stopped for lunch and were
rejoined by Ellen Wilkinson who had dashed off to Leeds
on Labour Party business. I arrive a little later than they did
after a fairly nondescript plod and take a look around. It is
a charming spot, although clearly that's helped by the name.
Everything in Bunny sounds cute; Bunny Village Hall, Bunny
Primary School, even the Bunny Trading Estate (home to Fine
Finish Kitchens, Appliance City UK, units available to let). An
information board on the village green details local walks in
the area that sound appealing – Sid's Seat, Bradmore Church,
the Pineapple Gate – but which will have to wait till another
day. I take a stroll down Moor Lane and Church Lane which
are delightful but for the first time on the march to date I
have a feeling of dislocation, homesickness even. I wonder if
the marchers ever felt this way, or whether they were always
buoyed by the camaraderie and adventure and the sheer selfish
pleasure of getting out of Jarrow for a few weeks.

In the bar of the Rancliffe Arms the lights are coming on.
A few tankards of foaming ale will be raised tonight and the
issues of the day debated at the bar. Roughly 60 per cent of
Nottinghamshire voted to leave the EU, although anti-EU feeling
was strongest in former manufacturing towns like Mansfield rather
than commuter villages like Bunny. Various signs tell me that
CCTV is in operation, not anywhere in particular, just generally
in the village. A man loading his Range Rover with rubbish for
the tip eyes me with interest. For the first time, I get the feeling
that I might be asked what exactly I'm doing snooping around
here, and not entirely out of idle, genial curiosity.

Then a cheering encounter. A nice curly-haired lady with glasses and a big scarf is selling kindling by the roadside for one pound a bag. It's a family tradition. 'My father started to do it when he was 90 for something to do really. We said, "Why don't you chop some of those old trees down and sell it for kindling. You could give the money to charity." We change it around from time to time. We've done it for the church and Rainbows. You're not from Bunny are you?'

'No. I'm from the north.'

'Ah, the north,' she says, with a little mysterious laugh, as if it were Narnia. She's heard of the Jarrow march but didn't know that they stopped for lunch in Bunny. 'Oh, at the Rancliffe?' Well, no, probably a tin mug of tea and corned beef butty on the village green. 'Well, there are worse places to have lunch. I'm biased as it's my home village but I do think it's beautiful.'

I agree and though I have no need of a bag of kindling I give this kindly welcoming lady a few quid for whatever charity she's currently supporting and head off. As I go, I reflect on how very old fashioned the encounter was – the travelling fellow, the roadside stall. Once, and not that long ago, travellers on the road were much more common than today and would pitch up in villages for work or leisure. Reading Alfred Wainwright's *A Pennine Journey*, I was struck by how the author, then a young man on a walking tour two years after the Jarrow march, would simply knock on doors and ask whether the residents could put him up for the night in return for a few shillings. He even offers some advice on this matter: 'Avoid the hotels, choose the lowly homesteads. Be one of the company, do as they do. If the family goes to bed early, be the first upstairs. If the host eats with his fingers, do the same. If he repeats loudly after his meal, make the attempt. He'll love you as a brother and take you into his confidence.'

In Loughborough, the marchers stayed at another drill hall. According to the nice lady in Bunny, Loughborough's is still here and I noted its address in case I got the chance to make a visit. The skies were darkening though and I wondered again how 200 men (actually 192 by this time) often managed to make better time than me. Perhaps I needed to get myself a harmonica band. Somewhere between Bunny and Loughborough, the marchers' supply bus driver stopped to help a motorist who'd broken down on the main road. He turned out to be an ex Jarrow man himself; 20 years a resident in the town who had left to find work like so many Tynesiders had been forced to do. Between the General Strike of 1926 and the Jarrow march, South Tyneside lost almost 100,000 people. London and the home counties gained a million.

As the Nottingham road finally slides into the outskirts of Loughborough, my eye is caught by two buildings. Firstly, a city pub that promises 'Netbuster Carp Fishing Here' (which brings forth visions of men in waders splashing about struggling with slippery tench amidst girls drinking spritzers and blokes watching SkySports). Secondly, a glorious building built around the time of the Jarrow march and a fabulous example of art deco thirties architecture. Lynne Dyer, who blogs about Loughborough, tells me this would have been newly opened when the marchers passed by and is still going strong as Beacon Bingo (a great-granny won a quarter-of-a-million pounds here a few months before I set off).

It's said that when a visiting Aussie saw Loughborough on a road sign he announced 'What kind of place is Loogabarooga?' This has now become the affectionate nickname for the town, which for me will always be associated with Human Groovers. Back when I was at college in the mid-1980s, the campus was a sea of tribes. There were swots doing chemistry who liked the Alan Parsons Project and Marillion. There was a new wave of British heavy metal-heads into the Tygers of Pan Tang, who generally got kicked out after a term. There were girls who loved Rush who wore cheesecloths and girls into Dollar who wore headbands, and pale young oiks like me with a copy of Camus's

L'Etranger in his overcoat pocket and an obsession with the first Human League album.

But perhaps most noticeable of all were the PE students who would come down to the bar en masse in tracksuits at nine o'clock, put Rod Stewart on the jukebox and drink pints of 'still orange'. Their course was officially called Human Movement but we hipsters obviously renamed them Human Groovers.

One of the few things I knew about Loughborough was that it had built a worldwide reputation as a capital of excellence in the field of sport thanks to the brilliant facilities at the university. Alumni include Paula Radcliffe, Seb Coe, Monty Panesar, Tanni Grey-Thompson and former Arsenal goalie Bob Wilson. Today, the university attracts Human Groovers from all over the world. I did see a few athletic-looking types knocking around in leggings and lycra but if I was expecting to see anyone lobbing a javelin down the high street or doing squat thrusts in Pizza Hut I was disappointed.

'Loogabarooga' is now the name given to a festival of children's literature, which was in full swing when I arrived. The local Waterstones was festooned with promotional materials and classic children's books from *Black Beauty* to Judy Blume. Sometimes festivals and their host towns have only the most tenuous of links but a jamboree celebrating kids' literature makes perfect sense in Loughborough, which was for many years the home of Ladybird books. There's a green plaque in Angel Yard at the site where books were printed from 1915 to 1973. Local printers Wills and Hepworth decided to try their hand at 'pure and healthy literature for children' during the First World War, and the publishing house grew to be one of the most distinctive and best-loved British brands.

Originally Ladybird published children's fiction of a rather folksy, cutesy bent like *Tiny Tots Travels* and *Hans Andersen's Fairy Tales*. Bunnikins and Downy Duckling were very popular comfort reading during the Second World War. But following this, Ladybird took a defining decision to expand into educational non-fiction. The Learnabout books of the 1960s introduced children to everything from metalwork to heraldry. Thanks to Ladybird, I became mildly obsessed with the latter whilst still at primary school and am still fluent in terms like sable, gules, chevron, dexter, sinister and lions couchant – knowledge which has thus far proved entirely useless outside pub quizzes. Ladybird's Keywords reading scheme taught generations of British kids to read.

There were other less predictable results. *How it Works: The Motor Car*, published in 1965, was used by Thames Valley police driving school as a general introductory guide for rookie cops. Their Charles and Diana wedding book in 1981 was the first to be published and on the shelves within five days. It sold one and a half million copies. Ladybird is now an imprint of Penguin books and publishes Peppa Pig and Hello Kitty. But the classic look of Ladybird lives on in the adult versions produced by the brilliant Jason Hazeley and Joel Morris using the beautiful original illustrations and covering such topics as *The Hangover, The Hipster* and *The Zombie Apocalypse*. By happy coincidence, the second tranche of these were published on the day I arrived and piled high on the tables of Waterstones.

It is possible then that the marchers' kids would have had a Ladybird book or at least have seen them. But they would have been spoiled for choice for a good read if they'd had access to a decent library. The 1930s were a boom decade for children's literature. One might even say it was the decade in which children's literature as know it really began; in the sense of novels and stories set in a believable world or a newly minted fantastical milieu and written by contemporary writers, rather than fairy stories and folk tales. Children's authors began to move away from producing dull, adult-approved morality tales to stories that would appeal directly to children. The thirties brought us *Swallows and Amazons, The Sword in the Stone, Professor Branestawm, Charlotte's Web, The Hobbit, National Velvet* and *Mary Poppins* as well as some classics of what was almost social realism for kids: Alison Uttley's richly evocative study of rural Derbyshire life *The Country Child* and, the year after the Jarrow march and perhaps influenced by it, *The Family from One End Street*, a sentimental but sympathetic account of life among the working classes in the fictional town of Otwell.

Beyond the metaphorical and actual warmth of the bookshop, a chilly Friday night in Loughborough was warming up socially. A smart middle-aged couple meet, kiss, embrace under a street light and he says 'Shall we see what's on at the pictures?' It could be a twenty-first century *Brief Encounter*, except the huge Cineworld here has a lot more to offer than a Lyons Corner House or a rock bun in the station waiting room, including a Bella Italia, Nando's and Pizza Express.

At the big Sainsbury's, I finally met two Human Groovers, sports science students Lucy and Dawn. They wear tracksuits and their basket is definitive (smoothies, filtered water, wholegrain baps) but Dawn is wearing a t-shirt of the uber cool German jazz label ECM records. This suggests far better taste in music than the rugger buggers on my course, who were Queen fans to a man. 'They're all into hip hop now,' laughs Lucy. 'They think they're gangsta rappers. But they still take their rugby gear home to Surrey for mum to wash.'

Whether Dawn, Lucy or the sports scientists of Loughborough Uni would have approved I doubt, but I decide to take the weight (and rucksack) off in the warmth of the Nepalese curry house and the Swan in the Rushes pub, both of which had been recommended to me. The advance press was no hype; the curry was breathtaking and the range of beers in the boozer mind boggling. But the saloon bar was raucous and crowded and I couldn't shake that feeling of being out of place and at a loose end. So I left Loogabarooga to its own Friday night devices. A good band called The Wave Pictures have a lovely, observational indie song called 'Friday Night in Loughborough' – witty, sad, pitch perfect. The line, 'With the girl from Bakers Oven holding back your hair,' is both brilliant and poignant; fans of the fast-food retail scene will know that Bakers Oven was taken over by Greggs in the mid-1990s. *Sic transit gloria mundi.*

LOUGHBOROUGH TO LEICESTER

22 October, 11 miles

With the same sense of purpose, though less sense of impending catastrophe, the Jarrow men left Loughborough bound for Leicester as the embattled Spanish Republican government moved to Barcelona, driven north before Franco's remorseless advance. Europe's other two leading Fascists, Hitler and Mussolini, were preparing to meet and sign the Rome–Berlin Axis and bring the Second World War a little nearer. If you were trying to forget all this and relaxing at home on 21 October 1936, Sherlock Holmes and Doctor Watson were attempting to solve the mystery of the Bruce-Partington plans in a new series on BBC Radio. Vying for column inches in the papers of the day was the Jarrow march itself; Scullion, Riley and Paddy the dog were becoming household names and Ellen Wilkinson one of the most famous women in Britain. The *Leicester Evening News* met the march en route and were much taken by Wilkinson's blue suede shoes. The coverage was extensive and constant but often trivial and even patronising. Five of the marchers had set up a committee specifically for dealing with the press and they were keen to maintain an upbeat, positive and non-political image of the march. It worked, but inevitably led to a lot of chattily inane columns about dogs and shoes.

The 15 footsore miles from Loughborough to Leicester as the main road are unremarkable to the point of a walking stupor. With two important appointments later this cold, bright afternoon, I make no apology for hopping on the Kinchbus No. 2 around Quorn (which is a real place) and letting it do the hard work for a few miles. Eighty years ago, when the Jarrow Crusade came to Leicester, the shoe workers of the town mended their boots overnight for them. When Ellen Wilkinson went to see them and thank them at 2am, she found them happy in the charitable work they were doing. 'There was such a gay enthusiasm for this unusual bit of help that it was fun to be among the men. One boot repairer, pulling to pieces an appalling piece of footwear remarked, 'It seems sort of queer doing your own job just because you want to do it, and for someone you want to help instead of doing it because you'd starve if you didn't. I wonder if that's how the chaps in Russia feel about it, now they're running their own show.'

Sidney Sterek, one of the reporters who walked with the marchers, reported, 'If the wives and families of the Jarrow pilgrims to London could have seen their men folk last night, they might have mistaken our sturdy and well-nourished army for a huge theatrical male chorus. The Crusaders have been rigged out in new flannel trousers, new boots and underwear. If Leicester had done no more than this for the marchers, it would have been said … that it just about topped the list of the most hospitable cities, towns and villages through which we have so far marched.' But according to the day's *North Mail*, back on Tyneside, Leicester did much more. 'It fell around our necks and hailed us as friends in dire need of assistance.'

Perhaps it could remember its own recent past and privations. While Jarrow's steelworks and shipyards were booming in 1905, Leicester's shoe and hosiery industries were being badly hit by a trade downturn and organised their own hunger march. A group of 440 men were sent on their way to Trafalgar Square by an estimated 20,000 townspeople. Many newspapers and commentators remarked on the similarities between the two marches. The Leicester men were well drilled and disciplined, much was made of their non-political and spiritual nature, and the Labour Party would have nothing to do with them.

In 1936, when the Jarrow marchers arrived in Leicester, one of the most curious aspects of the whole Crusade occurred, or rather probably didn't occur. The Church of St Marks is now, I discovered deflatingly, the Empire Conference and Banqueting Centre, having been 'decommissioned' as a place of worship in 1986. But in 1936 it was one of the main Anglican parish churches of the district and a strange, spurious tale grew up that the marchers had come here and had their feet symbolically washed in a religious blessing. They in return gave the church a crucifix made from wood hewn in Jarrow. None of this seems to be true, but the story gained credence to the degree that 52 years later, the Mayor of Leicester returned the cross (or at least, a cross) in a civic event attended by a hundred or so people including many parishioners (who said they had been at the original ceremony) and six Jarrow marchers, all of whom remembered something that seems to have been completely fictional. One marcher, Jimmy Foggon, even remarked, 'I don't remember it very well but it's part of the march and that's all there is to it.'

The resurgence of some of our modern cities often stems from some strange or unexpected seed. Manchester had the IRA bomb which kick-started a long overdue civic regeneration. When the City of Birmingham Symphony Orchestra appointed the youthful, brilliant Simon Rattle as its conductor, it gave the city new cultural clout and kudos as well as the best concert hall in Europe. Leicester has the discovery of the body of a long-dead much-maligned 'crookback' under a car park near Costa and Poundland to thank for boosting its profile and prestige. The sensational rediscovery of Richard III's burial site in the centre of Leicester, where he was unceremoniously and hastily interred after being dragged from Bosworth Field, has brought tourists and historians to the town and revitalised and smartened up a part of the city that several Leicesterians tell me was once very shady and shabby indeed. 'You would not have wanted to hang around the cathedral after dark ten years ago,' being a typical comment I heard.

Richard III, the final ruler of the Plantagenet dynasty, was killed on 22 August 1485 at the last major battle of the Wars of the Roses. Afterwards, his mutilated body, slung across the saddle of a horse, was taken to Greyfriars Friary in Leicester where it was buried in a crude, shallow grave. After Henry VIII, poster boy of the new Tudor order, dissolved the monasteries and Greyfriars was demolished, the burial place was lost and forgotten. Some said Richard's bones were tossed into the River Soar. The Richard III Society, indefatigable enthusiasts who've long campaigned to alter our negative opinion of the monarch, set in motion an archaeological project called 'Looking For Richard', which set out to find his remains on the old friary site, now a car park. On the very first day of the dig, a human skeleton was uncovered with both a severe curvature of the back and dreadful skull injuries consistent with a fatal blow from a halberd, which had sheared off the back of his skull and exposed the brain. After extensive tests, it was concluded that this poor fellow was indeed Richard III.

Leicester City Council purchased an old school building next door, empty since the grammar school moved out in 2008. This was to create a centre that would tell the story of the remarkable search for – and at that point unconfirmed discovery of – King Richard III. The resulting complex is a triumph for the city. Superbly done, it has just the right mix of gravitas and reverence with modern technological and cultural savvy. The audio-visual recreation of the battle is thrillingly impressionistic and there's a smart overview of both Richard's contentious reputation and longevity as a cultural trope, from Kevin Spacey to Laurence Olivier to Johnny Rotten, who's said to have based his onstage persona on Larry's twisted misanthrope on film. I urge you to visit it if in the area. I'd have spent longer but I had an appointment with some other guys who'd put modern Leicester on the map. Not a king this time, but King Power, the stadium where Leicester City, shock champions of English football, were playing this afternoon.

This wasn't just that I fancied a bit of footie. Honest. It was very much part of my plan to take in cultural or historical aspects along the route to compare Britain then and now; concerts, churches, restaurants, pubs, a theatre show, and very definitely a football match. Football was a vital, integral part of British culture then too, and the happy coincidence of me being in Leicester on a Saturday when the new Premier League champions were at home was simply too providential to ignore. There was just the small matter of getting a ticket for the sold-out clash with Crystal Palace. Thanks again to social media and a lovely woman called Lara (who once shared a squat with my old art editor at NME), I was put in touch with her friend Mark, equally terrific and equally generous. As a season ticket holder, he could get me a ticket and I was to meet him and his lad Sam at the ground. Which is how, by 2.30, I was sitting with Mark and Sam sipping a very decent IPA in the Fosse Lounge, a suite inside the splendid new stadium.

Much has changed in English football since I first went to the cowshed that was Springfield Park to watch Wigan Athletic wrestle – sometimes literally – with the likes of Goole Town and Gainsborough Trinity in the Northern Premier League back in the muddy, violent 1970s. Over the next three decades, plucky little Wigan climbed all the way up the tiers of English football to the very top of the Premier League, then won the FA Cup, and are now sliding joylessly back down again. That top tier is now called the EPL, formerly the Premiership, formerly the First Division. Times change, kick-off times change, but for some of us the thrill as three o'clock on a Saturday approaches never ages or fades.

Much of the barely believable money now sloshing around English football came in the wake of Sky's involvement and the setting up of the Premier League in the early 1990s. But even in the day of the Jarrow march, there were Cassandras and naysayers bemoaning the national obsession with football, the amounts of money in the game and the subsequent erosion of the pure ethos of amateurism. 'Shamateurism', as it was called, was rife, especially among the bigger clubs. Martin Pugh cites the case of Manchester United's Frank Barson who would routinely expect an envelope stuffed with cash waiting for him in the dressing room with his kit. 'Where's the doins? I'm not tekkin mi bloody coat off till I get it.'

The depression of the interwar years, particularly in the industrial north, made football even more popular and more important, a source of both romantic escapism and social cohesion in the face of the long dehumanising economic slump. Unfortunately, it also created an insularity. England were to go through the 1930s wrongly believing themselves to be world leaders at the sport, a notion they were to be humiliatingly disabused of after the Second World War.

When the Jarrow marchers came to their town, Leicester City, 'the Foxes', were top of the Second Division and heading back up having been relegated the year before. Many of the Jarrow men would have been able to tell you this since football was already a major part of working-class social life, much debated and discussed, if not the unhealthy, maniacal obsession it is for some now. The money involved in the game today has grown to an insane degree that no one in the 1930s would have found believable. The game's appeal now, while still strong in traditional working-class and industrial Britain, is far more classless these days. Purists and traditionalists complain the sport has become gentrified and detached from its parent culture. In 1936 though, the ravaged industrial north east was arguably the football hotbed of England, home to champions Sunderland who had just won the title for the sixth time. There'd been football at that summer's Olympics in Berlin, but it was a miserable tournament dogged by cheating and the baleful presence of

Hitler and Goebbels at some of Germany's matches. Britain sent a team who were put out by Poland but who took a principled stand by refusing to give the Nazi salute despite being told to do so by the British authorities and thus enraging the German hosts. Italy eventually won beating Austria in the final.

Mark's nine-year-old son Sam has been following football for one year, and in that year his team Leicester City became champions of the Premier League – the richest, most globally watched, most celebrated league in world football. 'I keep telling him, this isn't normal,' says his dad, ruefully. 'This isn't going to happen every year, you know. I don't think he realises quite how special and incredible it was.' Against all odds and defying the hegemony of the big glamour clubs such as Arsenal and Manchester United, or the bottomless cash reserves of Chelsea and Manchester City, Leicester City won the Premier League and the hearts of all neutrals with a brand of football that was fresh and exhilarating played by largely unknown players under the stewardship of the impish and genial Claudio Ranieri. Previously mocked in the UK as 'the tinkerman' for his ever-changing tactics when manager of Chelsea, Ranieri, smiling, bespectacled, was a refreshing contrast to the sullen, scowling self-importance of some of his managerial peers. He seemed to embody the club's self-effacing underdog charm. As Sam passed through JFK returning from his ninth birthday treat, a trip to New York (I think I got a Spirograph, by the way), one of that airport's notoriously sour immigration officials called, 'Hey, Leicester City! Well done you guys!'

Though Leicester are perhaps a more homespun club than their glitzier rivals in London and the north west, their well-travelled Italian boss still marshalled a team drawn from around the globe, from Japan to Mali and Austria to Argentina. Listening in the Fosse Lounge to a blazered Leicester City official read the team sheet and struggle with some exotic surnames, it is clear this new cosmopolitanism brings novel difficulties for the old guard.

'Number 19, Islam Salmani ... Slam ... Salami ...'

'SLIMANI,' roar back the crowd in amused exasperation.

'Sorry, Slimani ... Riyad Mah ... raz.'

'MAHREZ!'

'Mahrez ... and finally, the referee, Mr ... ah, who cares.'

Mark runs construction companies across the Midlands and is Leicester born and bred, although he now lives in the countryside between his home city and Market Harborough (my next destination). Mark has been Leicester City through and through, since he was Sam's age. 'My first game was the old Filbert Street, late seventies, Keith Weller, Jimmy Bloomfield, sitting on the wall. Then a season ticket in the family enclosure. I was there for Gary Lineker's debut. New Year's Day 1979, Oldham Athletic in the old Second Division. But last season was something else. There was a real buzz around the place. A spring in its step.'

By dint of the Premier League victory, Leicester are now in the Champions League, Europe's biggest and most glamorous competition and have made a good start with nine points, which is more than they have managed in the League in a miserable start to their title defence.

'It'd be funny,' says Sam, 'if we won the Champions League and got relegated in the same season.'

'No, it wouldn't,' says Dad quickly.

For today's match against mid-table Palace, Sam predicts that Leicester will win three nil and the unpronounceable Slimani will get a hat trick. We drain our glasses and take our places in the stand. This is always a thrilling moment, especially if you watch most of your football on TV; the sense of space, the vivid green of the turf, the crackle of noise and expectation generated by thousands of expectant fans. Leicester decided to augment this atmosphere by giving away cardboard clappers before every home game. It was a stunt they tried at a fixture with West Ham when they were bottom of the Premier League in 2015. They won and that was the turning point from which came last year's title, so it's a talismanic 'tradition' that persists. There's one on my seat and on every seat for the 30,000 home fans. Some think this barrage of percussive noise, like the rattle of an ack-ack gun, has been Leicester's secret weapon. Others grumble that it's yet another contrivance of contemporary football. Mark says that it's rumoured that they have paid more for the clappers than they did for bargain Algerian star striker Riyad Mahrez.

Before kick-off, there's another illustration of the changed modern game. Since 2010 Leicester City have been owned by the Srivaddhanaprabha family from Thailand, who run the King Power duty-free empire. That week the Thai King Bhumibol Adulyadej had died. Where once, the booming Tannoy announcements before matches would ask the owner of the maroon Vauxhall Viva blocking the hot dog stall to move it, the one before this match goes like this:

> Can we ask that you all join us in respectful appreciation of a truly significant figure in Thai history? The directors, management, players and staff of Leicester City Football Club extend its deepest sympathies to the Thai people during this period of mourning. The world's longest-reigning monarch, his Majesty the King was widely loved, revered and admired in the homeland of the Leicester City owners and we now ask that you help us mark the occasion with a show of unity and support for our owners and the Thai people with a minute's applause.

The Palace fans are in good voice, aiming some good-naturedly abusive songs at the new Leicester faithful ('where were you when you were shit?'), who respond with a defiant, 'We know who we are, we know who we are, we're the champions of England, we know who we are.' The match itself is fast and free flowing. Leicester start poorly, with new signing Musa particularly ineffectual. Palace are clearly on top with former

England man Andros Townsend looking sharp. But after Palace's Benteke heads powerfully against the bar, Leicester are stirred into action. The formerly inert Musa shoots home from the edge of the penalty area, Shinji Okazaki grabs one and a terrific left-foot volley from Fuchs completes the Leicester tally before Palace get a consolation goal in the last minutes. Three–one to Leicester. On social media, my presence is jokingly seen to be as talismanic as the clappers. 'You can come every week,' says one Foxes fan on Twitter.

We walk back along the main road with the delirious throng now augmented by Leicester Tigers fans leaving the rugby union stadium. Mark has never been to the rugby union ground and in his village pub there is a clear distinction between the two camps; football on the telly in the bar, rugby in the more comfortable lounge. Stacey Pope of Durham University chose Leicester to study class differences in sporting allegiances since the city has support fairly equally split between the two professional football and rugby union clubs and with their grounds barely half a mile apart. She interviewed 85 fans and their comments were enlightening. 'It's just such a class thing. I'm working class, that's why I go to the football. Posh people go to the rugby … I think in this village there's an "in crowd" that goes fox hunting and played rugby. And then there's, like, the other people that work in petrol stations and things … Now I look back on it I can see there is this kind of rugby and class divide.'

Interestingly, a small number of rugby fans asserted that their own 'local' attachment to the club was rooted much more in the shires – to the county of Leicestershire – rather than to the city where the Tigers played. As one put it: 'I love Leicestershire … I hate Leicester city centre, but I love Leicestershire.' And another, 'I don't feel as though I've got an allegiance to Leicester, the city. I don't equate the city itself with Leicester Tigers so much. Leicester Tigers for me is Leicestershire Tigers, not the city … they're not just playing for the city, they're playing for

Leicestershire … Like the cricket, it's county cricket, it's not city cricket.'

I have to say that I can't share interviewee R15's antipathy to Leicester city centre. As afternoon gave way to night, it began to throb with life and good humour. By nine it was positively jumping as I took my regular little solo promenade. A cheery East European bouncer tries to get me to come into his dingy-looking club for 'two for one shots' and 'great DJ. You like grime? Me neither. Awful. We play Katy Perry, Justin Bieber. Classy stuff'. Girls spill out of the Bossa bar on vertiginous heels and in sheer shiny tops to vape furiously, their elaborately piled hairdos wreathed in watery smoke. The Barley Mow pub is deserted though, perhaps because of the dentist-drill drum and bass music that is making the windows bulge. Two girls in micro skirts play balloon volleyball in the doorway of Fenwick's department store, in whose famous Newcastle sister outlet I bought the socks and flat cap I'm wearing. Removing the former, I have an American hot pizza and a big glass of Rioja in a restaurant down by the cathedral. The young waitress is originally from Skipton and loves Leicester but is jealous of my sojourn in North Yorkshire. 'My folks, my local, my dog … I miss 'em all.' England is small but sometimes, she says, a hundred miles can feel a long way. I know, I say, ordering another Rioja and thinking back to Harrogate and Northallerton, and further back to Ferryhill and the dog walker, and further back, to Fenwick's on that bright morning that feels like years ago. It was three weeks.

I decided to make sure I was back in my room with a warming whisky – autumn was beginning to bite across middle England – to watch the game I'd been at on Match of The Day, and also to see what kind of mood presenter Gary Lineker was in. One of Leicester's favourite sons was ending a turbulent week in which he'd incurred the wrath of the *Sun* newspaper for having the unmitigated gall to show some sympathy for the refugee kids in the Jungle camp in Calais. The *Sun*, the paper that defamed and wrongly accused Liverpool fans of pick-pocketing the Hillsborough victims as they lay dying, was now calling for Gary Lineker to be sacked from the BBC.

'Getting a bit of a spanking today,' he tweeted, 'but things could be worse: Imagine, just for a second, being a refugee and having to flee from your home.' The *Sun*'s splash of the previous day, 'Out on His Ears', splurged, 'Calls for BBC to sack Lineker after he peddles migrant lies.' Of all the mendacious and slippery tricks of shoddy journalism, alleging there've been 'calls' for something or other is one of the most irritating. It means either 'we are calling for it' or 'nobody is calling for it, but our jobs depend on producing this stuff'. Or often both. It is part of the flotsam of cliché, half-truth and banality that passes for news today, it seems.

Taking a long circuitous way back, via the Jewish Museum and the railway station, I experience two different Leicesters – the same dichotomy I guess I'd see in any big English city today. On his patch between the taxi office and the station I give some cash to a guy selling *The Big Issue* who happily tells me his real name but let's call him William. He is gaunt and red-eyed; about 30 I'd say but it's never easy to tell when people live lives this precarious and draining. His story is typical I imagine. He came here from Coventry with an ex-girlfriend, struggled to get by, dabbled in heroin, became addicted, lost his job, house, girlfriend and, he says, access to his kids who've been adopted by their stepdad. 'I want to fight it in court. But there's no legal aid. So my only chance of getting access is to go on *Jeremy Kyle*.'

For a moment I think he's joking. But then I realise that William actually thinks that wretched TV freak show is some kind of court. Which I suppose it is. 'Still, I've been clean now for two months ... apart from this of course,' and he indicates the can of Red Stripe in his shaking hand. 'It's tough, because, you know, all those people who sit down and beg, the people you see on the street, they're not homeless. Eighty per cent of them have got properties. That hurts me. And the foreign people who sell *The Big Issue*, the Poles and Romanians, they shouldn't

be selling it. It's British. Why don't they sell it in their country?'
Blaming immigrants for our ills runs from the top to the bottom
of our society, but it all feels worse when it comes from those at
the bottom. 'I just want to tell my story,' says William shakily.
'Hey,' he asks, 'is that one of those machines you can record
ghosts on?' No, I answer, nothing can, and shove a fistful of
pound coins into his unoccupied hand. 'Come back later, I'll
tell you some more,' he shouts after me, but by then I'm a few
hundred yards away, in a scene typical of the new Leicester.

At the 2011 census, Leicester was widely tipped to be the
British first city with a minority white population, but fell just
short of this landmark with 50.6 per cent describing themselves
as white. It does have one of the lowest rates of residents
who identify themselves as white British, at 45 per cent, and
the highest proportion of British Indians, at 28.3 per cent.
Narborough Road in the city has been described by academics as
the most multi-national road in Britain. The owners of the 222
shops along its one-mile length come from four continents and
23 different countries, such as Tanzania, Uganda and Zambia as
well as Pakistan, Iran and Afghanistan. There are shopkeepers
from eastern Europe, a fish and chip shop owner from Hong
Kong and a book shop run by a Canadian couple. (The *Daily
Star*'s headline read 'Foreign Nation Street', which you have to
admit is good work by the subs.) Leicester is getting younger
as well as more diverse. More than a quarter of Leicester's
population – 27 per cent – is aged 20 or under. At Taylor Road
Primary School, in Highfields, Leicester, the children speak 42
different languages.

Immigration has changed and is changing Britain. Rightly
or wrongly, whether based on legitimate concerns or concocted
hysteria, it informed the decision to leave Europe. It has led to
the rise of certain parties and individuals, along with resentment
of a perceived elite class and it is a major turbine in the engine
driving the new populism. Impressions matter more than facts
and statistics and as I leave behind wretched, sad, embittered

William with his can of Red Stripe and his misplaced faith in Jeremy Kyle, I pass by pavement cafés all along a neon-lit strip, where young people from India, Asia, the Middle and Far East, whose culture or faith or taste doesn't embrace alcohol, playing cards and drinking milkshakes and coffee, eating ice cream and baklava, laughing and flirting and chatting outside in what must surely be almost be zero degrees. Their presence, beautiful and lively, brings real warmth to the street and the night. This is how Leicester looks now; it has as much of the souk of Tehran or Tangiers about it as an old hosiery town of the English shires. The Jarrow marchers would not have believed it. But that doesn't necessarily mean that they wouldn't have enjoyed it.

LEICESTER TO MARKET HARBOROUGH

23 October, 14 miles

From the *Shields Gazette*, 12 November 2015:

A Scottish company has defended its decision to sell 'Jarrow Marcher' boots for a hefty £180 price tag. Aero Leather's website describes the boot as their 'version of the classic early twentieth century man's working boot, the type worn across the globe before WW2, made famous by such diverse and legendary characters as Charlie Chaplin and the Jarrow Marchers'. The website also states: 'While everyone knows Charlie Chaplin, the Jarrow Marchers might not be so well known outside the UK. In 1936, a group 200 men from Jarrow marched the 300 miles to London to present a petition to Parliament, asking the government for work, as the shipyard in Jarrow had closed down in the previous year leaving local unemployment at 70%. Period photos show that almost every last man wore a pair of boots like these; it's in their honour that we remember these fine men in the naming of our boots.'

Local historian Paul Perry said that it was 'disgusting'.

Resplendent in their re-soled boots, smart new flannel trousers and clean underwear, the Jarrow march left Leicester. While the welcome had been warm, the night was less so, spent in the bare stone cells of the Swain Street Institute. I had the luxury of a bed and a bath plus hot chocolate and a complementary Hobnob but still had a bad night. At 2.30 in the morning, with the crazed, disorienting whoop that is the constant subliminal fear of the regular traveller, the fire alarm goes off. I imagine all my neighbours along the corridor making the same vague desultory attempts at dressing, wondering how little anatomical coverage is acceptable and willing the noise to stop before we all admit defeat and troop down the stairs in variously surprising nightwear to stand in the freezing car park until the fire brigade arrive. 'It'll be some drunks smoking,' comes a familiar voice behind me and thus, weirdly, I bump into my old friend the comedian Jo Caulfield, who I haven't seen for years. She is on her own kind of march, a tour of the UK, and Leicester is always a popular stop-off for comics thanks to the comedy festival here.

And so in the morning, I wake myself up with something artisanal, hot and caffeine-rich in one of the many stylish cafés of the St Martin district; a maze of little streets down which a man will never want for granola, halloumi or sourdough. Choosing one at random, I refuel cheek by jowl with yummy mummies deep in the family section of weekend papers while their offspring crayon furiously and middle-aged men in expensive knitwear drink macchiatos and earnestly read slim paperbacks. Thus fortified, I set off for Market Harborough.

London Road climbs steeply past the Lansdowne pub and various large townhouses, once the residences of mill managers and shoe barons, now converted to house financial brokers or nurseries with names like Little Acorns and Tiny Tots. Up past Victoria Park carpeted in autumn leaves with the low sun glimmering through bare trees, on past the racecourse and, after the sprawling suburb of Oadby, the city falls away behind me and the countryside opens up into Leicester's own Great Glen.

Nothing like its Scottish namesake; it would disappoint anyone who's come equipped with crampons and carabiners, being a wide open tract of flat arable countryside where pretty villages loom up every mile or so. In one, the Pug & Greyhound pub advertises an 'adults only bonfire', which seems an intriguing idea.

I spot a few early poppies blooming on some of the lapels of the villagers in Kibworth Beauchamp, who I feel sure was the handsome but cruel cavalry officer opposite Margaret Rutherford in an early *Miss Marple*. Unusually, Kibworth's village trail leaflet mentions the passing through of the Jarrow march. A local blogger comments, 'The Jarrow marchers halted here on their journey and were addressed by Ellen Wilkinson. I like to think of her standing on the mound making her speech.' It may not have been the first time inflammatory words were heard here; for all its olde worlde charm, Kibworth was known locally for the fervour of its radical knitting workers, uncommon in this leafy and docile part of England.

These lovely commuter villages with their cottages covered in ivy, old churches and well-kept gardens suggest the loaded term 'quintessentially English'. No Conrad Ritblat or Hotblack Desiato boards here. This is Fine & Country country, the estate agents of affluent rural England. I think of the marchers coming through. Was it as delicious and desirable then, or maybe just a simple cluster of agricultural workers' cottages and a few farms?

It may have been simple but it would have been a kind of paradise after Jarrow. Agriculture fared far better in the mid-1930s compared to the heavy industry staples such as steel and coal which were beginning their slow decline. The farmer and even his ploughman were more secure in their jobs than the pitmen and shipwrights of the north east, even at the price of deference and a stifling social conservatism, nowhere better seen than in the red jackets and antique traditions of the hunt.

Leicestershire is fox-hunting country and Market Harborough stands at the heart of it. It was within Rockingham Forest where William the Conqueror and his successors would chase and kill whatever was about in these royal forests; hare, boar, deer, wolves, game, foxes. In the nineteenth century, the market town became a centre for hunting the latter with dogs. Mr Tailby of Skeffington Hall established a hunt in south east Leicestershire in 1856 and Market Harborough became a centre for the 'sport'. A hunting guide of 1904 states:

> Somewhat less expensive than Melton is Market Harborough, and, although you can hunt six days if you like, yet it is not considered necessary. The Cottesmore and Mr Fernie's will be the hunts you would follow. Owing to its admirable train service it is quite possible to spend a business day in London from Market Harborough once or twice a week. It is a charming old-world town, very quiet; the hotels are comfortable, and there are some delightful houses to let in its vicinity.

Another book stashed electronically in my pack, *A Week's Fox Hunting at Market Harborough* by one Louis Dieulafait, written in the 1870s, sings the praises of the town even more fulsomely. 'It is a pleasantly situated place and a perfect picture of a homelike English market town ... a very considerable number of hunting people have made the neighbourhood their permanent home. Market Harborough is not only a pleasant town, it is a convenient one for a man who has other occupations.' The author goes on to detail how one could be up here on a Friday evening and hunt all day Saturday and Sunday before returning to town, assuming that the gentleman had the inconvenience of a job rather than a private income.

The Jarrow men would not have been familiar with the stirrup cup and the tally-ho but they would have enjoyed a good day's sport of their own with dogs. Greyhound racing, though, was never imbued with the same romantic affection as the hunt. Then and now you were unlikely to find dog track scenes on a restaurant's place mats. The 1930s were a boom time for greyhound racing, though to the consternation of some in authority. They were keen to ban betting at dog tracks but could not, since to continue to allow it at horse racing meetings would have quite blatantly been an act of class prejudice. Betting on greyhounds was legalised in 1934 but strictly controlled. It was only allowed on 104 days a year and then only for four hours a day. Its popularity continued unabashed. The number of women gambling on it was particularly worrisome to some. One Glasgow track provided a crèche. A Harringay stadium had seesaws and sand pits to occupy the little ones whilst mum gambled.

Market Harborough's idea of canine sport remains in the field though. Even as recently as October 2013 (well after the ban on hunting with dogs), a travel piece in *The Times* still found Market Harborough ringing on a Sunday morning to 'the sound of hooves and barking'. More generally though, a local shopkeeper reported that through the week the town had become very quiet, testament to its new status as a dormitory town in a commuter belt. The trains are even more convenient than they were in Louis Dieulafait's day. London is only 50 minutes away by fast train and house prices have rocketed. But for a town that was forever sounding the hunting horn, it seemed loath to blow its own trumpet to the *Times*'s reporter.

> It could have been a display of East Midlands modesty, but when we asked our taciturn cab driver where we should visit in Market Harborough by way of sightseeing, his response was a ruminative silence, followed by the advice that we could always try Leicester, 15 miles away. Eminently commutable … the town is undergoing a kind of personality shift as a result. A new development of smart modern apartments offering 'landscaped gardens and secure underground

parking' sits next to Frank Hall Tailors, provider of
bespoke hacking jackets to the Prince of Wales ... but
in the town centre tweed-jacketed country gents and
their wives now rub shoulders with city-dwellers with
weekend homes and a fondness for expensive coffee.

In his magnificent survey of the nation, *English Journey*, J B
Priestley showed little warmth or enthusiasm for Leicestershire's
rural heartland, or Market Harborough in particular. 'I did not
break my journey to have another look at Market Harborough.
Hunting country and hunting people have their own literature
and I have no wish to add to it. I have only now and again met
hunting people and I do not understand them ... All I ask is that
they should not pretend to be solemnly doing their duty when
in reality they are indulging and enjoying themselves.' He went
on to describe fox hunting as extravagant, cruel and antisocial,
and local hunters as oafs. I probably wouldn't be giving an
impromptu reading of Priestley's book in any of the local pubs
where I was headed once I had taken in something of the town.

All day I've had in my head a snatch of a song by Paul Simon,
an earworm in the modern parlance. It's the line in 'Graceland'
that talks about travelling 'through the cradle of the civil war'.
I know that Simon was singing about the bloody American
conflict, but I'd felt the same as I moved along the quiet roads
of Leicestershire. When we talk of middle England, we imagine
something cosy and well-fed, ample and abundant, content and
even self-satisfied. In fact, these shires have seen dire conflict,
atrocities and bloodshed, a world turned upside down and torn
apart by violence, and sleepy Market Harborough was at the
centre of it.

In May 1645, the Royalists, buoyed by recent victories in
the field, laid waste to Leicester, killing hundreds of civilians.
News of the pillage and murder soon reached Parliament in
London who were appalled and alarmed at the atrocities

and by the loss of a strategically vital town in the heart of
the English countryside. They set out bent on revenge. The
Roundhead Thomas Fairfax lifted his siege on Oxford and
the Parliamentary forces marched towards Leicester. King
Charles, oblivious, was headed south to protect Oxford, his
capital. Exhausted and depleted, he stopped off at Market
Harborough to regroup. While here he learned that Fairfax and
the Parliamentary forces were on their way. At 11pm that night,
Charles was woken from a fitful sleep to be told that the village
of Naseby, just over the border in Northamptonshire, had been
captured by Parliamentary troops. Naseby thus became the
site of the last great battle of the Civil War and a triumph for
the Parliamentarians. Afterwards, the retreating Royalists were
caught by Parliamentary troops and brutally cut down. Four
hundred were killed altogether between Market Harborough
and Leicester and some 5,000 infantry were taken prisoner into
Harborough for the night.

It's a testament to the healing balm of time and the English
capacity for turning even the direst calamity to their advantage
that there is now, and here I quote the *Harborough Mail*:

> An eye-catching trail highlighting the town's links with
> the Battle of Naseby… The Market Harborough Civil
> War Trail will describe on six permanent information
> boards what happened in the town before and after the
> battle. The boards will be displayed at key sites in the
> town – in Church Square, Church Street, Coventry
> Road, Millennium Mile (near Northampton Road)
> and Welland Park. … John Liddell, of the Market
> Harborough Civil War Committee, said: 'We believe
> that 1645 should rank alongside 1066 and 1940 in our
> nation's history. We hope that these display boards will
> raise awareness in local people and visitors to the town
> of the importance of this battle to the development of
> democracy in this country.'

On the quiet street in the dwindling afternoon, as a few late shoppers load wine and pizzas and loo rolls into their estate cars, I reflect again how bloodsoaked England's history is and how short memories are. We assume wrongly that human history is an unbroken journey towards peace and perfectibility; a tale of improvement and progress. But the events of 1645 – and Jarrow's march too – prove otherwise. Starving towns, fascists on the streets, decapitated kings, towns like Market Harborough and Leicester aflame and ringing to the sobs and wails of townspeople butchered by their own kinsmen. That's our history as much as thatched cottages and courtly coronations.

In a sense, the shock of the Brexit vote brought this home to many who assumed that a progressive consensus was the natural state of our democracy, and only an aberrant few dissented from this. Political analyst David Runciman remarked that the Brexit vote was a blow to 'the benign liberal idea that if you open up things to the public, they are basically OK and will come to the right decision. It's a myth.' This is hard to swallow, especially if like me you are someone who travels the country seeking to see the best in people and write about them in a positive and uplifting way. It's hard to imagine, but maybe necessary to get some kind of perspective, to imagine the Leicester streets where I ate frittata and drank mocha, ablaze, running with blood and choked with corpses. Perhaps we should be a little more calm and reflective about our current schisms and divisions. England has seen worse.

Mark Bauerlein of Emory University does see in Brexit and the rise of Donald Trump, 'a reaction against the English Majorification of politics, where there's all this meta stuff about how to express oneself and what you can say. Endless discourse obscures actual policies and emotions. Trump gets this. And he's like the fool from medieval or Elizabethan drama, an idiot who says the unthinkable and some people like him for it as an antidote.'

The musician and thinker Brian Eno in a *Guardian* interview was soberly self-reprimanding. 'My feeling about Brexit was not anger at anybody else, it was anger at myself for not realising what was going on. I thought that all those UKIP people and those National Front-y people were in a little bubble. Then I thought: "it was us, we were in the bubble, we didn't notice it." There was a revolution brewing and we didn't spot it because we didn't make it. We expected we were going to be the revolution.'

Shivering in the gathering gloom of a cold Sunday in Market Harborough, the church clock struck four sonorously and I remembered something that I had to make time for. I wish I could say that it was a civic ceremony or choral evensong or cheese rolling or well dressing or anything rooted in the deep loam of these ancient agricultural shires. But in fact it was Chelsea v Liverpool on Sky Sports One, a top of the table clash that I was loath to miss.

I mooched about the cold darkening town looking for a likely spot to thaw out with the match. A thin, sluggish river runs through one end of the High Street and by it sat a couple of wheezing elderly men drinking from cans of cheap lager and a few kids kicking a plastic bottle around outside B&M Bargains. The church bells were still tolling and mixed in with them was the muted throb and drone of a mobility scooter, a very melancholy English evensong.

The tweedy gents and affluent commuters that *The Times* writer had found were nowhere in evidence. With my new enthusiasm, I tried the local Wetherspoon, and whilst it was warm, crowded and welcoming, it had no TV. I walked a little further up the road past a few similarly purist boozers until I found one from which the crackle and blare of televised sport with all its concomitant 'idents' and 'stings' was clearly audible above the low-level growl of male drinking. The pub was packed with loud men, most with their heads tilted upwards towards an enormous screen which had been secured to the wall just high enough to be uncomfortable. In the window, a table of drunk women was having some kind of shrieking contest. Close by, a partially demolished giant Stilton had been given a table to itself and various drinkers would weave and wobble over to it, carve off a chunk, balance it on a cracker and then return to their various perches leaving a trail of crumbs and cheese. It was like a corny comedy sketch set at a medieval banquet.

This was one of those pubs where a new face excites a surly kind of interest everywhere except behind the bar. There, a tough-looking woman with a severe ponytail studiously avoided my gaze. Eventually, by elbowing a couple of people aside and waving money ostentatiously I secured a pint as well as a hard look from a pugnacious little bloke in a tracksuit. He notices my recording device and regards it and me as if I'd brought a Luger or an egg whisk into his local.

'It's for making notes,' I explain, 'I'm researching a book. Maybe I could get a word with you. You could tell me what you think about Market Harborough.'

He nudges his mate, a tall thin chap with a shaved head.

'After a few more pints, I might tell you what I think about you.'

'Why not tell me now?' I say, way more aggressively than I intended to, and there's a weird, awkward, tense impasse broken only by loud cheering as Pedro scores for Chelsea. This confirms all my worse suspicions about the pub.

The back bar has a telly too so I decide to base myself at a table in there. It is just as unwelcoming as the main bar but in a different way. Soulless and spartan, there are two other occupied tables. At one, a mournful man with some kind of dossier is sipping an enormous glass of red wine. At the other are four young people, three lads and a girl, students I would guess, each with a different flavour of fruit cider. They are discussing British cities and the topic moves to Newcastle. 'Have I ever been to Newcastle?' says the girl. 'No. I'd get a nose bleed.' Chelsea score three more times. The Sky Sports panel begin a prolonged

debate about Jose Mourinho who is pictured sulking, bottom
lip thrust out like a toddler.

There was no analysis, no slo-mo, no goal-line technology
or satellite television in 1936 but the boffins at Alexandra Palace
were gearing up to begin the TV era. In late August of that
year, 7,000 people had queued to see the first talking pictures
on a television set at an exhibition at 'Ally Pally'. The broadcast
featured announcer Leslie Mitchell looking sweaty and awkward
and Paul Robeson singing 'Ole Man River'. The first TV sets
went on sale soon after costing around a hundred pounds at a
time when the average wage was three pounds a week. Even if
you could afford one of these luxurious, high tech items with its
walnut veneer and twelve-inch screen, you could only pick up
the snowy, flickering image if you lived within roughly 20 miles
of the transmitter. This led the *Spectator* to opine that it was 'a
mere toy or hobby for the well to do and will make little change
to social life'. It also had the dire warning that as well as being
able to enjoy 'Hammond bat and Larwood bowl' you would
have the comfort of your front room invaded and ruined by
'rebellions in Spain, concentration camps in Germany, misery in
the depressed areas'.

The men of one of those depressed areas would probably
not own a TV for another 20 years at least and they took little
cheer in Market Harborough. In contrast to the new world being
ushered in at Alexandra Palace, Market Harborough was the old
England; hierarchical, agricultural, conservative, the domain of
parson, squire, labourer where all knew their place, and I felt
that a sense of that remained. The marchers got a cool welcome
here; the worst of the whole journey they said. Not one member
of the council or representative came to meet them. There was
no reception, no public meeting and they were given the bare
stone floor of an unfinished workhouse to sleep in. This was of
course Market Harborough's prerogative and perhaps explicable
by the fact that the industrial downturn that had blighted Jarrow
had not touched them. Your child was three times more likely

to die in childhood in Jarrow than in Market Harborough. The people of this market town were by comparison well off, well fed and healthy with little natural kinship with the men of the north. Local papers took offence at any slur on the town's good name and claimed the men had been warmly welcomed and shown great hospitality.

I can't say that I or the Jarrow men could claim that about our visits, although in fairness some nice people from round about did extend the hand of friendship to me via Twitter. Perhaps the marchers and I caught them on a bad day. If I were advising the marchers now, I would tell them to go to Wetherspoon, whatever their views on Brexit. Market Harborough, incidentally, voted to leave in contrast to its large urban neighbour Leicester where the majority voted to remain. A lot can change along those 14 miles of English road I had found. For the first time, I felt in a different part of England, an England I didn't know and wasn't at home in. I was reminded of a famous anecdote about the absent-minded writer G K Chesterton who once sent a telegraph to his wife: 'Am at Market Harborough. Where should I be?' To which she replied, 'Home.'

STAGE SEVENTEEN

MARKET HARBOROUGH TO NORTHAMPTON

24 October, 17 miles

At the end of yesterday's big match, the one I'd watched with the aggressive cheeseniks and forlorn vinophiles of Market Harborough, I'd spotted (along with a couple of million intrigued others) the new Manchester United manager Jose Mourinho whisper something in the ear of Chelsea boss Conte. A few minutes earlier, the latter had been visibly encouraging the crowd into making more noise at the end of their four–nil drubbing of United (drubbing, like adjudged, is one of those words only ever heard in a football context). Mourinho apparently said to him, 'You shouldn't whip them up like that at four nil. It's humiliating. You should do that at one nil.' Incredibly, Mourinho's wounded feelings took up nearly as much space in the morning papers as reports of the 'Jungle' refugee camp in Calais which was cleared by French police last night amidst flames, tear gas and violence.

Eighty years ago, the vexed question of refugee movements across a dangerous and fissile world was a global preoccupation too. British colonial powers in Kenya were dealing with a huge influx of Ethiopians as Mussolini waged modern war on a third-world country in an act of grandstanding machismo designed to distract from his incompetence domestically. Essentially, it was a conflict between modern weapons technology and men armed with spears, bows and antiquated rifles. The Ethiopians were soon overrun and Emperor Haile Selassie driven into exile as his countrymen fled into neighbouring countries.

In Jaffa, rioting and clashes between Jews and Palestinians forced 6,000 people from their homes, many reduced to camping in public parks. In Oklahoma, drought across the dustbowl displaced thousands of poor Americans, events which John Steinbeck would soon write about in *The Grapes of Wrath*. Within months of the Jarrow march, 4,000 Basque children would arrive at Southampton docks fleeing the violence of the Spanish Civil War. They were housed at the rapidly built Stoneham Camp on land donated by a local farmer.

As the horror of Nazi rule worsened and became more apparent, the first Jewish refugees began to come to England. But as Louise London showed in her book *Whitehall and the Jews 1933–1948*, the same reluctance and indifference shown by politicians and press now was prevalent at the time of the Jarrow march. The Liberal politician Viscount Samuel said, 'out of that vast reservoir of misery and murder only a tiny trickle of escape was provided.' The government feared the usual catalogue of problems, real or imagined, such as depriving the native population of jobs, and social unrest. Lord Rothermere's titles were generally most hostile to the refugees. The *Mail*, one of whose more memorable 1936 headlines was 'Hooray for the Blackshirts', said, 'the way stateless Jews are pouring in from every port in the country is becoming an outrage'. Eighty years on as I marched, the *Sun* was still giving Gary Lineker 'a spanking' for his support for refugees.

I've left some kit behind in Gary's old stamping ground of Leicester so this morning I double back the ten minutes on the train to pick them up before setting off for Northampton. (It's both amazing and slightly dispiriting how slowly the miles go on foot, and what a distorted sense of distance trains, planes and automobiles give you). I get talking with a friendly young couple who were in Leicester last night watching a band. They're only vaguely aware of the Jarrow march ('Was there a song about it?') and when I mention Market Harborough she pulls a little face and comments merely 'Good charity shops'. Of today's destination, Northampton, they tell me to look out for one of the oldest churches in Britain and the Otis Lift Tower.

The couple came from Corby which is just down the road from here and home to the famous steelworks newly built when the marchers passed by. Ironically, it was partly the success of Corby that brought hardship to Jarrow. The plan for a new steelworks in Jarrow collapsed because competition was deliberately suppressed by the British Iron and Steel Federation to protect towns like Corby. Even worse, the BISF was part of an international cartel whose members included Germany, whose industrial strength was at this time still being propped up by some financiers and industrialists as a balance to Soviet might. All these factors conjoined to mean that in the summer before the march the Federation itself admitted, 'it is considered very unlikely that the scheme (the proposed Jarrow steelworks) will be proceeded with'.

I would be making my way to Northampton via the route of a defunct transport network where nature was slowly reclaiming the land from the technology of man. After a slightly confusing start with signage hidden in dense undergrowth around Britannia Walk and Scotland Road (where I ended up in a very surprised lady's front garden), I finally found myself on the Brampton Valley Way, which heads arrow-straight across the 14 miles between Market Harborough and Northampton. The walk literature promises pubs, local attractions like Kelmarsh Hall, Brixworth Country Park and Lamport Steam Railway but most intriguingly of all, 'two marvellously spooky tunnels' – surely a phrase that no one who has read Dickens' 'The Signalman' could possibly resist.

Many of the trails like this that you find now across the British countryside owe their origins to the infamous Doctor

Beeching 'axe'. In 1963, in cahoots with a transport minister with commercial interests in road haulage, British Rail chairman Beeching began the process of closing a third of British branch lines, becoming a bona fide folk devil in the process. But the Northampton to Market Harborough line, built by George Stephenson's nephew to ferry ironstone, survived remarkably until 1981. Then in 1993, it was opened again as what the council call 'a linear park'. After only a few hundred yards Market Harborough is left behind and the path becomes a gentle climb through open country. It's half term but even so, the way is quiet and unfrequented; the occasional family on bikes pass like a family of ducks gliding by, eyeing my enormous pack pityingly.

After the bitter, biting evening in Market Harborough, today feels like spring. The mild afternoon is full of birdsong, hazy sunshine and far-off children's laughter. I pass a small lake, and a lone fisherman raises a hand in greeting. I imagine his keep net, packed with fat carp and glistening tench and feel suffused with well-being at the simple pleasure of being out and alive and putting one foot in front of another on a country path in England. But then in quick succession, a man in upsettingly frank lycra aimed his bike at me, and soon after in the distance comes a sight that causes a small ripple of trepidation, like the rumble in the basses in the *Jaws* theme, like something worrying glimpsed out of the corner of the eye. A few hundred yards along the path, where the embankment narrows and the trees hunch over, is a small dark hole where the path disappears into blackness beneath the hillside.

Kelmarsh is the first of two tunnels, the other being Ovenden, that will bring up short any walker on the Brampton Valley Path. They're 322 yards and 462 yards respectively, and if you really don't feel like the long, dark, slow trek along the dank and darkened first tunnel with its dripping walls, you can take a diversion that promises pleasantly, 'Kelmarsh via woods and spinneys'. That, though, would add several miles to an already long day. So, loins girded, in I went for what seemed like a dripping, echoing eternity, stumbling occasionally, cursing regularly and trying to get the torch facility of my phone to project something more useful than a pale circle of milky light the size of my hand. Every hundred yards of so, a ventilation shaft soaring up above one's head provides a pool of welcome sunlight. This though can be a mixed blessing. On YouTube I'd watched a solo walker bask in the shaft's light and film it on his phone turning slowly around as he did to get a nice shot, and then not be sure which was forward and which was back, and whether he was progressing or retreating and would have to do the whole thing again. I don't think you ever find out what happened to him. Unless you fall down, or get hit by an unlit cyclist, or perhaps snatched by a hideous formless creature lurking in the shadows, you will probably emerge from the tunnel unscathed, but it is certainly an eerie experience (or rather two) and the old adage about the 'light at the end of the tunnel' will take on new and vivid meaning when you have watched the small disc of sunlight grow from a pinprick, promising the way back out into the very welcome fresh air and sparkling light of an October afternoon.

Between the tunnels I'd passed a middle-aged couple on a bench eating their sandwiches, sipping from their flask and clearly recovering from either Kelmarsh or Ovenden (I forget which). It was she who'd suggested I use the torch facility on my phone, unaware that my particular device possessed a weaker wattage than an ailing glow worm. As was customary now, I asked them about the Jarrow march and received the now customary response; a vague recollection of some struggle or protest. 'They came down the road, didn't they, past here? Weren't they coal miners? From Newcastle? I'm not clear as you can tell, but it was during the great Depression, wasn't it? This line would have been working then though.'

Though this is agricultural Britain, and its character 'parson and squire', heavier industry like those the Jarrow men knew had a presence here. The Midlands ironstone field stretched from Lincolnshire through Leicestershire, Rutland and Northamptonshire to Oxfordshire and the materials were moved from quarry to factories by many narrow-gauge railways like this one. The still and benign fields and pastures I'm now crossing, dotted with stiles and crossed with cow parsley hedgerows, would have once been a pitted and smoking industrial workshop. As the Nene Valley narrow gauge website has it, 'It is now hard to envisage that the pleasant rolling countryside in the East Midlands has been host to opencast ironstone mining on such a grand scale.' The quarries themselves are now nature reserves or landfill, or even suburban housing estates. Steel gave men work here for much longer than it did in Jarrow, but even here it disappeared as Britain abandoned its industries and began to lose its industrial culture.

I leave the track at Draughton Crossing bound for Maidwell village, halfway between Market Harborough and Northampton, and where the marchers took a break in 1936. It's deserted and silent; its residents all presumably hard at work at computers and counters in one of the above two towns. As it's half term, even the smart new school, built in 2000, according to its foundation stone, is shut up and quiet. There are pumpkins for sale in a neat garden but no one about to sell them. A phone rings unanswered in the rectory and the village has a newness and an unreality about it that's queer. The Old Barn is nothing of the sort, rather a newbuild a rock star might live in. Despite this, the village apparently has a long history; it has nine listed buildings and the church boasts 'interesting cupolas', but as in Bunny, I get the feeling that I'm being watched by suspicious eyes behind Laura Ashley curtains and so I pass quickly through and head along the mile or so to the main A road. It's been a good morning's walking, but a long one, and I can feel a tiredness in my legs and even a little sunburn on my face. The map shows a pint glass symbol just where I'll emerge, and I'm very much hoping that will mean a late lunch for me in a sun-dappled beer garden.

It didn't. A very apologetic young woman locking the door of the Stags Head tells me that if I'm prepared to wait for two hours, they'll be open and serving food again. But I doubt that the Marie Celeste-ish Maidwell could keep me occupied that long so I dump myself and the pack on a bench dedicated to Bob Lilley ('his favourite walk') and write a couple of postcards. While I'm thinking through my next move, which may involve foraging for nuts and berries and weeing in a hedge, a passing van pulls over and stops in the layby.

Kev and Jake of Windsor Windows of Northampton have been following my progress on Twitter as they've done their daily rounds and, knowing I'm behind schedule, hungry and tired, offer to help out with a lift or a mile or two to the outskirts of Northampton. I jump in and they prove to be fine company. Kev is a 6Music fan and listens to my shows. 'This is that bloke,' he says to Jake, the younger of the two and in his early twenties I'd guess.

'I make him listen to you, educate him a bit, wean him off all that dance stuff of Radio One. His dad's the boss of the firm and it's his van. But I'm the senior worker!'

Jake smiles wanly. If I regularly ruin his day, he is too polite to say. Kev's a season ticket holder at Northampton Town. He once saw a train on the Brampton Valley Line when he was a kid in the 1970s – 'Definitely still going then'. In their working life, the pair cover all the little towns and villages hereabouts. Work is plentiful and they are kept busy. When I tell Jake that some of the Jarrow men had worked two days in ten years he looks genuinely appalled. 'Were they on benefits?' Yes, but not much. Nothing like today. 'I'd hate to be on benefits. People say it's an easy life but I'd rather be getting out and about. Even with his weird music. No offence.' Their busy schedule is a testament to how our economy has changed. We manufacture very little now, but the cash-rich, time-poor, long-hours working middle manager or teacher or IT specialist has neither the free time nor the skills to plumb in a new bathroom suite or plaster a bedroom or install double glazing. And so people who can, like Kev and Jake, tradesmen as they would once have been known, are always in work. Good, reliable ones are as rare as neurosurgeons and spoken of and recommended in the same reverential whispers. Even as we're chatting a work call comes in on the van hands-free. I keep quiet while Kev and Jake's dad discuss the scenario: 'Thing is, the client, they don't want that door going in there … what with all the wheelbarrows going backwards and forwards … and I can see their point.'

As we near Northampton, they recommend a cheese shop, the old Saxon church at Brixworth and a pint at the Malt Shovel. 'Northampton's alright. Everyone slags it off but that's the British way, isn't it? There's worse places that's for sure. And we've probably put their windows in. If you see what I mean …'

Towns always feel complicated, crowded, strange and disorienting as I march in after the quiet of country tracks or even the droning anonymity of the highway. It's late on a very ordinary Monday afternoon but there's a detectable hubbub as I negotiate the traffic islands and pelican crossings and make my way into the heart of the town to be met by flashing lights, screams, whirling machinery and the unmistakeable tang of the fair. According to a leading online encyclopaedia, 'The St Crispin Street Fair is an annual fair held the town centre of Northampton England organised by Northampton Borough Council though it is not held every year.' I like an annual event that's not actually held every year, it adds a little frisson of unpredictability. Maybe we should try it with Christmas.

The St Crispin's designation sounds nicely ancient but the fair is relatively modern, erratically staged, and not to everyone's liking. A local fancy dress shop owner complained to the local paper in 2012 that, 'there will be a tremendous amount of noise which will make it difficult to talk to customers and the smell from the food vans will get on the costumes'. The smell from the food vans was certainly making an impression on a visitor who'd walked the best part of ten miles and not eaten all day. Within minutes I had my feet up at a plastic table in the square watching terrified townspeople flung high into the air on what seemed to be a gigantic piece of knicker elastic while I set about devouring unidentifiable but delicious meat slathered in fried onions and ketchup. From the Dodgems an enormously amplified, scratchy version of the Supremes' 'Baby Love' was blasting out. So far, I was greatly enjoying the shoe capital of the Nene Valley.

St Crispin's may be a contemporary invention but autumn is the traditional season for the great British fair, some of which have achieved world renown. Scarborough Fair lasted an astonishing 45 days in its Middle Ages heyday and lured merchants from all over Britain as well as Norway, Denmark, the Baltic states and the Byzantine Empire trading wine, silk, jewellery, lace, glass and spice for wool and leather. Some fairs specialised in single commodities, like Nottingham's famously riotous Goose Fair or the impressively niche Dish Fair in York. I'm not sure what St Crispin's speciality is; bingo possibly, or Hook-A-Duck, where you can win a giant banana that looks like a Rastafarian.

I got out quickly, pushed through the crowds at the Kentucky Derby horse racing game and back into town. Professional curiosity generally drags me towards a bookshop and in this one there was an interesting conversation going on at the counter. The young goth sales assistant was talking animatedly with a wizardish-looking man of about 60 with plastic bag and grey beard. They were discussing the short stories of Edgar Allan Poe, she enthusiastically, he more analytically, and I got the feeling that this was some kind of 'catch up' between a regular, perhaps eccentric customer and a pleasant, keen member of staff. She made a few concluding remarks about 'the surreal darkness' of 'The Tell-Tale Heart' and then brightly suggested, 'OK, well, if I get you a chair and a pen and a cup of tea, maybe we could put you over there and you could start signing some stock for us, Alan.'

Slowly, realisation dawned. Alan Moore is perhaps the most eminent and critically acclaimed British writer of speculative

fiction and graphic novels of our time, and I had bumped into
him in a suburban branch of Waterstones on a slow Monday
afternoon. Cognisance of this came to me by virtue of his
distinctive appearance and the fact that we were in his home town.
Northampton has haunted his work from his very first novel,
Voice of the Fire, which consisted of connected Northampton
stories from several eras of history, and the town is at the very
heart of his new book *Jerusalem*, a hefty tome here stacked into
piles, which he is now seated behind and signing.

Moore came to prominence in the British comic scene in
publications like *2000AD* and then succeeded in the American
mainstream, the first British writer to do so, with his work on
Batman and Swamp Thing. Moore's fiction, whilst thrilling
enough on a purely visceral level for any fan of superhero
schlock and action movies, generally has a deeper dimension
and darker purpose. His best work like *Watchmen* or *V for
Vendetta* has always been implicitly political, anarchistic and
anti-Establishment, preoccupied with the individual and the
state. In the latter, a fascist regime of Mosley-style Blackshirts
called Norsefire rule Britain, helped by big business and the
Church, exterminating their enemies in the minorities and on
the left. Ironically, the Guy Fawkes mask worn by the hero,
designed by David Lloyd, has now been appropriated by the
tendentious right wing blogger Guido Fawkes, which must
surely gall Moore immensely.

Jerusalem is not just his most major venture yet. It is
one of the biggest novels ever written. At 600,000 words, it's
considerably bigger than the Bible. He considers it his crowning
achievement and magnum opus and Northampton and its
people are at its centre. *Jerusalem* is not just an epic imaginative
exploration of several centuries of Northampton's history, it
is specifically about Spring Boroughs, the working-class area
where he was born and still maintains links with. The *Guardian*
described it as 'a sprawling behemoth, this teeming leviathan,
this pythonic mammoth of a novel'. Some have baulked at its

sheer size and ornate prose but most have agreed it is some kind of masterpiece. I haven't read it of course. Its bulk would compromise even my capacious litreage. But I decide that the coincidence of chancing upon the laureate of Northampton here in the streets he writes about, he and I the only non-employees in the shop, is too fabulous not to act upon and I go and introduce myself.

If he regarded this as an imposition or distraction, he did not show it. Gracious and genial, as anarchistic mavericks often are, he seems genuinely interested in my project ('How fantastic!') and warms to my suggestion that this centre of England, cradle of the Civil War, seems to have a secret darkness, even violence about it beneath the reassuring stereotypes about middle England.

'There's an insurrectionary tradition here. The Civil War kicked off around here, or at least came to its conclusion here at Naseby. Bedford, where you'll be going, is of course John Bunyan's home town. He was a Roundhead who spent the last 30 years of his life in Bedford prison. They'd let him out to do the odd bit of insurrectionary preaching because he was very popular. There were a lot of disenfranchised Protestant sects about round here. The Quakers, say, who were nothing like that nice man on the Oats packet. They believed in the violent overthrow of earthly monarchs to be replaced immediately by the kingdom of God, they'd tear off their clothes to make a public display.

'Yeah we had all of them. All around Northampton. I think you're right, there's a darkness beneath a lot of what are today very sedate English towns and villages, especially here around the middle of the country. This is the navel of the nation. This is where all the bad blood gathers. The main history of Northampton is of brilliant troublemakers … and that was before the Jarrow marchers turned up.'

I leave Alan to his signing. Sheepishly I admit that I don't have room to take a copy of *Jerusalem* with me, but Alan generously offers to put one by for me to collect later. Delighted by the encounter, I head back into the throng of St Crispin's fair, steeling myself against the smell of sizzling sausage and then out into the quieter streets. The Guildhall is a truly fabulous building and tonight, there's a performance of *Dracula*, more Northamptonian darkness. At the opposite emotional extreme though, Northampton has a Bar Hygge, a smart, upscale café founded on that Scandinavian notion of cosiness and wellbeing currently being simultaneously promoted and mocked in several hundred fey broadsheet articles. I like a spot of Hygge myself, but think it works best in Tromsø or Gothenburg so I pass by leaving the gravadlax, dill herring and cake untouched. A few doors down is the Saigon Vietnamese café, reminding one how cosmopolitan Britain has become in its dining. Next door to this is a vintage record shop with a collection of jazz vinyl in the window – Miles Davis, Terje Rypdal, John Surman – so achingly impeccable that it hurts. I pop in naturally just in time to overhear the long-haired owner having an involved conversation about who has shown the more genuinely experimental tendencies, Madonna or Kylie. Past the Shoe Museum, I notice a hybrid that speaks of modern Britain; a store named Sklep Na Rogu, the Polish for corner shop. I wonder how the mood behind the counter has changed since June.

Evening is coming on in the English midlands. The King Billy Rock Bar doesn't appeal with its twin connotations of sectarianism and Bon Jovi, so I make for the recommended Malt Shovel to read and make some jottings with a pint. Googling on my iPad, I seek out some of Alan Moore's recent interviews, and find one he did with his local paper the *Northampton News* about *Jerusalem*. We seem to have been thinking about much the same things.

> If people do talk about what we fondly call the working class then there seems to be a choice of two registers in which they talk about it: they either deplore it for

its vulgarity and, yes, I'm looking at you Martin Amis, and they produce spiteful parodies of the way that they perceive working class people living, behaving and thinking. The other mode is to pity these poor victims. Nobody sees themselves like that.

Jerusalem acknowledges that. It is saying these are people with lives, with histories, with stories that are as gigantic as any Royal family or bloodline. The Windsors, Bourbons, Spencers, Tudors – the aristocrats – are apparently entitled to their genetic mythologies, so this is a genetic mythology for people who have not previously had one … because when we talk about history we talk about the history of church, of state and maybe a dozen families. What about the rest of us? Weren't we doing anything while all that was going on, or were we minor players in their drama? This is insisting that everybody has their own drama and mythology and story.

Across the web, *Jerusalem* is being feted by many as the great speculative novel of 2016. At the time of the Jarrow march, those accolades were being bestowed on the newly filmed *Things to Come*, from a novella by H G Wells. This was a vision of the future clearly fuelled by the fears and hopes of 1936. Wells's story was typical of the kind of fiction and themes preoccupying the literary intelligentsia of the day; technology, war, free will, disease, propaganda and dictatorship. It is set in the British city of 'Everytown', in a world beset by a seemingly permanent global war that began at Christmas 1940 (remarkably, Wells was only three months out). The conflict drags on into the 1960s which in Wells's vision is not a blissed-out era of promiscuity, groovy sounds and kaleidoscopic kaftans but a new Dark Age of endless pointless war and a biological plague called the 'wandering sickness' which kills half of humanity and destroys the last vestiges of civilisation. By 1970, a warlord known as the

'Boss' or 'Chief' rules southern England by force and intends to conquer the 'hill people' of the north next to obtain coal and shale to fuel his machines. It's not hard to see something of the Fuhrer and Il Duce in the 'Boss', or something of Jarrow in the now-desolate hill people's tradition of mining and delving. Eventually a new world order based on a benign technocracy comes to power, and the film ends with a faintly fascistic speech about progress and conquest. Though inevitably dated now, the film's expressionist style and Arthur Bliss's strident music are hugely impressive. For a student of the thirties zeitgeist, it's invaluable. In the tremendous opening scenes, the phalanx of marching working-class men carrying placards predicting war has definite shades of the Jarrow march.

The big comic book sensation of the day was *Flash Gordon*, invented in 1934 and debuting at 'the flicks' while the Jarrow men marched. (They may well have seen it on one of their many free hospitality nights at the cinema.) Flash was basically the archetypal square-jawed, two-fisted adventurer of classic boys' adventurer yarns transplanted into the future in a somewhat unsafe-looking, cigar-shaped craft that showered sparks. Flash was a star polo player and Yale graduate, who becomes a sort of arch preppie in space. Played by the equally implausibly named Buster Crabbe in the 1936 movie, he travels to the planet Mongo where he encounters the evil Emperor Ming the Merciless, a tyrannical inhuman nutjob. Perhaps sensing a subtext, the Nazis banned the strip.

Flash Gordon was a child of the US depression and was embraced by thrill-hungry readers of 1930s Britain. In a world of shortages and murky morality, the unambiguous moral superiority of the handsome nice guy proved irresistible. And it was easy to read. Maybe even a Jarrow marcher had one stuffed in his overcoat pocket for when he dossed down on the next drill hall floor. Or, as in the case of Northampton, on straw on the floor of St James school after a rousing meeting at the town hall. Alan Moore's *Jerusalem* was going to prove less portable so thanks to the pub's free wifi I decided to download the ebook and take a look. Almost immediately, my eye was caught by a line that seemed to capture what I (and I think Moore) still see as the defining division in British society. It's the one that is still proving difficult for some to understand, the great social rift that drove the Jarrow march and may well be driving the flight into the political unknown now, away from consensus and towards demagogues and anger. 'Despite the very real continuing abuses born of antisemitism, born of racism and sexism and homophobia, there are MPs and leaders who are female, Jewish, black or gay. There are none that are poor.'

Of course, in their defence, it is hard to be poor with an income of £74,000 a year but the point holds I think. Despite a genteel nervousness about it these days, class supplied the great splintering fault line through British life in 1936 and the crack is still wide. As I ventured further south, I, and the men of Jarrow, would feel it between our feet.

STAGE EIGHTEEN

NORTHAMPTON TO BEDFORD

26 October, 21 miles

The great American cultural critic Greil Marcus came up with the resonant phrase 'the old weird America' to describe what his country was once like before the levelling and sanitising effect of modernity, before industry, homogenised culture and the mass media. America when it was still a place of dark secrets, odd corners, vast and unknowable. England is a great deal more ancient and complex than its colonial offspring. The old weird England is far older and weirder than America.

Even had I not had my conversation with Alan Moore, Northampton seemed to have very strong echoes of the old, weird England, especially on a damp, silent autumn morning. I walked through a shrouding mist up Black Lion Hill, down Chalk Lane, following the Knights Trail, a walk through the town that takes in some of its oldest and more storied crannies. Just by the railway station, there's a funny little hump with some railings around it and an information board. If you make your way up there, you'll find that this is not some old landfill or the remains of a shed for the locos. This was in fact Northampton Castle, mentioned in Shakespeare's *King John*, where turbulent priest Thomas à Becket was tried. At the parliament of 1381, the last to be held in Northampton, the hated Poll Tax was introduced. This led to the Peasants Revolt and was revived, you may recall, to similarly negative popular response by Mrs Thatcher's government in the 1990s. As Santayana said, those who forget the past are condemned to repeat it. And as Einstein said, doing the same thing over again and expecting different results is a good working definition of madness.

In 1662, the king knocked the castle down pretty much on a whim. Then the Victorians built a railway station over it. That's gone too now. So it goes. The plaque on Black Lion Hill also states that in 1349 when the Black Death came to Northampton the town was 'decimated' when 'half the town succumbed to it'. In my mind, I tried very hard not to be the sort of person who points out that this is not what 'decimates' really means. A kind of Pedants Revolt if you will.

Surrounded by dripping trees, mist hanging like lace across the Nene valley, in the heart of the old, dark weird England, it feels like it could be the fourteenth century rather than the twenty-first. If, that is, it wasn't for the National Lift Tower thrusting rudely and concretely 120 feet towards the sky just on the horizon. Even that has a strangely heraldic and Excalibur-ish feel to it, though only built in 1978 by Express Lifts, later Otis lifts for the testing of, yes, lifts. It's a Grade II listed building though, which is perhaps why the plans for a 100-seat theatre and café came to naught in what the late Terry Wogan called the 'Northamptonshire Lighthouse'. Do the people of this quiet shire look out for it as a beacon of home like Geordies look out for the Angel of the North? Twitter correspondent Phil Ashby suggested that, 'It's full magnificent grandeur is best viewed from up the road at Sixfields, from the car park by the rubbish tip'. But it looked strange and imperious enough rising in the mist from where I stood.

*

For days Ellen Wilkinson had been suffering from exhaustion and forced to convalesce. The men were publicly hugely supportive of her, but in private they worried that her insistence on leading the march was setting too slow a place. That was a particular concern today as this would be the longest leg of the whole march, 22 miles, and the day had dawned wet, murky and freezing. My day promised to be more clement if just as long.

Once en route, the villages fall away with the miles. Yardley Hastings ('Just starting on Radio 4Extra, a classic edition of *All Pals at the Parsonage* from 1955 with Yardley Hastings as the short-sighted rector ...') has four entries in the Domesday Book as well as the new and superbly incongruous Belgian Fries outlet. The first I'd ever seen, it offered a range of exotic sauces from Andalouse to Samurai to Hannibal. Had there been world enough and time, rest assured I would have tried some in the interests of journalistic rigour, and found who knows what backstory of someone's homesickness for the snacks of Antwerp or Ghent in commuter belt Bucks.

I cross into that county over the lazy, swirling river Ouse where sleepy swans dawdle beneath a bridge and the only sound is the rasp of carrion crows across flat, churned empty fields. There seems nothing but tilled acreage and scraps of woodland between me and the low, blue bar of the Chilterns.

Possibly the most significant thing to occur to the village of Lavendon since the war-torn mid 1600s might well have occurred 80 years ago today when the Jarrow march broke for lunch here. One of the very few pictures of the march on the road was taken here as the huge group, banners aloft, rounded the bend. I come around it myself and instantly recognise the spot. Just a little further on, on the wall of the church, I found the only plaque anywhere outside Jarrow commemorating the Crusade, quite a handsome thing too, erected by local unionists of the Association of Scientific, Technical and Managerial Staff (ASTMS), Clive Jenkins's famous old white collar union, now swallowed up into the

Unite behemoth. Quite why this village rather than any other should mark an act of northern protest is not clear, but it was an excuse to pause and get a selfie, that new act of commemoration.

The miles between Lavendon and Bedford are a miserable, rough, ankle-turning trek in roadside ditches with merely the occasional pub or post office or bus shelter to break the monotony. Every pub is gearing up for Bonfire Night, 'fun nights' and 'barbecues' to commemorate a major attempted act of religious terrorism and regal assassination, its foiling by treachery and state forces and the subsequent torture and execution of those concerned. What could be more British? I revel for a while in the sheer delightfulness of Turvey with its water mill and abbey, where a district nurse waved to me as she got into her mini outside the Three Cranes. A Twitter correspondent by the name of Hazel told me that I would enter into Bedford along the Bromham Road. 'My late mother watched the marchers from outside her home Windmill Lodge on this main route into town. She never forgot the courage and dignity of so many proud impoverished and exhausted men. Her harrowing description remains with me as does the awful irony of relentless social injustice still perpetuated by shameless men in power. Good luck with your march in their memory.' I imagine that for the most part the marchers enjoyed their trek, its camaraderie and change from routine. But the days were long, tiring and hard, men got ill and they were concerned about their families left behind. Or maybe by now the harmonica band were just really getting on everyone's nerves.

Listening to the Radio 5 Live news on my headphones as I rearranged my pack in Bromham, I heard a new definition of hardship anyway. The always newsworthy Jose Mourinho blamed his team's recent poor form on him living in Manchester's five star Lowry Hotel, which he said was 'a disaster'. A sympathetic caller said he had lived in a hotel for two years and moaned that he had exhausted the restaurant menu in three weeks. I fought hard not to let glib, judgemental phrases like 'first world problem' swim into my head. We are living in the first world after all and unlikely to encounter any other kind of problem – cholera or drought, say – but I did think of the marchers bedding down on straw in drill halls and workhouses, and pressed on.

I was pleased when the road signs and the out-of-town hypermarkets began to promise an entry into Bedford. The marchers, with Ellen at their head again, were met by a Conservative Alderman and a local headteacher, H W Liddle – himself a man of the north east. He had persuaded the local Rotary Club to 'adopt' a blighted County Durham village called Eden Pit. Sixty schemes like this were set up across the prosperous south, voluntary acts of admirable civic kindness. Of course, there ought to have come state support or drastic reform, but I found myself wondering if we could count on such generosity and fellow feeling now in the land. Given the sour and bullying tone that had dominated discourse in 2016, I was far from sure.

I'd never been to Bedford before and knew little of what to expect. Inquiries about it would be met with a shrug or some vague reference to John Bunyan, pasties called Clangers or vans. Thirty-five minutes from London by commuter train, it's the 'capital' of one of England's smallest counties, but even a cursory half-hour of research on the village green in Turvey suggested there was more to Bedford than any of the above, and that the visit of the Jarrow men might be just a part of an old, strange parade of history.

'Somewhere in England'. It's an evocative phrase, pressed into service by many. It's an album by George Harrison and a song by Al Stewart, an online adventure game, a play about the US Air Force bases in Britain and a hairdressers in Farnham. But however imprecise and nebulous 'somewhere in England' might sound, make no mistake, it's Bedford. In 1942, the BBC evacuated from London and relocated here in great secrecy, and began broadcasting entertainment and propaganda from the Corn Exchange in the town. For the duration of the war, in these broadcasts, Bedford was referred to only as 'somewhere in England', a neat mixture of pragmatic secrecy and mythic symbolism.

Bedford housed the school where the Bletchley Park codebreakers were trained and the airfields from which Churchill wanted to 'set Europe aflame'. Bing Crosby, Bob Hope and Glenn Miller came here to make radio shows. The Czech government in exile ran its official radio station from here and, in perhaps the town's greatest act of wartime subterfuge and chutzpah (let's use the Yiddish word, it feels appropriate), a multinational team based in the surrounding villages of Toddington, Aspley Guise and Woburn Sands created radio programmes like 'Atlantiksender' and 'Gustav Siegfried Eins', designed to convince German civilians that they were listening to a genuine German station, playing the latest German pop hits and American jazz outlawed by the Nazis, as well as giving misleading and contradictory news and instructions. They did this so well that Goebbels raged about them and at least one German U-boat surrendered as a result of Bedfordshire's black propaganda.

There's information about all this in various places in the town such as the excellent Higgins Museum and at Holy Trinity Church, which has stood in the centre of Bedford for a thousand years. The bustle of the town goes on around, but encircled by trees and choirs of thrushes and blackbirds it's remarkably peaceful and a fine place to sip a decent coffee and watch Bedford go by. Dropping by a low green wooden hut adjacent to the churchyard to get my coffee, I was alerted to another strand of Bedford's rich story.

The name La Piazza Café needn't necessarily signify anything. Exotic, alluring, ersatz café names are commonplace in England, usually for a chain with its head office in Letchworth or Croydon or owned by a carbonated drinks giant out of Atlanta or Fort Lauderdale. But not La Piazza. Here, asking for your espresso interrupts a conversation between owner and a regular patron in quick fire Italian. A *grazie* will earn you a smiling *prego* or *ciao bella* and you can sip a strong, tiny cupful and nibble a biscotti while you take in the posters of AC Milan's great side of the late eighties; Van Basten, Gullit and Baresi side by side with Bobby Moore lifting the World Cup. Libby Lionetti has been running the café here since that Milan heyday. He's here at six every morning for Bedford's cappuccino and macchiato devotees. He was born in Bedford's big maternity hospital but did two years' national service in Italy, and returned twice yearly to Foggia. He and his family – recently featured as typical Italians in a TV ad for Aldi pizzas – are part of a fascinating Bedford story that began soon after Jarrow's men has passed by here, coming as part of a new Europe rebuilding itself, and a story I would pick up later. First though, I wanted to check in with a son and daughter of Bedford, visionary non-conformists or troublesome zealots depending on your point of view, whose legacy lives on in buildings that face each other across staid and everyday Newnham Road.

Lynn, the lady who greets me at the door of the John Bunyan Museum, is small and twinkling and somewhere between 70 and 80 I'd say. She is wonderfully bright and nimble nonetheless, full of enthusiasm and energy and takes my arm only once at the top of a flight of steps that slowed me up too, especially after 20-or-so miles of Buckinghamshire asphalt. We've come upstairs to an exhibition about the life of Bedfordshire's most famous former resident, much-beloved of some like this lady, who keep alive his most famous book and his spiritual mission at the centre of a global branch of Protestantism. Some earlier Bedfordians weren't quite so keen on John and, perhaps with one eye on future tourism marketing opportunities, didn't run him out of town but, in 1660, threw him in Bedford nick for what turned out to be a very long if productive sojourn.

'I can show you around or you can wander at will,' chirps my guide and I think I know that the right answer is the former as she leads me gently around the upstairs room. She indicates an impressively severe mannequin of a stern puritan. 'The great man himself. He was over six foot, big for the time. Do you know his story? Born at Elstow just south of here, his father was a tinker, which meant he repaired pots and pans. John used to say he was born into poverty but he wasn't really as his father owned his own cottage and could send John to school to learn how to read and write.' There's a facsimile of John's cottage and home life. 'A fire, so you could stew but not roast and these plates—' and here a slightly pained expression crosses my guide's features at the inexactitude, '—well, these are pewter but to be honest John wouldn't have had these. You drop pewter, it bends. If it bends you have to have it repaired. John would have used wooden cups and plates I think. Drop wood, it bounces. Now these barrels … salt fish, possibly corn …'

We move slowly around in this delightful fashion and while there's not room here to tell it all, highlights included Bunyan's actual anvil. Like the windlass in Chesterfield, one gets a real charge from seeing an actual object – not a gilded treasure but a working tool – used physically by human hands, Bunyan's hands, four-and-a-half centuries ago. There's a violin that he made and a chair he sat on, much repaired. My guide points out on a map of Bedford the various local landmarks that made their way into *The Pilgrim's Progress*, all still there, though in various states of ruin and disrepair, such as Houghton House, 'the house beautiful' at the top of Ampthill ('the hill of difficulty') near the marshy part of Elstow that Bunyan turned into 'the slough of Despond'.

Joining the army at Newport Pagnell, Bunyan became a Roundhead. ('People are now fed up with the king, you see, so they chopped his head off' is Lynn's admirably brisk summary of the English Civil War.) 'John had been a bit of a lad in his youth, he swore, he played football on Sundays, he played tricks on neighbours. He was a thorough nuisance actually. But one time he was playing football on the green, he heard a voice saying, 'Are you going to carry on like this, young man? Are you going to go to heaven or go to hell?' and eventually, he thought he had nothing to lose so he started to go to St John's church. The rectory's still there, St John's ambulance own it now, you can have a look in but you have to make arrangements.'

People come from all over the world to do just that. Bunyan went on to become one of the great voices of Protestantism with his sermons of 'plain piety' and force, which of course were fine while Oliver Cromwell was in charge but after the Restoration, the wilfully obtuse Puritan Bunyan was *persona non grata* in an England newly back in love with ritual and ceremony. Bunyan wrote the bulk of the great Christian allegory *The Pilgrim's Progress* whilst in prison for 12 years in Bedford.

'The gaol was at the bottom of Mill Street,' Lynn explains. The family were at the bottom of St Cuthbert's Street and his blind daughter Mary would walk through the town every day to take him food to the gaol. She smuggled out his books and pamphlets which a printer in London was willing to take a chance and print. An awful lot of pamphlets. I think, and I say this with great affection, John was the sort of person who had something to say about everything.' Bunyan stands thus revealed as a seventeenth century tabloid columnist forever manufacturing fake outrage and proto-Twitter storms about the irritating bendiness of pewter plates or *The Book of Common Prayer*.

The Pilgrim's Progress is still one of the world's most popular books in history with over 200 translations, making it second only to the Bible. Foreign editions are kept in a glass case here. At a quick glance I spotted Swedish, Afrikaans, Welsh, Indonesian, Hebrew, a Korean manga version and one in Dutch, the first language it was translated into. I'm not sure Bunyan would have been my sort of fellow with his dour piousness and cussed awkwardness, but finding out about him in such a charming way from gentle Bunyanite Lynn was lovely after the relentless drudgery of the road, with my own burden on my back, through underpasses of despond and flyovers of difficulty.

About a century and a half after Bunyan wrote his big seller, a woman called Joanna Southcott was working on her own, scorching religious text. This would prove much less popular, largely due to it being locked up in a sealed box for centuries and thus becoming the centre of one of the strangest of all the global cults. As I left the Bunyan Museum, the museum and headquarters of The Panacea Society was just across the pelican crossing in a comfortable suburban detached house on the other side of Newnham Road. Behind it, backing on to Albany Road, was the Garden of Eden. The actual Garden of Eden.

The lady on reception seems preoccupied in a jolly way. 'It's chaos here today I'm afraid! We're all getting ready for the Children's Book Festival tomorrow. But the museum's open. Do you know much about the Panacea Society? Would you like to watch a video? It's about eight minutes. It's quite useful.' In truth, neither an eight-minute video or the space here afforded can really do justice to the tale of Bedford's Panacea Society. But here's the bare bones of a bizarre British story.

The Panacea Society formed in Bedford in the 1920s. Mabel Barltrop and 12 female disciples were inspired by the teachings of aforementioned Devonian mystic Southcott who'd attracted some attention a century before with her apocalyptic visions and prediction of the coming of a new messiah, Shiloh. Barltrop adopted the name Octavia and believed, or at least announced herself to be the Shiloh messiah of Southcott's prophecies. The community in Bedford grew and for several decades, they lived and worshipped in relative seclusion whilst acquiring disciples across the rest of Britain and its colonies. But the Panacea Society – so named for their belief in the universal healing properties of tap water infused with Octavia's breath – gained national and international notoriety through their campaign for the Church of England to open the writings of Joanna Southcott.

Joanna had left a sealed wooden box of prophecies, usually known as Joanna Southcott's Box, with the instruction that it be opened only at a time of national crisis, and then only in the presence of the 24 bishops of the Anglican church. This became an obsession of the Bedford Panacea community, attracting international publicity and no little mirth. The Southcott Sealed Box became for a while a cherished and silly meme of English life, appearing in cartoons about Churchill and Baldwin, newspaper ads for shoes and batteries and an early Monty Python sketch.

In 1927, a psychic researcher named Harry Price claimed that he'd come into possession of the famous box and arranged for it to be opened in the presence of one reluctant Bishop. In it were a few irrelevant and random documents, a lottery ticket and a horse-pistol. Octavia and her Bedford community declared this box inauthentic and continued their campaign on billboards and national newspapers through the 1960s and 70s under the catchy, upbeat slogan, 'War, disease, crime and banditry, distress of nations and perplexity will increase until the Bishops open Joanna Southcott's box.'

But all the genteel daftness cast darker shadows. In America, rival Southcottian sects, claiming their own Shiloh messiahs, harboured sexually predatory male leaders, some of whom were jailed for sex with minors. At home, Octavia's Panacea Society, formed in the dramatic, divisive decade before the Jarrow march, were nearer to Mosley than Ellen Wilkinson, implacably right-wing and brazenly inegalitarian. Class distinctions were rigidly observed in the community. Lower-class believers were accommodated as unpaid servants with no status and little time off. Octavia believed that the monarchy, capitalist big business and empire were instruments of God and that trade unions and even the meek Labour Party were in league with Satan. In 1934 however, the society's confidence took something of a knock when Octavia died, never a good career move for an immortal daughter of God, and the community went into decline. By 1967, it numbered just 30 members and the last adherent, Ruth Klein, died in 2012. Small and marginal though it might have been, the Panacea Society was rich, owning £14million of properties in Bedford, which it was forced to sell when, no longer able to claim to be a religion, it became a charity. The museum is now run by this charitable trust and their remit is to sponsor academic research into the history and development of prophetic and millenarian movements and to support the work of groups concerned with poverty and health in the Bedford area.

The whole story is told with clarity and candour in the museum, which is genuinely fascinating. I tell the helpful trust member on reception that the Jarrow march would have passed down this very Bedford street when the Society was still a going concern, but just after Octavia's death. She laughs wryly. 'Probably just as well she wasn't around. She was very conservative in her social attitudes. She thought socialists were "reds under the bed". She did have a couple of Suffragette members but she wasn't very nice to them. She threw one of them out in fact. She wasn't very progressive at all.'

If you should find yourself in Bedford with some free time on a Thursday, Friday or Saturday between mid-February and the end of October, I can recommend the Panacea Society Museum as another peek into the old, slightly weird England. When you have taken in the wireless room where the members would listen communally in the evenings whilst knitting, or the chapel or the bedrooms and rehearsal room where the Bishops would prepare for the opening of the box (once they had seen sense and agreed), you can take a turn in the actual Garden of Eden of Book of Genesis fame, the handy Bedford location of which had been revealed to Octavia in one of her frequent communications with God. In a shady corner of the pleasant suburban lawn, you'll find an impressive tree the society believed to be 'Yggdrasil', the tree of life in Norse mythology, showing that the Panaceans were nothing if not eclectic in their outlook.

It was darkening as I left the Garden of Eden and even if there had been any forbidden apples on offer, I'd already decided in favour of a pizza and a big glass of red. In a town of 15,000 Italians (some say more), chianti and calzone are as prevalent on the menu as the much vaunted yet untasted Clanger. Why is this Bedfordshire town full of Marios and Marias, Fabios and Francescas, why as many posters for Fiorentina and Napoli than Luton or Leicester? Why is almost a fifth of Bedford's population Italian or of Italian descent? There's a short, unromantic answer: bricks.

After the war, Bedford's Marston Valley Brick Company was desperately short of the labour needed for the huge reconstruction boom and drive. A few thousand miles way, in southern Italy, they were desperate to put the ignominy of Mussolini's era behind them – and more to the point, they were shockingly poor. Unemployment was far worse than in the prosperous north, and many villagers, and even the post-war Italian government, began to see emigration as the best solution. In 1951, the Marston Valley Brick Company established an office in Naples, sending two employees to recruit 250 men. This was just the beginning. Between 1951 and 1960 over 7,500 Italians were signed up for the scheme. Each man who volunteered from the *Mezzogiorno* to work in Bedford was given a medical examination, a paid passage to England and a bed. They were lodged communally in a converted prisoner-of-war camp. The English weather and food and sheer homesickness meant that over 60 per cent returned within four years. But many stayed. They worked their contracts, bought their own houses and paid their families' passage to come and join them. By 1958 around 85 per cent of new arrivals in Bedford were married Italian women joining their husbands. An Italian/Cumbrian friend of mine Guilliano remembers visiting Bedford in the 1960s; 'It was amazing, full of delis and trattorias, like a little Italian provincial town.'

Again, social media was proving invaluable in uncovering the story of Bedford's Italians. Tweets chirruped into my devices from native or exiled Bedfordians. Tony Malone told me that at one point Bedford had its own Italian consulate. James Coyne recommended Club Prima Generazione and Amalfi cakes, adding 'virtually everyone in Bedford has one Italian relative or another'. But as I was on Newnham Street and its 6 o'clock opening time was fast approaching, I was noting hungrily the many mentions of Pizza Santaniello, 'a proper Italian family pizzeria'. In fact, I could see it. Its bright red frontage spilling enticing light on to the pavement and its white painted slogan 'Bedford's Number One Pizzeria' had a bold machismo that was irresistible. *Andiamo*!

'My parents came after the war, early 1950s,' says Antonio, whirling a disc of pizza base in his outstretched fingers. 'A four-year contract and then they were given the choice to stay or go. And we stayed. Five couples in one house, that's how close the communities were. Mostly from southern Italy – Campagna, Foggia, Sardinia.' Antonio is now head chef at what was Bedford's first pizzeria, opened by Fiorangelo and Ida Santaniello and now run by their son Geraldo, busy behind the bar as I make a nuisance of myself by the hot maw of the stone baking oven. 'There were three queues for the Italian men, my dad would say, one for Brazil, one for Venezuela and one for Bedford. We ended up here, at the brick works in Stewartby.' Geraldo's son, the younger Fiorangelo, is now the third generation to be here offering 'the best hand stretched pizzas outside of Naples, as you'll soon find out' he says as he passes by with several carafes of wine.

It's a few minutes after opening time but I still only just manage to squeeze into a corner table. It's mainly families on half term, but there are a few dining adults like me, an Indian businessman boasting to a pretty younger girl, his secretary maybe, about his friends in St Petersburg and Riga; a quartet of Scottish women swapping stories very entertainingly about their disastrous honeymoons; a white-haired man with a hefty paperback into his second carafe. It is busy, loud and hot, and by now full of delicious pizza and house red, I decide to make way for one or two of the potential diners queuing by the door, presumably being driven nearly insane by the aroma of sizzling garlic and the popping of another cork. I go to say goodbye to Antonio. He's shovelling another two pizzas into the oven's fiery recess and, pushing back his bandana, drags a forearm across his dripping brow. '*Ciao*, I hope you enjoyed it my friend ... where are you from then?' I tell him I'm from the north and have been on the road for two-and-a-half weeks on the trail of the Jarrow march. Antonio hasn't heard of it, but when I tell him the story and how they came to Bedford 80 years ago tonight he cocks his head and says, 'Like my dad then, like Geraldo's parents. They just wanted work. They were desperate. They made sacrifices. Working people, you see, same all over the world. They move and they make new homes. There's still lots of Italy here. There's an Italian church that the community built. There are community centres. There's a few Italian bars ...'

Really? How would they feel about a stray Lancastrian Italophile dropping by?

'Try them!' he laughs. 'Club Italia, up on Alexander Road by the railway station, bit hard to find down a back street, but if you fancy a late grappa ...'

I'd been wondering how to spend the evening and had narrowed it down to the open mike music night at the Standard or the monthly meeting of Bedford Electronic Organ Club (est. 1972). Both now paled before the prospect of Club Italia. *Ciao ciao* Pizza Santaniello! *Allora*, Club Italia.

BEDFORD TO LUTON

28 October, 19 miles

On a fine warm morning, or a still balmy night, should you take your *amante* or *tesoro* for a *passeggiata* down the riverside banks of the stately Great Ouse, where the ducks and rowers glide by and the lamplight ripples; you will surely find Bedford as lovely as Bath if perhaps not *Venezia*. The concrete enclave of poundshops and snack bars around the bus station, however: not so much. Although, that said, Venice's bus station is pretty grim, and Bedford's is at least brand spanking new, all curved glass and burnished chrome – 'a travel point the borough can be proud of!' – including real-time display screens, a travel centre and a new departure hub. 'A major regeneration project which has transformed the local area,' is how the leaflet trills it, and I have no reason to cavil.

It's 9am, and I'm digging out the Nurofen again at a café in Bedford's Bus Station over a mug of hot brown builder's tea. I have the address of a shop where I can find a proper Bedfordshire Clanger, and I will, as soon as my head stops banging and my vision clears. I took Antonio's advice and headed off to find Club Italia. I went across town, up Midland Road by the railway station, Bedford's own 'Via Roma', and into Alexander Road. Where Club Italia is tucked away is a parade of slightly seedy looking international drinking dens; here a Polish one, there an African, there Turkish. Across a darkened car park I glimpse an

Italian flag and, in a pool of light, two silhouetted figures lit by the orange tips of their cigarettes. I had come this far, I had expert local knowledge and I was emboldened by several glasses of slightly rough Chianti. I took my chance.

'Who you looking for mate? You wanna drink?' said one of the men. He wore a paint-spattered overall that was definitely not one of either Signor Armani, Dolce or Gabbana, and he pushed open a nondescript hardboard door to reveal a scene of frenetic drilling, hammering and sawing. The bar was open for business though and the barman beckoned so I took my place alongside a couple of other drinkers, cradling small grappas and bottles of Nastro Azzurro. 'We're having some work done as you can see,' said the barman, a doughty fellow in his late fifties with glasses and a salt and pepper moustache, 'but if you don't mind that ...' Having come this far, and feeling more foolish were I to leave, I ordered both a beer and a grappa to be on the safe side and took my place at the bar.

The welcome in Club Italia was more cautious and cagey than in Pizza Santaniello and understandably so. I doubt they get many strange northerners dropping by even if 20 days of road walking have given him a distinctly walnut complexion. Club Italia clearly had a community function but that was presumably during daytime and weekends. On a dark Monday evening, this was a place for men to drink and swap stories of the old days, play scopa and drink grappa under posters and murals of the great Italian World Cup teams and their maestros, Gianni Rivera, Luigi Riva, Paolo Rossi. It was a place to crowd round the TV on big football nights draped in the tricolore and sing on the Azzurri, shouting, '*Dai! Ma stai scherzando arbitro! Mandalo a casa!*' or 'Come on, you're having a laugh, ref, send him off!'

As we drank, we shared our stories. I told them of Jarrow and my walk in those men's footsteps. They told me of their fathers and grandfathers coming to Bedford from much further away in the ravaged post-war world. This time though, the recollections seemed less sunny and celebratory than they had in the pizzeria. 'My brother was born in 1953 and I was born in 1958 and my parents had been here a few years then and they were amongst the first ones to come. After your four years in the brickworks hostel, well, if you were good, you were allowed to stay. If not you were on the boat back. You were on probation and if you were a good worker, you were OK, but if not they could send you back at any time. They were like slaves really.'

'Yep, they were slaves,' one of the young workmen, job done and settling back with a beer, chips in. 'They were sold by Italy for 400 quid. The Italian government was paid 400 pounds for each person they exported. My dad turned 18 on the boat and because he didn't have his papers, he thought he'd be sent back. They detained him for a while. Britain was desperate for labourers though, and they were desperate for work.'

'It was exactly like the Poles and the Romanians now,' says the barman with an equivocal shrug. 'They're poor. Italy was poor. The brickworks may have been hard work but it wasn't hard compared to their lives back there. No food, no money, no decent housing, no warmth, no toilets. Italy was bad. The husbands came, the wives followed. They all came with the intention of working hard, making their money and going back. It doesn't happen, does it? You have kids. There's a good 20,000 Italians here now I reckon. Most of them have got properties over there that they built that have just gone to waste. They just stayed here.'

'Bedford has this effect on you. I came for a weekend ten years ago and I'm still here,' says a well-spoken man at the bar with a cravat and ponytail. Another voice, a young bloke in a baseball cap and tracksuit, joins in. 'My granddad was a prisoner of war, they captured him in Africa, Tripoli. Then they sent him to Yorkshire working on farms for a couple of years. After the war was all done and dusted, they let him go. He came down and joined all the Italians in Bedford.'

'Don't get me wrong,' says the barman, sliding another Nardini across the counter to me, or possibly a Fernet Branca. 'They weren't resentful. They were grateful. You and I couldn't have stuck it. We couldn't just move to another country 'cos we've got everything here. But it's like these Africans. They have nothing. Wherever they go, they're grateful even if you treat them like shit. We can't share these people's perspectives.' An old boy gets up from his card game to leave, the barman breaks off to embrace him and there follows a quickfire exchange in Italian with the odd English word standing out as if by highlighter pen: 'cooker', 'worktop', 'microwave'.

After these discussions and more like them and more grappa and Nastro Azzurro, the evening unravelled somewhat. More people, all men, came and went and gathered at the bar. 'People come here for a drink late. Not just Italians. Albanians, Rumanians, Poles ...' Brexit was discussed and there was no consensus. The well-spoken man turned out to be the grandson of an infamous Scottish writer. He had been 'in the clothing game and a GP in another life', and now he talked of his mental health problems and wondered if I could help him get some help from social services. The stocky leather-jacketed man on my left turns out to be from Albania. Tirana, I guess?

'No.'

Shkodër? I guess again. I know the names of several Albanian cities and have decided as a point of honour that this will not beat me.

'No,' replies Rudi again.

Hmm. 'Durrës?'

'Durrës! You know Durrës! Half an hour south of there!'

I've never been to Durrës, or Albania, but it was an obsession of mine during the crazed, insular, appalling regime of Enver Hoxha when it was Europe's very own North Korea. I buy him a grappa and we talk. 'Fifty years of communism my country had under a man called Enver Hoxha. What? You know of him? How?'

It's a long story, to be honest, and you'll think I'm weird.

'Well, we are small country and Enver Hoxha made it even smaller. You could say nothing. You could be arrested at school. If you did not agree with Hoxha, or you upset him, you were jailed for life ... if you were lucky. You could be shot in the head. You could be hung in front of your family. I was very young. But people tell the stories. We change in 1990. We change for better. But I still come here. I came for better life. I get married. But then I get divorced, and she make a hard life for me. Now my life is over. I haven't seen my son for three years. He is 13 now. Game over. Everyone is married but not me. It is very sad.'

Rudi went on like this for some time, darker and sadder with every *slivovitz*. My head was spinning by now but even through the haze of grappa, I knew that this hard-working man was lonely; lonely enough to talk to a complete stranger for a long time while all around noisy card games were played and worktops were ordered. We had talked all night about migrants and borders but loneliness and sadness are countries without borders. My obsession with Albania's craziness and otherness now seemed very callow, even shameful.

At different times in our history, we have been very happy to allow the free movement of people to our shores when we have needed them, be it German mining engineers to the Lake District of the Elizabethan era, Nigerian cleaners to our midnight office blocks or Polish receptionists to the Malmaisons of our revitalised cities. Brexit and the reasons behind the seismic vote of the summer had cropped up in conversation but not as I thought it would, with entrenched views and clichés. Over the evening, 'somewhere in England' had proved itself the perfect description of this English town. It was both typical and utterly unique, full of the same things that we find across the modern country, the ubiquitous, the homogenous, the mass produced and, then again, full of weird secrets and stories, heroism, mystery, madness. 'Somewhere in England' was the perfect description, both prosaic and enigmatic, and echoing around my head, along with the wine and grappa, as I crossed the wide lamplit river, through reception and the bar with its change-jingling, late night business drinkers and the lift up to bed.

Before they left for Luton, the marchers went to look at Bedford's fine new brickworks at Stewartby. This was the sort of new industry their own deprived town badly needed and surely they must have looked at it with envy. They couldn't have known, however (though a few of the more gloomy might have feared it) that within three years the world would be at war, and the brickworks of Bedford would then need legions of vanquished men from the Mediterranean to help rebuild England. Bedford had been good to the marchers during their stay. The local Rotary Club and Christian charity Toc H had given them cigarettes and tobacco and put on a night's free entertainment at the town hall. So warm had been Bedford's hospitality that the Conservative mayor said that he had been accused of being 'a convert to Labour, a rigid socialist and even a communist'.

At the bus station I picked up an intriguing magazine. It was called *This England* and there was something soothing about its lovely cover of a warm russet sunset in an English wood. Being unashamedly of Attlee's patriotic leftist strain, I can be something of a sucker for this kind of thing and as the magazine seemed to consist of little else except nostalgia and anniversaries, I felt sure the autumn number would have some mention of the Jarrow march. But having scoured the magazine from cover to cover, I could find nothing – though I did find a gloating editorial about leaving the European union, a eulogy to the late TV presenter and extreme right-winger Norris McWhirter and a fun piece condoning violence against 'atheist teachers with links to the Civil Liberties Association'. Like the Panacea Society, there was a cold meanness underneath the moist-eyed middle England niceties and a kind of ignorance too; the kind that uses Battle of Britain imagery to celebrate Brexit, forgetting that we won that with heroic help from Czech and Polish pilots; or presumes that

Vaughan Williams's music embodies their world view when the socialistic, knighthood-refusing giant of English music would have loathed them. *This England* would have probably not had much time for the Jarrow marchers and may even have thought the mayor of Bedford was a communist, embodying that particular kind of English sense of fair play, justice and tolerance that wants Rudi the Albanian builder to go home but they to be allowed to retire to Magaluf. Quite how its expatriate readership would fare in the next few years as we pulled up the drawbridge to Europe would be diverting to say the least.

I'd woken that morning with a new earworm, a song from The Clash's *Sandinista!* album called 'Something About England'. A sort of potted radical history seen through the eyes of an ageing tramp who missed out on the First World War but 'not the sorrow afterwards'. It goes, 'They say it would be wine and roses/ If England were for Englishmen again'. (An ideal strapline for *This England* magazine, I'd have thought.) I liked 'Something About England' far more than *This England*, but though The Clash meant well, they too got Jarrow wrong describing the Jarrow marchers as 'hunger strikers'. The Jarrow men weren't on hunger strike; in fact they hadn't eaten so well in years. But no matter. It was a good song to keep time too as I left town.

As I did, finally I found a Bedfordshire 'Clanger', the local pastry delicacy with savoury filling at one end and sweet at the other, thus providing both dinner and dessert for the hungry agricultural worker of yesteryear. These ones came recommended by Jamie Oliver no less and the proprietor's manner suggested I was highly honoured to be served with one (I was once treated with similar guardedness buying 'rowies' in a back street in Aberdeen. I must bring out the worst in regional bakers). Anyway, it was horrible. I can't remember which of the fashionable filling combos in this new artisan version I plumped for; pulled pork and banoffee must have been there and salted caramel and ricotta too I imagine. But in any event, I couldn't discern which end was which as both seemed filled with wallpaper paste mixed with Quaker Oats. As I was decanting it into a bin, the delicate, troubled writer's grandson from last night passed by with a cheery wave and a curious look as I hurriedly disappeared into the transport point/departure hub that Bedford can be proud of.

I was going to take a bus for some of the way to Luton just to buy myself a little time as I had another appointment to make, again thanks to the social media. So far I had been lucky with Twitter; only two trolls and they had been mildly useful, and lots of help, encouragements and offers to meet or walk with me. I'd been touched by many of these but had accepted few in order that I could stay flexible and agile, able to change my mind or act on a whim. But today's from Rachel Hopkins was irresistible.

'A Friday in the Brickies (by Luton Station) with a bunch of left-wing types?! A must surely?!'

I had to agree and so I took the 81 out of Bedford via Progress Way and through Elstow, Bunyan's birthplace and location of the Slough of Despond. On we went via Bunyans Mead to the 'no cold-calling zone' of Wilstead and, just after Houghton Conquest (surely the chiselled RAF hero of the wartime love story *Wings Over Waterlily Lane*) I jumped off in order to walk the A6 for a while.

The A6 café, shuttered and quiet, doesn't seem to have served a hot sausage bap or milky coffee in a good few years. Before motorway service stations and catering vans, these were the much-loved fuelling stations that broke journeys and marked the miles. I wondered if some incarnation of the A6 café had been here when the march passed by. It was just here that a contingent of Mosley's Fascists asked to join the march and were given short shrift by the men, although this should be balanced against the fact that the day before marcher Fred Harris had been rather furtively sent home for expressing 'communistic' beliefs, proving that a certain forelock tugging fear of giving offence still informed the march organisers, whatever their personal beliefs.

Having sent the Blackshirts packing, the oldest marcher, 62-year-old George Smith told the reporters, 'I'm going strong and the rest of the march is going to be a cakewalk.' As I pounded the noisy, dirty fringes of the A6, I envied George's confidence.

From time to time, my path had merged and flirted with this famous old English arterial road, one of the great north–south highways of England. But after Bedford, it generally veers and swerves left and west, thundering up through the Midlands and my patch of the industrial north west headed for Carlisle. It would make a good long walking project one day, I thought, if not a scenic one, as I negotiated the swirling confusion of the Barton-le-Clay bypass fork, a kind of whirlpool as I neared the source of this mighty, dirty river of tarmac; Luton.

Luton did not offer the marchers a grand civic welcome. This was not through any coldness or antipathy, but because the new town hall was only being opened that night by the Duke of Kent. The Duke may well have known what few ordinary Lutonians or Jarrovians did; namely that that afternoon Wallis Simpson had been granted a decree nisi at Norwich assizes and the looming constitutional stormclouds gathered ever nearer. Nothing dampened the enthusiasm of Luton towards the aristocracy that day though. Children's choirs sang, fireworks roared through the dusk, flags were unfurled and bunting draped. The crowds welcomed the Duke warmly and then many stayed in the streets to cheer the marchers into town as well in a very British display of camaraderie.

I should make clear here though that the reason Luton needed a new town hall was that the townsfolk had burned the other one down in 1919 in a quite astonishing outpouring of rage. *Luton Today*, the local newspaper website, has footage of the conflagration under the glorious headline, 'Luton Town Hall burnt down during Peace Day riots', a sentence as cherishable as the famous line from *Doctor Strangelove*, 'Gentlemen, you can't fight in here! This is the war room!' The full story is worth recounting, shedding light as it does on how England's dissenting nature has not only been shown in supplicant crusades. Sometimes we go cap in hand to our superiors. Sometimes we burn down the town hall and try to kill the mayor.

The Peace Treaty concluding the Great War was finally signed in June 1919 and Luton Town Council planned various civic celebrations followed by a sumptuous 'mayor's banquet'. This was to be paid for from the civic purse but invitations were strictly limited to the mayor, councillors and close friends, none of whom had seen active service. No ex-soldiers, sailors or airmen were included in the lavish council celebrations. This prompted various veterans groups and their supporters to boycott the council's celebrations and hold their own event in a local park. The council refused them permission, and so the ex-servicemen's groups decided to make their anger known.

At first, the protest was quiet and controlled. Maimed and disabled ex-servicemen lined the procession route under a banner that read, 'Don't pity us, give us work'. When the officials processed by unmoved, they were followed by the irate ex-servicemen. On arrival at the town hall, the soldiers barracked the mayor's platitudinous oratory and when he tried to patronise them, the mood turned really ugly. The 20,000-strong crowd suddenly surged forwards, sending the mayor scurrying into the bowels of the town hall as they tore down the doors. Once inside, the crowd wreaked havoc, hurling the contents of the town hall through the windows onto the street and trying to get at the mayor and his party who were barricaded into his parlour. Their lives were probably saved by the arrival of a contingent of police. The townspeople then turned their anger on them and fought a pitched battle with policemen in the street. By now, the rioting and looting had taken on something of carnival atmosphere and 20,000 people gathered at the town hall (with petrol stolen from Hall's garage) and razed it to the ground singing 'We'll Keep the Home Fires Burning Here'. The mayor was spirited away and the police turned savagely on the crowd, beating women and children with sticks. Four days and nights of rioting followed before order was restored leaving the town centre in ruins and looking like a war zone.

The Bricklayers Arms was nothing like this lively, but it was packed and noisy even for a late Friday afternoon. Some kind of speech was being made, and pictures of a smiling man adorned the pub walls. It was evidently some kind of wake and the young woman who pushed her way through the throng to appear at my elbow, explained more. She was crying a little as she indicated another picture of the man, this time above a stool at the end of the bar. 'My friend Steve. That was his seat. A lot of these people here have come to pay respects to him because of his work and his art. But he was just my mate Steve. I met him five years ago when I first started coming in here. He was just your classic decent bloke.'

Steve Dillon, a Lutonian born and bred, was one of the biggest British names in the field of comic book art. He began his professional career at the age of 16 on Marvel's Hulk Weekly before moving on to *Nick Fury, Warrior, Doctor Who* and *2000 AD*. He co-founded the influential *Deadline* magazine in 1988 which brought comics to the attention of many an indie kid thanks to its pop cultural savvy and hip NME-style credentials. In recent years, he had invented the series *Preacher* which had transferred successfully to TV and was in New York doing some work for a comics charity when he died suddenly from a ruptured appendix. 'He was cremated today at 10.30 in New York, which is why we all came here at 3.30 our time to raise a glass to him.' The pub is full of colleagues, friends and fans, and the range of t-shirts, adornments, hair styles and piercings is impressive.

I might have felt something of an interloper into other people's grief but Rachel, who'd been following my progress on Twitter, had wanted us to meet up anyway. She's a Labour councillor, her dad is Luton's Labour MP – one of only two in Bedfordshire – and she had a Jarrow tale for me. 'As an idealistic 14-year-old, I went down to the drill hall in 1986 when a group of unemployed marchers were passing through Luton recreating the march and I made them their breakfast. The week after, we were visiting my granddad and I told him this proudly and he smiled and said, 'Well, guess what, I did the very same thing for the original marchers when they passed though Leicester.'

I'm liking 'The Brickies' very much. It's an old-school boozer in Luton's 'High Town', a favourite with football fans, real ale drinkers and lefties alike. Rachel's boyfriend, a cheery soul and I think a little less political than her, nudges me and says, 'All the politburo are in here,' with a grin. I fall into a conversation about progressive rock with a genial man in a well-filled t-shirt featuring the cover of Emerson, Lake and Palmer's *Tarkus* (the concept album about the war between the robot scorpion and the giant mechanised armadillo. You remember.) I feel I am amongst friends.

Another local councillor, Mark, offers the thought that, 'Luton is essentially a northern industrial town in the south of England'. Politically it has never been as conservative as the rest of the home counties, although it did return Tory MPs at the high imperial phase of Thatcherism. Drawn to work in the town's Vauxhall car factories, it has a Kashmiri population of 40,000, a quarter of its population, and is sometimes cited as officially 'hyperdiverse', i.e. more than 50 per cent of its population are black or minority ethnic, although definitions of the term seem to differ. Rachel checks her phone. 'There's a reception for the Kashmiri consul tonight and my dad's going to be there. He says he'll pop in here and have a beer if you can hang around for a while.' It would be rude not to, I say, as the chap in the *Tarkus* t-shirt goes to get me another pint of Centurion.

Not long after, I am in the quieter back bar with the only man in the pub wearing a suit. Rachel's dad Kelvin has been the Labour MP for Luton since 1997. 'There were 22 of us from the region then but we've declined ever since … till now. There were a lot more socialists then. That was exceptional but at each election since then we've been cut back, we nearly only had me. The Margaret Moran scandal cost us lots of votes.' (The

former MP for Luton South was convicted of fraud in 2012.
Moran's claims for expenses 2004–05 were £73,198 higher than
Kelvin's.) 'But we go on. Jeremy's been elected leader by the
membership not by Parliament, thousands of people are joining
the party, tens if not hundreds of thousands left because of new
Labour. But that's all history now. I'm in a progressive mood and
I think there's a real chance we can have a progressive Labour
government next time round.'

I'm forced to say that I don't agree, even though I find
Kelvin's positivity and optimism laudable. I also don't share
Kelvin's view – a widespread one admittedly – that Blair was an
enemy of the people and his leadership a toxic one. The Iraq War
was a dire misadventure but making mistakes in war situations is
not, I suggest, a problem Jeremy Corbyn will ever have. Didn't
Kelvin concede that the Blair administration did a lot of good –
like Sure Start schemes and the minimum wage – and that 1997
seemed for a while to mark the rise of the forces of good? He
sighs.

'I have to say I didn't believe that myself. I felt that the people
wanted a Labour government and wanted progressive change
but they didn't get that. What they got was another version of
Conservatism. Blair and Mandelson were free marketeers who
wanted to privatise and carry on with the neo-liberal revolution.
I know many people welcomed it. My wife in fact said, "Isn't it
wonderful, now we can do all the socialist things we've always
wanted," and I said, "No dear it won't happen." The day I was
elected, at the count just down the road, people kept asking me,
"Why are you looking so sombre and reserved?" And I said,
"Well, I'm very happy to be in Parliament, thanks to all these
wonderful people and their votes but I'm contemplating the
struggles to come against the forces of darkness in our party,"
and now people know what I was talking about.'

Kelvin's optimism for Jeremy Corbyn's new left-wing
agenda was tempered by one thing. 'The boundary changes are
going to ruin us. We'll lose 20–25 seats before you even talk

about swings. But Scotland's the real problem. We have to win
back Scotland to stand any chance of a majority government.
You would hope that the Scottish Nationalists wouldn't want
to sustain a Tory government. But we shall see. That's four
years away.' (It wasn't.)

Kelvin's clearly a man of principle but I put it to him that a
jolt of pragmatism is also needed on the left. Competency and
power is a precursor of change, and the metropolitan left has lost
touch with its working-class base, just as it did in 1936. Marches
and rallies are good for the soul, but they change nothing.
Ask the Jarrow marchers. 'But Jarrow resonates still,' counters
Kelvin. 'It may not have achieved anything directly back then
but it has echoes and meaning. Sometimes even a defeat can
inspire; the miners' strike, the general strike, the split in 1931
when we were sold down the river by Ramsay MacDonald who
joined the Tories. All those things remind us that we have to
fight. Things do change. Take South Africa, I was a campaigner
in my youth and we often thought that nothing could ever really
be done. But eventually things change although there will always
be forces of darkness and conservatism in the world.'

He give me a wry smile. 'When I was a student I worked in
Potters Bar, 1962 it would have been. At the works there was an
old man who said, "When those Jarrow marchers came past our
town, I went out and jeered at them, the communist bastards."
I could never believe that, that a working-class man could do
that.' Britain's first troll, maybe, I suggest and remember the
statistic that I used to pass on to my sociology students back
in Skelmersdale. A third of the working class routinely vote
Conservative. Without those working-class Tories, there
would never be Tory governments. It is not a peculiarly British
condition or even delusion either. John Steinbeck once said,
'Socialism never took root in America because the poor see
themselves not as an exploited proletariat, but as temporarily
embarrassed millionaires.'

I take my leave amongst much kissing, handshaking and laughter. I liked Luton's rugged individualism, fierce sense of self and ornery distinctiveness. I liked the Brickies and its draught Centurion. Rachel shows me to the door and I thank her, her dad and her friends for a lovely afternoon. I ask her if she'd like to follow in her dad's footsteps and become an MP. She smiles coyly. 'Maybe, who knows? It'd be nice to do something for people, ordinary people,' she says and there's another hug or two and then I have to be on my way, onward to St Albans.

'We have to look after our own Stuart,' she calls to me as I head purposefully up the darkening street.

'Oh and by the way, Stuart, you're going the wrong way. St Albans is that way,' she points behind her and, laughing, disappears into the happy cauldron of warm companionship that is the Brickies.

LUTON TO ST ALBANS

29 October, 10 miles

As autumn hardens into winter, and the dark nights close in, so the mother of Parliaments finally has to go back after the mother of all summer holidays, now as in 1936. On the morning that the marchers left Luton for St Albans, Ellen Wilkinson headed for the Commons and the reconvening of Parliament after the recess. When she got there, she asked Prime Minister Baldwin how many resolutions and messages he had received about the Jarrow march. Quite a few, he grudgingly acknowledged, but he was still refusing to receive them when they reached London. Historian Dominic Sandbrook has said of Baldwin that his 'emollient and media-friendly' manner make him in some ways the first modern prime minister. Possibly so, but surely his pointed refusal to meet the men was a PR disaster that a contemporary spin doctor would have advised against, however distasteful he might have found it.

Over the last week or so of trekking, I had decided that I should like to try and succeed where the Jarrow men had failed and be met and taken into the Commons, if not by the Prime Minister herself, Theresa May (elevated unelected after David Cameron's resignation in the wake of his Brexit humiliation), Jeremy Corbyn, Tim Farron or whoever was UKIP leader on the day I arrived, then at least by an MP. I tweeted to this effect asking if any Member of Parliament would care to meet me.

Almost immediately I had received a charming reply from a new MP Tracy Brabin saying that she'd be delighted to meet me when I arrived on 31 October, and to get in touch when I was approaching Marble Arch.

When I mentioned this in the pub in Luton, Rachel, Kelvin and the councillors had been impressed, delighted and a little moved I thought. 'That's fantastic. Do you know her from the media?' No, not at all, I replied a little confused. 'She's an actress,' laughed Rachel. 'Didn't you know? She was in *Coronation Street*. She's just become an MP because, well, it felt right. It was a brilliant, amazing thing for her to ...'

'Sorry?' I say. Maybe it was the three pints of Centurion but I genuinely wasn't following this.

Rachel looked closely at me 'You haven't realised, have you? Tracy was a friend of Jo Cox. Tracy Brabin is the new MP for Batley and Spen.'

Batley and Spen is a political constituency in West Yorkshire created in 1983 and unremarkable until the summer of 2016 when a far-right extremist killed its MP, Jo Cox, outside her office. Thomas Mair, 52, stabbed and shot Jo, a Batley girl and the mother of two young children, whilst yelling 'Britain First'. There was no doubt what Mair's motivation was, nor his affiliations to white supremacist and neo-Nazi groups, or his fascist sympathies, but the majority of the British press chose to ignore these, describing him as a lone lunatic. This was an approach in sharp contrast to these papers' treatment of murders by Asians and Muslims, who were uniformly presented as radical Islamists. No newspaper called it an act of fascist or extreme right terrorism, which it quite plainly was; one presumably perpetrated in twisted response to Jo's support for the Remain side in the EU referendum. While the immediate reaction was dismal, there was worse to come from spokesmen of the far right. Nigel Farage attacked Jo's widower in a radio interview saying, 'Well, of course, he would know more about extremists than me, Mr Cox ...'

Others of a similar cast of mind soon joined in. 'When are we allowed to say that Brendan Cox is a total arse?' tweeted *Spectator* and Breitbart fulminator James Delingpole. UKIP bankroller Arron Banks contributed, 'I'm sorry about his wife but he chose to massively politicise it. Who does that?' Even in the enormously debased political discourse of 2016, these remarks represented a new low. It took either monumental stupidity or sheer wickedness to not acknowledge that the murder of a Member of Parliament by a neo Nazi shouting 'Britain first' seemed to have quite a political dimension already. So it was with a mixture of anger and pride that I picked up the pace as I left Luton. Whatever happened in the next few days, I would be there to meet Tracy at the Houses of Parliament on 31 October.

That Farage, Delingpole and Banks's remarks were contemptible was beyond doubt. But beyond that given, the situation in Batley and Spen was complex, awkward and revealed much about the chaotic and febrile state of our political culture in 2016. At Jo's memorial service in London, husband Brendan Cox's words were broadcast live back to Batley.

> Across the world we're seeing forces of division playing on people's worst fears, rather than their best instincts, trying to divide our communities, to exploit insecurities, and emphasise not what unites us but what divides us. Jo's killing was political, it was an act of terror designed to advance an agenda of hatred towards others. What a beautiful irony it is that an act designed to advance hatred has instead generated such an outpouring of love. Jo lived for her beliefs, and on Thursday she died for them, and for the rest of our lives we will fight for them in her name.

In a brilliant piece in the *New Yorker* though, British writer Ed Caesar went to Batley to gauge the response. Many wept in the streets at the mention of Jo's name, but in the main room of the Conservative Club,

Two members, named Darren and Stuart (they declined to offer their surnames), sat at the bar discussing how they had both voted Leave. Darren knew Jo Cox from school and said she was 'a lovely lass'. But both men spoke repeatedly about how they had been let down by politicians, particularly on the issue of immigration. Their complaint did not just concern the recent migrants from the E.U. but the older Muslim residents of Batley. Darren put his wish to leave the E.U. partly down to 'the change in the town and the feeling in the town. There are certain people who don't integrate.' Stuart said that, 'it's a sad thing what happened last week,' but added, 'we just want our country back.'

Both drinkers thought that the 'Jo Cox thing' would have some influence on the result. But both thought, unlike the professional pollsters and commentators, that Batley's region of Kirklees would vote to leave the EU. They were right, professional informed opinion was wrong, and as I walked along old Luton's streets of its famous blue Victorian brick – now highly desirable for the townhouses of Hampstead and St John's Wood – the fallout from that detonation was still settling gently on Britain, a cloud of unknowing that obscured the familiar and made the way ahead difficult to see.

The Jarrow marchers and I were now crossing over in the heart of the home counties, from one England to the next. The stretch between Luton and St Albans is only ten miles but it feels more, at least culturally, as the polyglot urban sprawl of a railway and car town falls away and a different England comes into view; older, leafier, smarter, richer. My drinking mate in the *Tarkus* T-shirt had said that most people thought Luton was 'a hellhole', which was not strictly true and certainly not the impression I had taken away. But no one would ever say it of St Albans, rightly or wrongly. We are not quite in Betjeman's Metroland yet, but we are moving into the ample bosom of the affluent commuter belt; golf courses, tankards, roses, stripped-pine gastropubs and garden offices.

Betjeman wrote some of his defining verses in the mid-1930s often rooted in very English locales, as in 'Death in Leamington', 'Distant View of a Provincial Town' and 'Slough'. The latter shows something of how untouched and untroubled by hardship some lives were. Drafted while the marchers were on the road, it says much of Betjeman's privilege and pursed lip that while the Jarrow Crusade held the attention of most, bringing the plight of workless men and their towns to the nation's conscience, Betjeman's major poem of the period was an etiolated sneer at one town's drab aesthetic and lack of pastoral charm. 'Come friendly bombs and fall on Slough, it isn't fit for humans now,' he pleaded; not because of slums, hunger or poor sanitation, but because he didn't like the vulgarity of its Tudor houses, sports cars and hairdos. It is snobbery – much anthologised snobbery, but snobbery none the less. If any town deserved friendly bombs to fall on it because it wasn't fit for humans, it was Jarrow, not Slough.

Fortunately, Betjeman in this unappealing register was far from being the typical voice of the most exciting decade of the twentieth century for British poetry. Those voices belonged to writers who were altogether tougher, more colloquial, more engaged. 'Even before they were quite over, the thirties took on the appearance of myth,' as critic Robin Skelton put it. The architects of that mythic significance were young poets like Stephen Spender, Louis MacNeice, Cecil Day Lewis, William Empson and Wystan Hugh Auden.

I have my battered copy of Skelton's classic paperback Penguin anthology *Poetry of the Thirties* in front of me for reference now as I write, but I could probably quote accurately from memory. This 1971 edition of the 1964 original with its striking red and white modernist cover design by Stephen Russ carries a recommended retail price of 35p, but I am ashamed to say that it cost me nothing as I stole it from an English

Lit store cupboard at St John Rigby Grammar School when I was 12. It has come with me to college, back home again and through every flat and house move over four decades. It fired my love of poetry and in particular the poetry of the thirties. I'd go on to love the poetry of Larkin, Gunn and Hughes and the generation of poets who followed after the Second World War, but I'd never have got there without Skelton's slim, dense volume, as packed with explosive force as a hand grenade.

To the best of my knowledge, there are no poems of the period specifically about Jarrow, but the best of them address and explore the world and the systems that made Jarrow poor and the world more dangerous. This was a time when, as Skelton remarks, 'mass movements were in the air and quite explicably. Hunger marchers were out in England. The militant unemployed were reading the *Daily Worker*. There was a need and a clamour for social justice'.

The media loves a movement; from Bright Young People to Britpop. They fill supplements and make good copy in high art as well as low culture, in the salon as well as the streets. The 'Auden Group' was something of a journalistic creation but there was something meaningful there too. The poets who have come to embody the spirit of the 1930s were of roughly the same Oxbridge generation and shared a demotic, forceful style and a vaguely left-wing outlook. Four poets were central to the 'group'; MacNeice, Auden, Spender and Day Lewis, satirically lumped together as a single fictitious hydra-headed beast called MacSpaunday by the Franco-sympathiser Roy Campbell, who was no friend of the group. (Campbell is an interesting figure; one of the few poets of the time to support the fascists. Some apologists like Joseph Pearce and Roger Scruton deny that he was one himself and say that he merely loathed Marxism. But a line like 'The chill, webbed handclasp of the Jew' suggests a deeper, darker affiliation to the far right.) MacSpaunday was a sardonic dig of course, and in truth the 'Auden' group never held meetings, were probably never even under the same roof and had no shared agenda beyond making poetry more vital and connected with the world. But there were connections between individual writers, as friends, travellers and collaborators. They had something else to bind them too. What shocks me now about Skelton's collection is that while many of the writers were gay, not one was a woman.

Spain loomed large in the lives and work of this group as it did in the newspapers of late October 1936. The Civil War caught the romantic imagination and fired the verse of the thirties poets but it spurred some to more direct action as part of the International Brigade. Auden and Spender both went, the former as an ambulance driver and stretcher bearer, the latter as a radio reporter, and Auden returned from Spain more philosophical and nuanced in his views than he had gone. His poem 'Spain' – which Orwell described as 'one of the few decent things to be written about the war' – with its notorious line about 'the necessary murder', later fell out of favour with its writer. He removed it from future anthologies on the grounds that it was 'dishonest', espousing views for effect that he did not really hold. But many of his poems from this time and later do embody the period and stand as brilliant individual works. He had begun 1936 with the celebrated 'Night Mail', a poem written to the music of Benjamin Britten and the visuals of Humphrey Jennings. He would end the decade with the doom-laden and valedictory '1st September 1939', written at the fag end 'of a low dishonest decade' and on the eve of a devastating war.

That was a few years away still though. On 26 October 1936, as Franco's troops approached the southern and western suburbs of Madrid, the Jarrow marchers neared the rather more placid outskirts of St Albans. As I made the same progress, uneventfully (with all due respect to Harpenden) following the old Roman road of Watling Street through Hertfordshire's undulating chalk downs and vales, flat pastures, and eventually its well-tended gardens and neat hedges, I wondered if the change in the country had been as apparent to the Jarrow marchers as it was to me.

A journey south through England via the route I've taken at least is one through increasing prosperity and growing attractiveness. St Albans greets you with the contentedness of a town in the heart of comfortable shires. At least it looks that way if you've walked from Jarrow. Perhaps it felt like that in 1936 too, although the enormous, swirling, centrifugal pull of London, its wealth, privilege and real estate, was less powerful then. But I could feel it as a real presence now. For all St Albans's distinct character and independence, its fine visage is tilted towards the capital, as if turning its face gratefully to the sun.

Once though, when Watling Street was a new transport project, London wasn't even in St Albans's league. Osbert Lancaster in his curious 1961 travel guide *Here's England* wrote, 'If you have a pleasant day for the journey to St Albans, you can stand on the bank of the little river and suddenly feel yourself touched, saddened by the great passage of time – Romans and Saxons and Normans and Lancastrians rode across the stream. Galloped up that hill and disappeared into the centuries.'

How steeped in, how packed with history every cranny of this nation is; sometimes the least likely, most prosaic or overlooked crannies. I spent the first 18 years of my life in Wigan but never noticed until a few years back that there's a chunk of old Roman wall down by a discount store on a town centre back street, or that in the door frame by the bar of the Grand Hotel, there are two bullet holes from a Civil War skirmish (or was it the Jacobite one?) When I walk into Manchester down the Ship Canal from the BBC in Salford, just before the fantastic chip shop on Liverpool Street, I pass a small Roman amphitheatre. As opposed to America, where the Trump Tower counts as an ancient monument, in Britain, we have history to burn, and we often do.

Unruly ancient Brits razed St Albans to the ground in AD 61. But eventually the Romans subdued them and rebuilt it. This time they wisely did this in stone not timber and named it Verulamium, one of the first places in Britain to be identified by its own name. The titular Alban is thought to have been a Roman-Briton of the third century who gave shelter to a Christian priest on the run, the religion still being outlawed then. When the authorities came for the refugee priest, Alban changed places with him, which turned out to be a bad move in every respect – except for his claim on posterity. Alban in disguise offered himself to the authorities and was taken to the pagan temple at Verulamium and presented to the judge. Enraged, the judge demanded that Alban renounce Christianity and offer sacrifices to the gods. At this, Alban spoke the words quoted in the prayer still used at St Albans Abbey: 'I worship and adore the true and living God who created all things.' Again, not the wisest of responses. Alban was scourged and sentenced to death. On his way to the place of execution, Alban had to cross the River Ver and, to speed things along, prayed for a quick death. At this the river dried up, allowing Alban and his guards to cross on dry land. When Alban's executioner witnessed this he baulked at carrying out the deed, so both he and Alban were beheaded. But as Alban's head fell to the ground, the eyes of the second executioner fell out too. The judge was so moved by all this – it must have been quite a morning after all – that he ended the persecution of Christians and began honouring saints. In perhaps the only nice touch to this grisly tale, the fullest and most definitive account of Alban's life and death was recounted by a famous son of Jarrow, the Venerable Bede.

St Albans Cathedral now stands on the very site of these gory and outlandish events, and is still the big draw in town, even if it is surprisingly easy to lose or never find, shyly hiding behind obscuring thickets of the everyday; cafés, pubs, delis. Prince Charles once opined that the clutter around St Paul's was like a carbuncle on the face of a much-loved friend. The architecture of St Albans is not a carbuncle but it is a fairly effective mask. I approach listlessly, summoned by bells through the town's back streets, which are fine as back streets go, but confusing. I pass Empire Records and Chaos City Comics – which amuses me since whatever St Albans may be, Chaos City it certainly isn't – until there it is, suddenly and gloriously. Osbert Lancaster was a little sniffy and backhanded in his compliments: 'St Albans is interesting, if not as grand as some of the other more famous English cathedrals.' Well, Osbert, I thought it was tremendously impressive and so it appeared did the genial babel of German, Dutch, Spanish, Italian tourists who had flocked to it.

In a little basement room, a choir is rehearsing a lovely version of 'Amazing Grace'. Inside the cathedral itself, a clearly supremely gifted organist is playing one heck of a flashy toccata (my notes read 'this dude can play') and the effect is cumulatively amazing. Of course, there will be some who say that this tremendous edifice is built on nothing but fairy stories and superstition. But, and I speak here as an agnostic, the mischievous part of me thinks that might make it all the more magnificent. Here are layered centuries upon centuries of history, human stories, politics, hubris, layered like geological strata, or the butter cream and jam in a Victoria sponge; Briton, Roman, Viking, Anglo–Saxon, Norman, Tudor, Civil War, Regency, Georgian, industrial, technological.

The marchers arriving in chill, heavy rain must have been cheered by the warmth of the welcome. A civic delegation was there waiting on the steps of the grand white town hall, including the Chief Constable and the mayor, eager to show the king Saint Alban's shrine, even then the town's main tourist attraction. Though the people of St Albans shared little of Jarrow's plight and discomfort, they knew of it and even the sceptical changed their minds and were moved by the men's testimony. The porter at the town's workhouse said, 'I had heard about Jarrow but quite frankly I was inclined to put the stories down to exaggerations. Now I know that what I thought could not possibly be true does in fact exist. If you can only convince everyone of those terrible conditions, as you have convinced me, I do not think that anyone can refuse you the work you ask.'

Also in the crowd was an old woman who had lived in Jarrow 20 years earlier and had come here with her son to find work. 'I have visited the old town several times in the last few years and I have tried to tell my friends how terrible things are in Jarrow but it's no use. They can't understand.' Much debated and pored over today, the 'north/south divide' was as real and unbreachable as the walls of St Albans Abbey in 1936. Baldwin was no 'one nation' Tory and he presided over a shockingly divided Britain.

When I arrive at the town hall I find a solitary man in his 60s loitering in the disused entrance of what looks to be an abandoned building. 'Is this … was this … the town hall?' I ask. 'I reckon so,' he says in an accent forged many miles north of St Albans, 'but they've 'ad for't close it darn cos it's full of asbestos'. It turned out he and his wife come down to watch the big NFL American football game at Wembley every year, staying somewhere on the outskirts of the capital. 'Last year it was Hemel Hempstead. This year we're in Tring,' he says morosely, suggesting Tring has not been all he might have hoped.

St Albans's Saturday market is as busy as Barnsley's but of a different character. Less cheap Spiderman duvets and *Fast and Furious* DVDs, more military memorabilia and varieties of marinated olives. An enthusiastic Asian lady approaches me waving a leaflet. 'When you've carved your pumpkin, don't throw it away. We have lots of ideas here! Sustainable St Albans! Can I interest you in some pumpkin soup?' Noting that the marchers would certainly have availed themselves of this generosity, and it looking and smelling delicious, I readily accept and someone takes a picture of my benefactor ladling out the pungent, gingery soup into a styrofoam cup for me.

I've been on the road for three weeks now, and as night comes on in the home counties, colder and rawer than expected, it begins to feel like it. Maybe it was the unfamiliar town, or a low-level cold threatening to come on, scratching at the back of my eyes and throat. Maybe it was just the relentless miles with the pack. Perhaps it was the long, full, satisfying but exhausting days, the constant note taking, negotiating and route finding, or the nights at hotel desks or on beds, reading and tapping at the laptop. Whatever it was, as I sprawled in my room at the top of Holywell Hill, (down which St Alban's head had once rolled, causing the well to spring) I felt weary and disoriented. I wonder how the marchers were feeling at this stage. Was it still a great adventure? Or just cold, hard, tiring graft? They walked every inch of the way, unlike me, and unlike me they couldn't text, tweet, call or email. Some will say of course that that's a good thing but I wouldn't agree. For all its potential for abuse, I know without it my trip would have been harder and less rewarding, and this book would have been thinner, and less well-informed.

With a supreme effort of will, since the room was warm, the bed soft and the newscaster's voice on the TV lulling, I got up, showered and headed up Holywell Hill to sample the weekend nightlife of St Albans, or a section thereof. If your name is Victoria, you get a free prosecco every Friday at the Victoria pub St Albans. Mine isn't and I don't think I could pretend otherwise, so I push on. I'd actually heard about the Horn when in Luton. It is known locally for its live music, and since I hadn't heard any of that since choral evensong at Ripon and Debussy at Leeds, I decided to try a new experience on my route. The Jarrow march had an 'embedded' three-piece mouth organ and, however keen one is on the braying of the harmonica, by St Albans that must surely have been a pleasure that was wearing thin.

The Horn is a big, solid pub on the bridge by the station, the one adorned with the mural of St Albans's favourite sons. This includes Alban himself (still with head), sole English pope Nicholas Brakespear, Stephen Hawking and Stanley Kubrick, the latter represented by a stylised 'Hal' and 'Dave' interchange from *2001: A Space Odyssey*. On the way there, I was delighted to see that St Albans can also boast one of those lovely traditional sewing machine and telescope shops.

Whilst the Horn is 'just' a pub, the back room plays host to bigger names than I'd have guessed. Upcoming attractions included The Bluetones and China Crisis (both sold out) who will be familiar names to any reader who knows their 1980s and 90s British pop. Tonight though, it's the turn of Maxwell Hammer Smith, a covers band whose name is a rather convoluted pun on an old Beatles novelty track. They promise 'harmony rock … Fleetwood Mac, Eagles, Queen' which to me (and this is personal and subjective of course) is a selection that in turn appeals and terrifies.

A common refrain of the last few years has been the valedictory lament for the English pub. We are losing them in droves across the land it appears, and the pub is now threatened with extinction. But even in the 1930s, a period one might assume was a golden age of the English local, some 1,500 pubs were closing every year and another modern malaise, that of binge drinking, was causing concern then too. In the poorest areas, mothers left their prams outside the pub while they drank, nipping out to placate the baby with a shot of whisky. At the very bottom of the drinking ladder, desperate folk drank Red Biddy, a potent, lethal mixture of cheap red wine and meths. At the top of the social order, Churchill was bet £120,000 by his chum Lord Rothermere that he could not go through 1936 without a drink. He refused the wager, probably sensibly on balance, as Winnie's drinking day began at 9am with a whisky and soda, continued with a pint of champagne at lunch and then would be topped up with amontillado, gin and brandy through the evening, often ending with the best part of a bottle of cognac at three in the morning.

English popular music in 1936 was dominated by the sentimental or the humorous in various different registers of class and region. George Formby was cleaning windows with lubricious intent while Noël Coward was picking his way daintily though several arch ditties. But the most illustrative hit song of late 1936 was Sam Coslow's 'If You Can't Sing It, You'll Have to Swing It, Mr Paganini'. All forms of music, popular and highbrow, were starting to feel the heat of a new music coming out of America. As Jarrow marched, America swung.

'Swing cannot be defined,' said the American jazz magazine *Metronome* in 1936. Fats Waller tried though; 'two thirds rhythm and one third soul' – which is more impressionistic than useful. Swing was more than just music anyway; it suggested a whole generational culture at least among the leisured and affluent with its own dances, tunes and clothing styles. But while audiences in the States (and increasingly Europe) were being wowed by the new offbeat rhythms and irresistible energy of Benny Goodman and the constantly touring, pioneering bandleaders of the new idiom, not everyone was keen. Novelist Compton Mackenzie said it was 'the wriggling of a child with an overcharged tummy'. Others were more savage; 'Musical Hitlerism' read one review, ironic since jazz, swing and associated music had been banned across all German radio since 12 October 1935. That day, Eugen Hadamovsky, conductor and Third Reich official, announced, 'As of today, I am placing a definitive ban on the negro jazz for the entire German Radio.' Swing was unstoppable though, and would have been the music most enjoyed by the Jarrow marchers and their dancing partners had they had time for music. I doubt music was laid on at St Albans's workhouse that October night in 1936, but the men got a hot meal from the sympathetic master of the institution.

I treated myself to a big glass of red wine at the bar of the Horn. The band weren't scheduled to be on till half ten, which felt very late for someone beginning to feel the fatigue of his journey. When they took to the stage of the back room though, there were still only a few of us in there, though I assume things filled up later. I stuck around for the first 20 to get me to stay in the same room as the music for the entirety of 'Somebody to Love' by Queen, something no one has ever managed before.

That's unworthy perhaps, but tonight I was feeling more road weary than battle hardened. I trooped back up the hill into the centre of St Albans. There were a couple of police cars outside the Slug and Lettuce and a young PC in a body armour gilet was gently trying to keep apart two women in sparkly dresses. A shaven-headed man with a short-sleeved white shirt, presumably the cause of this physical and emotional exchange, sat on the kerb with his head in his hands. My night, like my march, was ending, but there was certainly still some life in theirs.

STAGE TWENTY-ONE

ST ALBANS TO EDGWARE

30 October, 11 miles

On the morning of 30 October 1936, two days away from journey's end, the Jarrow marchers woke to find that they were the victim of 'fake news' or perhaps 'alternate facts', or as they called them then, lies. Even in 1936 though, the pure and simple truth was, as Oscar Wilde pointed out, rarely pure and never simple.

A phone call to the St Albans workhouse where they were lodged claimed that two marchers, Jos Bradley and Ralph Smith, had actually spent the night in the Barnet workhouse. This came as something of a surprise, not least to the two men concerned who were in fact with their comrades in St Albans. There may well have been a perfectly innocent explanation for all this; the two men in Barnet may have belonged to a different hunger march or were merely tramps who thought that claiming to be Jarrow men would give them better treatment or celebrity. But, typically fearful and suspicious, David Riley assumed yet another secret plot by communists to infiltrate the Crusade. 'If anyone attempts to crash in on the march, he will be met with the boot,' he told the press. There may have been a similarly reasonable explanation for the arrival of a taxi whose driver said he'd been booked to take a marcher to hospital. A simple case of crossed wires, perhaps. But the marchers suspected a plot to kidnap one of them, and both of these sinister explanations were widely featured in the press.

We don't know what the word or phrase of 1936 was. They didn't guess or vote on such things but if they did then, globally, it may well have been one of the words that have echoed through this book; 'Spain' or 'Swing' or 'Nazi'. In Britain specifically, perhaps it would have been 'Abdication' or 'Blackshirt' or 'Formby' or even 'Jarrow'. But in 2016, Oxford Dictionaries chose 'post-truth' as the international word of the year, after the contentious 'Brexit' referendum and an equally divisive US presidential election saw the word gain global currency. As the *Washington Post* put it, 'in this case, the "post-" prefix doesn't mean "after" so much as it implies an atmosphere in which a notion is irrelevant.'

I read or heard the phrase almost every day as I walked and initially it gained purchase in the States, during the last days of gruelling and vindictive presidential campaign. 'We concede all politicians lie,' wrote the conservative *Washington Post* columnist Jennifer Rubin. 'Nevertheless, Donald Trump is in a class by himself.'

'Post-truth' was selected after Oxford's dictionary editors noted a roughly 2,000 per cent increase in its usage over 2015 and 2016. But not just in the States. They also talked of the enormous increase in the frequency of mentions in news articles and on social media in the United Kingdom. British intellectuals and commentators, of the right and left if truth be known, still tend to exhibit a snooty, paternalistic high-handedness towards the supposed crassness of American taste and mores. The rise of Donald Trump could support such an attitude, but only as long as one was prepared to overlook the similar ascent to prominence of his friend Nigel Farage. The events of summer 2016 showed that Britain had moved as far 'post truth' as anywhere in the world.

Take, for instance, one of the most visible and emotive central planks of the Leave campaign; a trumpeted promise that the supposed £350 million a week the EU was costing us would be spent on the NHS if we voted out. Both ends of this statement were lies; the figure was imaginary, and the NHS stood to gain nothing. But still it was emblazoned on the sides of buses – buses paid for by millionaire donors – and supposedly respectable politicians such Boris Johnson, Kate Hoey, Michael Gove and Nigel Farage were happy to stand alongside and peddle that untruth. Once the Leave vote was won, all instantly acknowledged that the figures and claim were false and that nothing of the sort would be done. Even by the standards of modern politics, there as something in this brazenness that was new and quite breathtaking.

By 2016, the word 'lie' had all but disappeared from our political lexicon. But extinction had loomed since as long ago as 1759, when Edmund Burke wrote instead of being 'economical with the truth'. Winston Churchill may be many an Englishman's idea of a straight-talker, but it was he who invented the euphemism 'terminological inexactitude' to cover his own porkies. Lyndon B Johnson was guilty of a 'credibility gap' and then with Richard Nixon we enter a new golden age of slippery deceit, of 'inoperative statements' and 'strategic misrepresentation'. Alan Clark wrote shiftily in his diaries about being 'economical with the actualité'. Hillary Clinton 'misspoke', rather than 'invented', coming under gunfire on a trip to Bosnia. But in late 2016, Carl Bernstein, who along with Bob Woodward had exposed the lies of Watergate, said that 'Nixon had nothing on Trump'.

In Britain, barefaced and gleeful lies like the one about the £350million for the NHS promised by the Brexit lobby are rarer than a kind of 'building of one's part', as actors say. This is often to claim purchase on some romantic and emotive element of our shared past. Thus as I was writing this book, the then-UKIP leader Paul Nuttall got into hot water over claims on his website that he had been at the Hillsborough disaster and 'lost good friends there'. These claims turned out as resistant to verification as the one about him having been a professional footballer with Tranmere Rovers.

'Jarrow' has its own murky legacy of half-truth, partial truth and downright falsehoods. The old northern term 'romancing' seems appropriate here, as most of these myths are attempts to appropriate the teary romance and sentiment of the Crusade. Brexit minister David Davies said in 2005 that his grandfather had led the Jarrow march from York to Aldermaston. His grandfather was not part of the Jarrow march, which in any case never visited those towns. The *Guardian* claimed that the left-wing folksinger father of UB40's Ali and Robin Campbell had been on the Jarrow march. He hadn't. There's the incident of the cross in Leicester and the disputed whereabouts of the Jarrow Crusade banners today. It's easy to judge, or even mock, but as I found as I walked and talked and read, something as drenched in significance and emotion as the Jarrow march will inevitably create false memory, Chinese whisper and hyperbole, and not all of it ill-intentioned.

Elstree, like Jarrow, carries a certain antique, faded, very English glamour. In our time, Elstree has been home to Muppets, *Star Wars, Morecambe and Wise* and quiz show phenomenon *Pointless*. When the marchers passed in 1936, it's likely that *Drake of England, Dandy Dick* (starring Will Hay), *Invitation to the Waltz* or *I Give My Heart* were being filmed there. The *News Chronicle* carried a story that as they passed, the men were unnerved by the presence of scores of policemen who turned out to be extras in the making of a gangster movie (the nearest thing to this description I can find is *Living Dangerously*, filmed at Elstree though set in New York; it seems unlikely to have been *McGluskey The Sea Rover*). The marchers had every right to be nervous; whether they knew it or not, Special Branch had been tailing them either openly or clandestinely since Jarrow, a fact which only emerged much later.

*

When the marchers reached Radlett, halfway to Edgware from St Albans, the town council provided them with a crate of oranges and some welcome, hot mugs of tea at the Congregational Hall. Even then Radlett was comfortable. Now it's one of the most prosperous towns in the south of England. Lovely too, although we are now deep into that part of the country where the dizzying, lung-grasping, vertiginous height of the house prices make your head swim. A five-bedroom house here will cost you £2.5million, although a little place in Letchmore is a snip at £600,000. But this for a solid suburban house, not a gravel-drived country seat, which I still dozily expect for that kind of money. At the time of the Jarrow march, only a quarter of the British population owned their own home, and whilst sometimes this might have put them at the mercy of unscrupulous landlords or living in hostels, it meant we didn't have the uniquely toxic obsession with property we have today. From here until London, I will wonder at every estate agent's window I pass, and there are many, how any ordinary working person can live here, whether they're a carpenter, a cook, a nurse, a teacher, a roofer, or any of the jobs without which society can't function but seems to view as valueless rather than invaluable.

Dusk now, chilly too, and as the lights come on down the main drag, I'm envious of the late stragglers in the well-lit bakeries and bookshops, the milkshake bars and delis. In the Red Lion pub, at a scrubbed and notched faux-rustic table filled with food, young Mum and Dad are happily plying their little girl in a high chair with french fries from a battered metal cone. They look cosy, happy and presumably mortgaged to the hilt. The Radlett Centre has a colourful, enticing and diverse list of forthcoming attractions; Mark Steel, Think Floyd, Annie, an H P Lovecraft adaptation, *The Wiz* and Psychic Sally (Feefo Gold Trusted Service Award; 'deluded but essentially harmless' – *Guardian*).

On the garage forecourt, a Middle Eastern cabbie called Kerem notes both my huge pack and weary tread and astutely makes the connection. 'Hey, my friend, you look tired, man. Where you headed, London? I'll give you good price. You off to find your fortune?' I tell him that that would be cheating and why, but he is so convivial and funny, and I am so comprehensively knackered, that I accept his offer of a lift to 'the best kebab shop in Edgware, I should know. I worked there, my friend. There are many, but this is best. Also cleanest.' Fireworks streak across the sky as we ride the few, dark, hibernal miles to Edgware, a gentle profound reminder of how Britain has changed since 1936. Then those fiery trails could only have meant Bonfire Night. Now they might augur Diwali too.

'Ecgi's weir' is the pond where Ecgi the Saxon and his people would fish. By 1422 it had become 'Eggeswere' and by 1489, the Tudors had added a T, making it almost the name we have today. There's no Domesday Book mention but we know that the Edgware Road follows the same line as ancient Watling Street, an important Roman road later used in the medieval period by pilgrims headed to Canterbury. One of Dick Turpin's most infamous crimes was carried out here on 4 February 1735, when he and five of his gang broke into a farmhouse owned by elderly Joseph Lawrence. Turpin and his louts beat him with their pistols and tortured him by setting him on a fire whilst naked, before pouring a boiling kettle of water over his head announcing that they would amputate his legs. During this ordeal, one of the gang forced a servant girl upstairs and raped her. This is vile stuff, and I include the details for one reason only, to make a point about our national culture. While bemoaning the lawlessness and incivility of the modern world, we've sanitised and glorified Dick Turpin, turning a brutal, murderous thug into a Carry On film rogue, a dandy highwayman of pop songs and a tea towel icon. The British capacity for forgetting, let alone forgiving, is boundless. I expect a rosy, joshing article on Dick in *This England* magazine soon. Perhaps they've already done the Krays.

The coming of the railways and trams transformed Edgware from a hay-producing rural backwater into a crowded adjunct of London itself. In 1932 the parish became a part of Hendon, and Station Road rapidly developed in the early 1930s, with cinemas and stores opening all along a busy thoroughfare.

Born the year after the Jarrow march, a resident called Brenda Franklin told the BBC People's War site, 'Our address was 7 Millais Gardens, Mollison Way, Edgware. Edgware was right on the edge of London then – a sizeable sprawl of the mid-thirties house building explosion. Miles of mostly terraced, Bauhaus-influenced, wide-windowed houses occupied by respectable upper working class families with aspirations. I think that most were quite happy in their brand new easy-to-run houses in the leafy suburbs.'

The marchers would have walked down some of these new streets and emerged along burgeoning Station Road, finding Edgware in the grip of its feverish transformation from outlying village into London's maddening vital edge itself. It must have made them wonder what Jarrow would feel like when they returned, as they soon would. Homesick as they may well might have been, this was a prospect that still evoked dread. One confided to a journalist, 'The first morning is what I'm afraid of. It'll be getting up and looking out of the window on the same old sight – Jarrow – knowing that there's nothing, nothing at all to do. My feet hurt terribly, but all the same it's been a holiday. While you're marching, you don't think.'

After quietly comfortable Radlett, Edgware feels hardier, edgier, noisier. There's no pretty, languid sedate Sunday mood here. This could be any day in the rough hinterland of the city, the buses and cabs elbowing for space, honking and revving; the cheap convenience stores fluorescent and crowded. I realise that I've never felt entirely at home in the London suburbs, affluent or otherwise. Perhaps it was my bad experiences at the eastern extremities of the Central Line during a glum, brief sojourn there in the late 1980s but I'll think I'll always feel unmoored

and out of sorts here in the transient, fragmentary, ad hoc nature
of these places, by the crowded streets of people who always
appear stressed and unhappy and just passing through. Or is
that the three weeks on the road talking, in a tired, whiny little
voice? Possibly.

Happily, the distinctive neon outline of a rotating kebab tells
me that I have found Keren's old alma mater, the cleanest kebab
shop in Edgware, which shall diplomatically remain nameless of
course. I find a table in the midst of the diverse urban bustle of
teenage couples, Turkish cabbies and the odd solo oddball like
me, shoving his massive rucksack awkwardly under the table and
ordering expansively, randomly, hungrily in a way that makes the
small dark-eyed girl behind the counter laugh as she repeats it,
'OK, so that's large doner, kacik, sucuk sausage, patlican, large
Efes beer, pitta, salad ...'

These are always strange but nicely meditative moments,
these, becalmed somewhere new after the relentlessness of the
road. I cover the table in books and notes, devices and maps
but end up paying attention to none of them, drinking in the
changing atmosphere of the café instead. A smart, neat older
woman comes in slightly diffidently, one hand on her pearls and
the other dipping her glasses as she peers at the laminated menu
on the wall as uncomprehendingly as if it were the shattered
frozen landscape of a Jovian moon. Her awkwardness is not
assuaged by the large, burly, moustachioed Middle Eastern
proprietor behind the counter asking, 'Do you live nearby
then, love?' as he sharpens and wipes a huge, glistening blade
of obscure function, entirely innocently but unnervingly. A little
girl and her dad, clearly regulars, enter and are welcomed warmly
by all ('Hello Princess! Give us a kiss!'). They begin an order
of great length and complexity with much discussion. Princess
turns out to be boisterous, wildly voluble and just the charming
side of irritating.

'This door is rubbish [swinging on door] – you need to get
a new door,' she pouts.

'Will you give me the money, Princess?' says the blade-wielding owner, sweetly.

'No! Ask your mummy and daddy for the money!'

'Ah, (sadly but tenderly) my mummy and daddy are in Turkey. Do you know what Turkey is?'

'Yes, it's like a chicken you can eat.'

Leaving some time later, I find the White Hart hotel where the Rotary Club of Edgware treated the marchers to tomato soup, steak and kidney pud and apple pie. It's still there though it has changed its name. To the Change of Hart. Whether this is hilarious or dreadful, I find myself no longer able to tell. But I do know that tomorrow, Halloween, will mean the end of my long, strange trip and that London, tricking or treating, awaits.

STAGE TWENTY-TWO

EDGWARE TO MARBLE ARCH

31 October, 8 miles

London is the most dynamic city in the world today. Sure, it has always been an international hub … but it has never sizzled like it sizzles today. Other cities in the UK make grand claims and have their devotees and champions but Manchester, Edinburgh, Leeds etc pale before the might, sight, sounds, churn and fire of London. And those who disagree are just expressing the politics of envy.

Dylan Jones, *London Rules*

The thing is, most people in London are tired of life. You've only got to witness the queues in the Westfield multistorey or the reaction to a crying baby on the Tube to realise that this is a city that exists permanently at the end of its rope … It's the last metropolis in a sinking country on a starving continent, an island within an island oozing out into the Home Counties like an unstoppable concrete oil spill.

Clive Martin, 'Reasons London is the Worst Place Ever', *Vice*

I'm in a bagel shop in Cricklewood on the hottest Halloween since records began, reading up on my iPad about London, whose swaggering presence has been waiting for me like an unpaid bill since Jarrow. I feel that this might be the strangest day of a long, strange trip. The bagel shop promised free wifi and air conditioning, and, fair enough, you might not normally need the latter on the last day of October in England, but it can deliver neither. So having walked from Edgware already this morning, I sit, a glaze of damp across my chest, arms and forehead, having emerged out of the maze of dead residential backstreets, onto Cricklewood Broadway (formerly Watling Street).

I like the difference in tone of the above quotes, the second from Clive Martin in *Vice* magazine, sour and sharply truthful, the former from *London Rules* by Dylan Jones (who I know and like, if rarely completely agree with) full of the breezy superiority that so annoys us troglodytes of the north. Almost 200 of those came stomping through Cricklewood 80 years ago this morning, and now I follow belatedly in their wake; hot, sweaty, thirsty but not I think, *pace* Dylan Jones, envious.

Of all the queasy, weaselly, mealy-mouthed lickspittle dismissals in modern English, nothing compares to that phrase the 'politics of envy'. Effectively, it reduces people's desire for proper schools, houses, jobs and health care to no more than a jealousy for some nice brogues they once saw in *GQ*. It is both smug and vacuous and it is, of course, partly why Brexit Britain gave Islington a bloody nose though Islington still doesn't have the common sense or humility to see it.

Today is the last day of the Jarrow march. I was up and off early because I had a date at Westminster. If I could be there before noon, Tracy Brabin had very kindly agreed to meet me at the Commons and for this last day, I wanted the feel of the Jarrow marchers' entry into London, albeit that theirs was in the torrential rain and murk of a thirties Halloween and mine is in shirt sleeves, perspiring, under a freakish late October sun on the warmest morning of my 22 so far. I wash down the last of the salt beef and dill pickle with some sweet, scorching black coffee and push through the door into simmering Cricklewood.

Like Balls Pond Road, Golders Green, Surbiton or East Cheam, Cricklewood is one of those London locales that were once staples of British radio and TV comedy. *The Two Ronnies, The Goodies, Hello Cheeky*, all would regularly use these venerable names as handy ciphers as suggestive of tedious, drab London suburbia as Cleckheaton, Wigan and Goole were of northern bleakness when used by Les Dawson or Norman Collier. Cricklewood: is it the sound of the name with its evocative English tweeness, or could it be the place itself that has made this commuter backwater a synonym for genteel nothingness?

Peter Capaldi made a spoof documentary about British cinema called *Cricklewood Greats*, but its comic laureate was undoubtedly Alan Coren, writer, TV and radio panellist, former editor of *Punch* and *The Listener* and father of the modern media personalities Victoria and Giles. Coren styled himself 'The Sage of Cricklewood' and used the unloved area as a neglected eyrie from which to view the foibles of the world in hundreds of columns and parodic books such as *The Cricklewood Tapestry, The Cricklewood Diet, A Year in Cricklewood* and more. In their tribute to him, website *This Is Local London* said, 'Coren almost did for his childhood home what the Brontes did for Haworth'. The London *Evening Standard*'s obituary writer made plain that finding out that Coren actually lived in Cricklewood had to be 'a joke, I thought; so eminent a man could not possibly live in this mocked corner of north-west London, this nowhere between Kilburn and Colindale'.

Cricklewood follows the same spatial arrangement that's been common on the last, southern leg of the journey, one that's very different from northern towns. There the shops and offices and enterprise cluster haphazardly around a market square or town centre. Cricklewood, like Edgware and St Albans, comprises a single parade of commerce stretched out for a mile or two along the sides of an arrow-straight major road. It's linear rather than ganglia, with terraced streets stacking up behind in a residential hinterland. Apart from its very heart, nowhere in London feels like a town to me in the way that northern towns do, confirming my (not entirely negative) view that Greater London is 50 or so little hamlets held together by a tube train system.

Perhaps it was the heat, or our old friend the pack, but it was hard to tell where Cricklewood ended and Kilburn began. There was no greeting sign, no border patrol, just an elision from one unremarkable bit of the capital to another and one prevalent old ethnic tradition to the next. From the late nineteenth century onwards there was an influx of Jewish immigrants to the area and by the time the Jarrow march passed through, three new synagogues had been built in a district which even acquired the jokey cod-Yiddish name Cricklevitch.

Kilburn though is, or was, the raucous heartland of London's Irish community. They may now represent just 5 per cent of the population, much less than the Italians of Bedford, but their influence still permeates the district. Kilburn was prosperous briefly in the late 1860s and 70s when handsome villas abounded and a private school founded by A A Milne's father was attended by both his son and H G Wells. But then the area faltered and became much poorer later in the century. The posh schools closed and the large villas were broken up into flats or took in lodgers, mainly Irishmen coming to work as labourers. These new Kilburnians were pouring in when the Jarrow men marched by and continued to do so for the next four decades. Their story is essentially that of the Bedford Italians and a thousand immigrant communities around the world; young men (and women) come to a new land desperate for work intending to make money and take it home. Instead they work hard, build lives and families here and keep alive a dream of the old country while bringing colour and energy to the new.

Those days seemed to have gone. A reporter from the *Irish Times* had visited over the summer and found the same surly resentments that were making themselves felt everywhere. Kerryman John O'Sullivan told him, 'You go up the road there now and you don't see one English, Irish, Welsh or Scottish face working.' Kilburn's dominant ethnic minority groups were once Irish and West Indian, now it is Somali and Polish. Almost all of the Kilburn Irish interviewed in the piece had voted to leave the EU. This ran contrary to the perceived geographical split over Brexit, the one that said that London was an island of internationalist liberalism while the north and Midlands had been lured towards UKIP and the right. The opinions of Kilburn, whose parent constituency Brent actually voted to remain by 60 per cent, showed what I had long thought to be the case, that class not region was the significant variable, and that the commentators of the metropolis had little notion of life or the mood of depressed, post-industrial England. I might have popped into the offices of Hampstead and Kilburn Labour Party to chat about this, but as I passed it was closed and shuttered.

With all due respect to Dylan Jones, this didn't feel like any kind of international hub to me. Perhaps that ritzy marketing speak applies to a few postal codes around W1 or the City, but there was nothing here of the upscale vibrancy of Leeds. It was a dull plod from the fringes of London's grubby urban edges to its congested heart, though of course with a certain ragged liveliness and colour. But no hills or rivers, no views nor trees, no stone-deep history, just a long strip of commerce, cheap and tatty. That can't be helped of course; the same applies to

Smethwick or Levenshulme or Hebburn. But none of those places make claims for themselves as London does or seeks to mythologise itself quite so desperately, dismissing everywhere else as envious and 'chippy'. In fairness, novelist Zadie Smith, a former Kilburn resident who set her book *NW* here, wrote proudly but candidly of its unprepossessing nature when she wrote, 'Kilburn bloody High Road. Not everyone wants to be a national treasure, after all, nor to be knighted, and not every building longs for a blue plaque or to be held up as a shining example of the "Best of British". Not everything has to be part of the "national conversation".'

There are a few memorable highlights of my late morning in Kilburn though. Jessica, a long-standing Kilburnian of Jamaican descent, spots me marvelling at a grand art deco building across the road, shielding my eyes from the dazzling sun to take in its impressive white tower.

'Great isn't it? Ian Dury and Kilburn and the High Roads played there a lot.' It is the Gaumont State Cinema and for Jessica it has memories not just of late 1970s funk punk but 'Saturday morning cinema for ten pence. It's got one of those amazing pop up organs and a gorgeous art deco staircase that's all curving brass. Every now and then they open it up to the public and let you have a look.'

They, I ask?

Jessica rolls her eyes. 'The Happy Clappies, they've had it for about 15 years.'

More properly, 'they' are the Ruach City Church who offer 'lively, multicultural evangelical ministry with faith and bible classes'. Had I known it then, I would have impressed Jessica, who had by now gone into the Al Rouche Super Market to do some shopping, by telling her that you could add to Ian and his Blockheads, Larry Adler, Gracie Fields and George Formby, who all played at the Kilburn State on its opening night of 30 December 1937 in a concert broadcast by the BBC. When it

opened it was one of the largest auditoriums in the world, a
colossal piece of Italianate architecture whose art deco skyscraper
frontage was designed to ape that of the Empire State Building.
('Ape' I think is a good King Kong joke here. No? Oh, please
yourself, as Frankie Howerd would say. He played here too by
the way.)

Kilburn was once renowned across the capital as a lively
and popular place for public entertainment. Entrepreneurs
established several variety theatres and the High Road rang
with a good-natured rowdiness that it became famed for. Ian
Dury's first band were named Kilburn and the High Roads in
its honour.

It is quieter now. In the noughties, the London Tourist
Board tried to brand Kilburn High Road 'Music Mile',
specialising in Irish and country music played live. But most
of the famous pubs, like the legendary Biddy Mulligans, are
now gone, reborn as discount stores, gyms or computer repair
shops.

The A5 London to Holyhead trunk road winds on to
Maida Vale. When the marchers passed along this road, the BBC
had not long acquired the Maida Vale skating rink a few blocks
away for orchestral purposes and it is now the home to the BBC
Symphony Orchestra. It was where most of John Peel's radio
sessions were recorded and every significant talent (and quite
a few insignificant ones) in British alternative and progressive
music recorded such sessions here. A blue plaque above a studio
door will tell you that this is where Bing Crosby recorded his
last session in 1977. I was once showing rock superstars REM
around the studios and pointed this plaque out. Mike Mills and
Peter Buck were genuinely interested but singer Michael Stipe
barked, 'Can we just get on please!' Buck and Mills gave me a
collective apologetic look that suggested to me the band was not
long for this world, and it wasn't.

On the other side of the A5, you will find perhaps
the world's most famous zebra crossing outside the EMI

studios on Abbey Road in St John's Wood. As the marchers passed, Pablo Casals was headed here to record Bach's Cello Suites. Four years before, Elgar had conducted the teen prodigy Yehudi Menuhin in a performance of his own violin concerto. Over the next few years, everyone from Fats Waller to Vaughan Williams would beat a path to this corner of north London. Had I time, I would have taken a detour to see what bizarre, touching, inappropriate new graffiti had been written on its low white wall. This is a place of pilgrimage for Beatle obsessives from around the world who come from São Paolo and Tromsø and Lagos to have their pictures taken walking in step on the crossing as featured on the Beatles' *Abbey Road* sleeve. They then normally write something quite odd. 'John! Happiness is a Warm Gun, from Mexico!' was particularly unforgettable. I'm not sure even the language barrier accounts for thinking a gun reference an appropriate tribute to the shot and slain Beatle.

Those few miles along the A road take you, if you'll allow some poetic licence, from the Holy Land through the Emerald Isle to the Levant. Soon after Maida Vale, in appropriate temperatures, I reached the bustle and sizzle and scents of the lower Edgware Road, it's sudden exoticism a thrill. Three hundred years ago, it provided refuge for Huguenots fleeing persecution under Louis XV. Later it became a destination for successive waves of Middle Eastern immigrants. New trade with the Ottomans brought an influx though the late nineteenth century.

In the 1950s, many Egyptians moved to the area to establish businesses, but it was conflict and unrest that drove or drew people here from the seventies onwards; the Lebanese Civil War, the Soviet Invasion of Afghanistan, the Iran–Iraq War, violence in Algeria, the Gulf Wars. Some call it Little Cairo or Little Beirut. Less charmingly, a *Spectator* piece I read as I dallied over a thick Syrian coffee called it 'The Arab Street'.

Quite a few of those refugees had held skilled professional posts in their home countries such as teachers, programmers or doctors. But denied the same opportunities here, many went into catering or started businesses in the food industry. This may have been a tribulation to them but, from a selfish point of view, for me it has made the Edgware Road the best place to eat in the whole of London. The food of a whole diverse but connected swathe of the world is here from the Dardanelles to the Khyber Pass – Damascene cuisine, Kurdish cuisine, Afghan cuisine, shawarma, Arabic dates, labnah yogurt cheese, tangy zaatar bread, oozing baklava. But I have mentioned food enough and I had a pressing date (not that kind). Tracy Brabin, the MP who had so kindly agreed to meet me at the Commons, had a debate in the afternoon and so I had promised to be there by noon. Damp with sweat and steeling myself against the sizzling and incense of 'Arab Street', I pounded down the Edgware Road until the familiar shape of Marble Arch swam before my eyes.

Technically, Marble Arch was the end. The end of mine and the marchers' journey. They arrived here in teeming rain to be met by large crowds and the assembled press. The harmonica band played some of the tunes that had kept them going over the last three-and-a-half weeks; 'The Long, Long Trail', 'Tipperary', 'Annie Laurie'. I arrived to the sound of a passing boy racer playing grime and some construction work, took a selfie and grabbed a black cab by the swanky hotels of Park Lane. In my time, I've been to these scores of times for various awards do's. I wouldn't be dropping in this morning I didn't think, in my battered walking trainers, flat cap and gigantic rucksack. I was going to look odd enough in the palace of Westminster.

The Jarrow marchers carried a petition of 10,000 signatures from the north east in a wooden box the 300 miles from their home town to London. Each night it would be placed under lock and key in the council offices and drill halls of Ripon or

Mansfield, Darlington or Bedford. The petition asked very politely for a new steelworks to be built in their town; for anything to alleviate their dire, workless situation. Prime Minister Stanley Baldwin refused to see them. Later they trudged in their sodden capes to the Houses of Parliament to see the king in a Royal Procession to Parliament. Because of the rain though, the procession was cancelled and the marchers, standing four deep in the downpour, watched him swish by in his chauffeured car into the House. The mood of the capital's elites is brilliantly captured in a painting by Thomas Cantrell Dugdale, titled 'The Arrival of the Jarrow Marchers in London', in which a young woman with a cigarette holder eyes the Crusaders languidly from a salon window whilst her foppish male companion looks elsewhere. I had no petition, no request, no axe to grind or whet on my 'politics of envy'. But I had decided not long after setting off that I should try to do what the marchers failed to do. Get inside the House of Parliament and speak to a Member of Parliament.

Tony Benn, one of the great Parliamentarians whatever one thinks of his politics, said of the last stage of his life that it was being lived 'in a blaze of autumn sunshine'. It's a lovely phrase, something to hope for and it was very literally what had brought hundreds to Westminster that lunchtime. There are always crowds at the Houses of Parliament but there were more than usual that morning; smiling groups from Tokyo and Tampa having their pictures taken beneath the huge cliffs and crenulations of the palace and the imperious gaze of Big Ben. Again, whatever your politics, it's hard not to feel a little shiver of pride at moments like these. We do palaver well, and the Houses of Parliament are pure palaver, writ large in gilt and honey-coloured Rutland limestone.

It takes an age to get in, even with George, Tracy's assistant, at my side. There are security checks and re-checks to be queued for, but who could baulk at that after the events of Batley this summer. George is a lovely young man about a foot taller than

me, as is customary amongst the youth of today. It's his first day
in this job and I am his first official duty. He and I both pale
a little when I realise I have a Swiss Army knife in my pocket,
essential for my march but less welcome here. But we sort this
out with the guards just as the new MP for Batley and Spen
comes down the hall to meet us, beaming, blonde and sunny in
a bright red tunic.

'Well, day five in the Big Brother house,' she laughs 'and all
is going well.' It's Tracy's first week and I wonder whether, to
try another analogy, it's like first term at big school. 'It's pretty
full on. I've sharpened a lot of pencils, and I do keep getting lost
which is what happens when you go to a new school, isn't it? But
no one's flushed my head down the toilet yet ...'

She was born in Batley, West Yorkshire, in the constituency
she now represents, and educated at Heckmondwike Grammar
School. She studied drama and then did a Master of Arts
degree in screenwriting. She had a long-running nineties role
in *Coronation Street*, also appearing in *Holby*, *EastEnders* and
Emmerdale. She's a writer too, and has written episodes for
Heartbeat, *Family Affairs*, *Crossroads*, *Tracy Beaker*, *Hollyoaks*
and *Shameless*. But in parallel with this she has long been
politically active.

'There'll be people thinking, oh, you're just some actor off
the telly, but I've been a campaigner and activist for 30 years,
initially for the Writers Guild and Equity. I spoke at the European
Parliament about gender, I've campaigned for refugee rights.
I've done a lot of stuff which people wouldn't know about, but
they do know about *Coronation Street*, which is fine. Nobody
wanted this obviously. I wouldn't have wanted to be here under
these circumstances. But I'm from the area and Jo was a friend
and I campaigned with her over closures of libraries and the like.
So when the Labour Party asked me to do it, to stand as MP, I
thought I can't say no, I have to step up.'

We sit beneath a bush in the lobby and famous faces pass
by, politicians, journalists, TV presenters. If the Jarrow march

arrived today, would they be interested? Would anyone be clamouring for a soundbite from Ellen or Marshal Riley? A quick woof from Paddy the dog? Apart from the crowds in Trafalgar Square and the press, Westminster itself was cool and awkward toward the Jarrow men. Some thought it 'a bolshie show' but others surely knew that these 200 sodden men from the north were a painfully visible sign of their own failure. I ask Tracy what that word Jarrow means to her.

'It means working-class protest. It may have been in the end just a gesture but it was a gesture that says together we're stronger. But it's about poverty too. Batley food bank has given out 8,000 meals and that's not going to get any better. Are we not on the verge of a Jarrow again, with the poor literally having to choose between heating and food?'

I liked Tracy a lot. She is bright, brave and passionate and I could have stayed a lot longer. But to be honest, my journey was over now and after the long miles and the procession of towns and cities and days, I felt slightly overwhelmed in the vast lobby with its busy chatter. Staying around to eat cake at Westminster felt like prolonging the inevitable, which was turning around, making my way to Euston and heading back north, home. Tracy was going to be busy this afternoon too. 'The Orgreave debate is today, we'll get some kind of conclusion.'

Orgreave is a place like Jarrow that casts a long shadow and tolls like a bell in the political history of Britain, in particular the story of the English industrial working class. In the summer of 1984, at the combustible height of the national miners' strike, members of the National Union of Mineworkers picketed a coking plant at Orgreave, South Yorkshire. When they tried to persuade lorries not to leave or enter, a force of around 6,000 policemen turned on them savagely. A former officer present that day, who asked to be anonymous, told the BBC that the police were told to use 'as much force as possible' against the miners and that the police 'were anticipating trouble and in some ways relishing it'.

After Hillsborough, Orgreave was seen as another open wound in the British, or at least northern psyche. The behaviour of the police and the role of government in the attacks on the miners is something many still want proper answers about and satisfactory explanations for. South Yorkshire Police had told the BBC they would 'fully participate' in any enquiry. The day that I arrived in London, Amber Rudd, the Conservative Home Secretary, was to announce whether there would be a public enquiry or not. There was a definite feeling in the air that, with the truth about Hillsborough slowly emerging, the other great symbolic attack on the working class, Orgreave would be next to be opened up to the light of scrutiny and the fresh air of honesty. We would know in a matter of hours.

I walked back into central London via the House of Commons souvenir shop to pick up some postcards as souvenirs. As I walked past the Cenotaph I bumped into another Labour MP, Alison McGovern who I recognised from her Twitter picture. She too was rushing back for the Orgreave verdict but she'd been following my progress and we had a congratulatory hug and picture ('I wouldn't normally do this with no make-up on, you know') before she dashed away back to Westminster. Around Leicester Square, the heat and tiredness finally became too much and I flagged down a black cab to take me the last few miles of London's clogged streets to Euston.

'You look done in, mate,' said the cabbie cheerily into his rear view mirror, surveying my slumped figure. 'You come far?'

'Jarrow,' I said, eyes closed

'Jarrow? As in the march? From Newcastle?!'

'That's right.'

'Bloody 'ell, mate. No wonder you're knackered. What was all that actually about then? Was it something to do with the general strike, or later? I seen pictures and you hear the name. But what was the protest? What did they want? Were they miners? Who were they?'

I pause. It's a good question. But I can't summon either the energy or expertise to answer it fully or properly.

'They were just some bloody left wingers coming down here to make trouble.'

The driver gives me a long, amused look in the mirror, trying to work out if I'm serious or not. He's wondering what response to give when I suddenly ask him to turn the radio up, as there's breaking news crackling through and a familiar name. Orgreave.

> The Home Secretary Amber Rudd has just told the house that there will not be a public enquiry into the Orgreave clashes between police and miners during the 1984 miners' strike. The announcement will come as a bitter disappointment to campaigners. She said, 'This has been a difficult decision to make, and one which I have thought about very carefully. But I have now concluded that there is no case for either a statutory inquiry or an independent review.' Ms Rudd added that 'policing is very different' now to what it was 30 years ago.

It was a perfectly proper, fitting and bitter end to the trip. On arrival in London 80 years ago, the crowds were large and warm. Even Rothermere's right wing mouthpiece newspapers gave 'Three Cheers for Jarrow'. The harmonica band were offered a recording contract. But Parliament largely ignored them. As Ellen Wilkinson reported, despite many MPs being bombarded with requests for support for Jarrow from their constituencies, 'A few questions were asked … and the house moved on to consideration of other things.'

Sir John Jarvis MP did announce, however, that he was negotiating for a new steel tubes mill on the Palmer's site. But this was largely a ruse. Jarvis paid for a boat trip for the men on the Thames, ostensibly as a reward for their efforts, but actually to avoid any ugly scenes in the House. When they returned, they were told by the Special Branch that the petition they had carried 300 miles had been 'presented in their absence'. They were sickened. No one knows where this piece of people's history is: lost, burned, discarded, perhaps at the bottom of a cupboard in New Scotland Yard.

No new steelworks was ever built in Jarrow. The tube works opened a year later and the brief, fleeting hope that it sparked in the men is sad and touching. When Ellen Wilkinson walked through the site when the men were laying the concrete foundations of the rolling mill, she was greeted with, 'This is what we marched to get.' But the pathos and irony was not lost on her. She commented: 'The grim reality is that the workers have no share in these mills. When the works are built they will still be subject to the toll of profit, the exigencies of a system where they can be closed at the will of people far away to suit a financial policy.' In any event, the tube mill, dreamed up primarily as a face-saving ruse by Runciman, employed only 200 men and then only briefly.

When the money from their various collections was totted up that day, there was a profit of £100. It was decided to buy all the men a new suit with this since, if it were given in cash, the Unemployment Assistance Board would probably take it out of their benefits. As well as the suit, there was enough for each for a train ticket home. Otherwise who knows? Maybe they'd have been expected to walk back too.

My train was leaving in eight minutes. I gave the cabbie a handful of pound coins and, on a whim, a postcard of the Mother of Parliaments, floodlit and grand against an indigo night. Then I hauled my pack onto the escalator and thought about what the marchers Billy McShane and Con Whalen, the last surviving marcher, had said many decades on. 'When we were turned down at the House of Commons … that was it, you knew you were finished. It was a waste of time … but I enjoyed every step.'

The youngest marcher never came back. John Farndale stayed in London to work as a baker's assistant. But the harmonica band didn't get that record deal. They went back to Jarrow and waited for the call from London that never came, and then quietly broke up.

POSTSCRIPT

October's a blink of the eye, the apples weighing down
the tree a minute ago are gone and the tree's leaves are
yellow and thinning … the days are unexpectedly mild
… but the nights are cool to cold …

Ali Smith *Autumn*

Thou watchest the last oozings hours by hours …
sinking as the light wind lives or dies …
… And gathering swallows twitter in the skies.

John Keats 'Ode to Autumn'

October 2016 seems a long time ago. St Albans seems a
long time ago; Bedford, Luton, Market Harborough, Ripon,
Ferryhill, Jarrow, all of them, long ago and miles away. Autumn
froze and hardened into winter, and with each passing season,
the unthinkable became the norm.

Do the Chinese really have a curse that goes 'may you live
in interesting times'? It might well be one of those fictitious pub
'facts' like the Great Wall of China being the only man-made
structure visible from space. (It isn't. You can see lots of stuff
from the moon, from Bedouin campfires to power stations to
football stadia.) But the few months since I retraced the march
have been about as interesting as we could bear, interesting to
the point of fevered insanity.

Nothing felt quite as seismic and surreal as Trump's
astonishing and frightening elevation to the White House.
Trump won the US election, though not the popular vote, and
within days, mad and unprincipled executive orders were fired
off from the White House where our Prime Minister scurried

to curtsey and hold his hand. He appointed several far-right
demagogues and white supremacists into his closest circle of
advisers. One of his friends and supporters in the media called
Alex Jones has a radio/TV show *Info Wars* that Trump often
appears on. Jones said that both Hillary Clinton and Barack
Obama were literally demons from hell who wreaked of sulphur
and who were haloed with a ring of flies indoors at all times
of year. David Icke, wearing a turquoise tracksuit, used to say
these kinds of things on the Terry Wogan show in the 1980s
and we would chortle, perhaps uncharitably, at how the ex-
goalkeeper and *Nationwide* presenter had gone so demonstrably
and spectacularly nuts. Now such people are in the spheres of
influence of the most powerful man on earth. As of early 2017,
Icke is mildly resurgent with a quarter of a million subscribers to
his YouTube channel. He has wisely toned down the stuff about
Blair and Bush being pan-dimensional lizard overlords in favour
of much raging about, naturally, 'the mainstream media'.

One of the things I like about the mainstream media, for
all its undoubted faults, is that it uncovers, say, the Watergate
scandal – which is why Trump fears and loathes it – rather than
disseminating some juvenile garbage about the Queen being a
super intelligent reptile in a rubber mask. But that kind of abject
nonsense is thriving like a poisonous mushroom in the dampest,
darkest corners of the Net. Technology and politics writer John
Naughton says that the rise of the new angry populism, of Trump
and to a degree Farage, is perhaps because 'once upon a time
people angry about globalisation, cultural change, immigration
or whatever had to fume impotently in small local circles, but
now can crowd-source their indignation'.

Just as in 1936, the world seems to have fallen in thrall
to 'strong men' again, all promising action as an end in itself
however rash or backward. For Franco, Mussolini and Hitler
read Trump, Erdogan and Putin. The far right in France is in the
ascendant again. The engineer of this has been a young thinker
called Florian Phillipot. He has had the ear of *Front Nationale*

leader Marine Le Pen for several years now and his two main
strategies, both successful, have been to move the far-right party
away from taints of racism and anti-semitism (to the extent of
expelling Marine's father Jean Marie Le Pen) and making it a
populist party appealing to the ignored and discounted working
class of the northern French rust belt. Its English collorary,
the post-industrial north and Midlands, similarly abandoned
by liberals and globalists, is exactly the heartland Labour have
lost and must regain if they are ever to become electable again.
This is less an opinion than simple psephological truth, however
unpalatable it might be to the north London caucus. Unpalatable,
that is, if you are of the opinion that Corbyn and Momentum
actually want to win elections. This is a serious point; I suspect
that there are some now at the ideological helm of Labour who
find the purity of permanent opposition far more attractive than
the messy, difficult compromised business of government.

The romance that I felt in the stands at the King Power
stadium that Saturday afternoon, dissipated swiftly in February
when eight months after the greatest achievement in club
football, manager Claudio Ranieri was sacked by Leicester City's
billionaire Thai owners. These are the ones whose royal family
we had dutifully clapped in October like the saps we are amidst
some homily about respect and tradition. Fenwick's in Leicester
closed too, though the one in Newcastle where I bought gin,
socks and a flat cap still thrives. The happy and hardworking
Santaniello family of Bedford have appeared on the *Hairy
Bikers*, cooking spaghetti bolognese and touring the Stewartby
brickworks. Perhaps emboldened by our Twitter exchange,
Michael Gove was granted an audience with the new US
President. Rupert Murdoch sat in, just visible in the shadows,
baleful as the Mekon.

Three-and-a-half weeks. Three hundred miles. Roaring
arterial highways that arrowed to the horizon, B roads that
snaked down the shallow tray of a valley; up ahead, the bulk of
a city or the silence of trees; the growl of haulage, silent lanes

under canopies of leaves, abandoned railway lines, village inns lighting up at four, market days, candlelit cathedrals, darkened tunnels, steamy restaurants, the bright lights of the fairground, blue remembered hills, angry men in bad pubs, limpid French impressionist music in intimate salons, vast flat fields haunted by rooks. Britain in 1936 was a land of beef paste sandwiches and drill halls. Now we are a nation of vaping and nail salons, pulled pork and salted caramel. Some things have returned though; old-fashioned barber shops and hot towel shaves, allotments and baking.

I walked from the top to the bottom and into the heart of England. I looked it in the eye from morning till night and I never grew tired of it. Like the marchers, I learned something from those long days, evenings and nights that no amount of TV news or opinion pieces or well-meant documentaries could have given me. I learned about England now, about England then, and about England's secrets, its scraps and footnotes. I hope I have done it justice. Sometimes it baffled me, sometimes it irritated. But I came to know that, to quote that old maxim, yes, it is my country right or wrong. It seems to be wrong about something almost every day now, but I understand some of its discontent, it's bristling dissatisfaction with how it has been ignored, patronised and marginalised.

When it is right, it is still cheery and industrious, generous and tough, patient and dependable, rugged and gentle, mysterious and fascinating, charming and funny. It is not yet become solely the ruddy faced, shouting, unpleasant enclave of *This England* magazine, Piers Morgan and Nigel Farage. No, it is still the England of the warm, lovely Santaniellos and Inderpal the earnest, decent young Sikh in Beeston. It's the England of generous Mark and his little lad Sam in the stands at Leicester and kindly ladies like Lynn in the Bunyan Museum.

On leaving choral evensong at Ripon, after a few glasses of good Italian red, I took a turn around the town in the gathering gloom and found myself down by the bus station where I recognised two members of the congregation. They had seemed incongruous among the Barbours and tweeds and headscarves then; his raincoat too shabby and trousers too short, her coat too thin. He had pushed her out of the cathedral in a wheelchair, a worn plastic supermarket bag dangling from the arm. Now they were sheltering from fine drizzle under the plastic roof of the shelter. She was coughing violently and he was crouching to comfort her. They both peered at the illuminated yellow ticker that told them to 'await further information' about their bus home.

Seeing that couple, not young, not strong, ill-looking and sad in a chilly bus shelter as dusk began to fall, made me wonder; who is speaking for them? Who is fighting their corner, the weak and insecure and vulnerable? Who will make their lives better? Not bullies and narcissists like Farage or Trump for sure, nor Corbyn, scuttling in fear from every journalist's question. Maybe it is no bad thing if that consensus has been shattered if that is what makes the comfortable of left and right easy in their superiority. Maybe it might make them wonder what the lives of others are really like, whether they like them or not.

That last full marcher Con Whalen said that the Jarrow march had made 'not a ha'porth of difference' to the town's fortunes or its people and had been 'a waste of time'. But, according to Tom Pickard in his book *Jarrow*, a Sir Charles Allison, a politician of the north east, was asked about the Depression and the Jarrow march in 1965. He said, 'It's not bloody well going to happen again. There is a feeling, yes, a feeling in the minds of those who have experienced it that it could happen again. But if it did, there would be an armed revolt. Men would not go in supplication to the lord. They would take what they wanted.' Perhaps next time then, Geordie actually will go and burn them down.

Was 2016 like 1936? Will 2017 be like 1937? And so on and so on until disaster awaits a few years down the line. I saw and heard chilling echoes, not from the Jarrow march route but not too far away, that made me think. Domineering men telling lies, big lies, and snarling at the judges and journalists who try to hold them to account. Contempt for women. Contempt for decency. Banter instead of wit. Cruelty in place of compassion. The age of the troll and the snowflake, people reduced to stereotypes, and the newspapers once again denouncing 'enemies of the people' and printing their names and pictures. In 2016, for the first time for me, it was not glib chatter or student drivel to think that something very like fascism was arising again out of the depths of history, a rough beast slouching towards Bethlehem to be born.

Looking at the toxic venom and gainsaying between right and left today, you might despair. But don't. In 1936, Mosley's Fascists moved comfortably around the towns of England assisted by the police, championed by the press and tacitly supported by the aristocrats and royals. The Jarrow marchers, now fabled and romanticised, were spied on and bullied by the police, abandoned by the Labour Party and the TUC and mocked by the church. They were lied to and cheated and eventually ignored. It was ever thus. There may well always be people who lord it loudmouthed and self-satisfied: whether leering bullies or dreary puritans, over-entitled man-babies, privileged pub bores or ineffectual commissars, they are brothers under the skin, self-absorbed and impervious.

But they are not the best of us. The Jarrow men and Red Ellen were. Like her, like them, we are a mess of contradictions, a desperate, striving hotch-potch who are flawed and human and try our best to make the best of things. I'm not sure I want a nation entirely at ease with itself. We're not altogether the peaceful and compliant land we appear. We've cut the heads off kings and taken axes to each other in the streets and pastures. We've done wicked things to ourselves and to others. So no, not a nation at ease with itself. Better a nation always arguing amongst itself, civilly but passionately and endlessly restless in brilliant, angry, loving, vital cities and hard, defiant little towns, in market squares in the long afternoons and empty fields at evening under a huge, darkening sky of clustering, darting swallows or teeming with starlings. And in the distance, out of the past, the ghostly clatter of boots coming again down the long English road.

THANK YOU...

...to the following generous and lovely people, largely in order of appearance:

Matt Perry
Tom Kelly
Joanne Hackett-Smith, all at Jarrow Council Fun Day
Rowland at Opera North
Clare Hudson
Inderpal and all at the Gurdwara, Beeston
Nadia Shireen
Rowland at Opera North
Dan Jackson
Ian Stringer
Lara Skinner and Foxes fans Mark and Sam Pausey
Peter, Veda and Amanda at Chesterfield Museum
Mansfield Museum
Kev and Jake at Windsor Windows
The Chuckle Brothers
Tracy Brabin and George

And everyone who kept me company and made valuable suggestions via my blog of the journey or social media.

FURTHER READING

Jarrow Protest and Legend, Matt Perry, University of Sunderland Press (2005)

Jarrow, Tom Pickard, Alison & Busby (1981)

The Thirties: An Intimate History, Juliet Gardiner, Harper (2011)

We Danced All Night: A Social History of Britain Between the Wars, Martin Pugh, Vintage (2009)

The People, Selina Todd, John Murray (2015)

Britain in the 1930s, Andrew Thorpe, Historical Association (1992)

Britain in the 1930s, Noreen Branson and Margot Heinemann, Panther (1973)